D1067869

PERCEPTS, CONCEPTS and

THEORETIC KNOWLEDGE

Percepts,
Concepts

HAROLD N. LEE

and

Theoretic
Knowledge

A STUDY IN EPISTEMOLOGY

MEMPHIS STATE UNIVERSITY PRESS

121
247p

Ne

Copyright 1973
©

MEMPHIS STATE UNIVERSITY PRESS
Memphis, Tenn.

Library of Congress Card No. 73-82796

Manufactured in the United States
by NAPCO Graphic Arts, Inc.,
New Berlin, Wisconsin 53151
ISBN: 0-87870-014-5

PREFACE

Much of contemporary empirical epistemology proceeds on the implicit assumption that the world is made up of an innumerable variety of ready-made things, which in turn are composed of ready-made parts. Knowing the world, on this assumption, is finding out about the things and their parts. Thus, empirical knowledge is founded on an inventory of "the furniture of the universe"a phrase dear to the hearts of English empiricists.

The present study rejects this assumption. The world is not a furnished apartment which we come to know, use, and leave somewhat the worse for wear. The world is more like a garden where we get patterns and plans, flowers and fruit only if we formulate patterns and plans or cultivate flowers and fruit. There is no fixed world and there are no definite things except as mind contributes the definition. Mind delineates what it uses and in delineating knows; but mind is not a thing, nor does it view the world from outside. Mind is a way of doing something: it is a process and is part of the world process even though it too lacks structure and definition until it gives them to itself. It is not a nonnatural something imported from without.

The present study assumes that the world is flux—reality is continuous process—and mind arises in the course of the process. Changing parts of process interact and react with other changing parts, and highly sensitive centers of response arise.

v

HUNT LIBRARY
CARNEGIE-MELLON UNIVERSITY

MAY 15 73

The world is flux, but as Heraclitus proclaimed, the word introduces order into the flux. Language is of the essence of mind: mind is symbolic process. Mind is part of the universal process, but a part which uses other parts as surrogate for what is beyond the immediate sphere of direct interaction. When the symbolism becomes articulate and discursive, it is language. Without language there is no developed mind. By means of language, process can be symbolically stopped, and things—objects—are carved from the ongoing flux.

As process precedes mind, so action precedes thought. Similarities in reaction give rise to a rudimentary generalizing tendency, and this is the source of conceptualization, which is completed through symbolic activities. The generalizing, conceptualizing element in action is the source of the structuralizing, enforming powers of the mind. Action, carried on in the light of primordial generalities and the ensuing dim concepts, when refined by language, becomes cognitive and is the basis of the knowledge process.

The point of view of the study is fundamentally Kantian, but only in the way that American pragmatism is Kantian: order is introduced into the world of conscious experience by the activity of mind. The study rejects all the details of Kant's architectonic, and there is no structured mind to begin with as in Kant's theory. It has learned much from Bergson but rejects his doctrine of intuition, and with the rejection goes his *élan vital,* his reputed anti-intellectualism, and his mysticism. It owes much to Whitehead but rejects his doctrine of eternal objects and of the atomicity of actual entities. The pragmatic side of C. S. Peirce's philosophy has been a source, but the two main sources in recent philosophy have been C. I. Lewis and G. H. Mead. Neither of these, however, laid enough explicit emphasis on the place of process and continuity in their philosophies.

The usual epistemology among English-speaking philosophers today is some variant of the sense-datum theory. This is Hume warmed over and served with the embellishments of contemporary phraseology. Theoretic knowledge has advanced since Hume, especially in mathematics, logic, and the natural sciences. Knowledge is not simply the apprehension of the structure and operation of a ready-made world. Knowledge is the formulation by means of action and reaction of a process of which it is a part. No absolute divisions, distinctions or limits, internal or external, are part of the process without respect to knowledge, but process as known is process formulated and structured by the mind.

Many students and colleagues over the years have contributed in one way or another to the development of the ideas in this study. One especially should be mentioned. I received much help and stimulation from endless conversations and arguments with H. M. Johnson, late Professor of Psychology at Tulane University over the topics treated in this book. We had the same general direction of thought although we seldom agreed on details. His objections always had a point, however, and as soon as I clearly saw the point I had achieved an advance in thought.

The permission of many publishers to quote from their publications is gratefully acknowledged: to Dover Publishers, Inc. for quotations from W. E. Johnson's *Logic* and William James's *The Principles of Psychology*; to Farrar, Straus & Giroux, Inc. for Louis de Broglie's *The Revolution in Physics*; to George Allen & Unwin, Ltd. for Bertrand Russell's *Mysticism and Logic*; to Harvard University Press for C. S. Pierce's *Collected Papers* and W. V. Quine's *From a Logical Point of View:* to Humanities Press, Inc. for D. W. Hamlyn's *Sensation and Perception*, J. Piaget's *Judgement and Reasoning in the Child*, and for Ludwig Wittgenstein's *Tractatus Logico-Philosophicus*; to The Macmillan Company for A. N. Whitehead's *Adventures of Ideas* and *Process and Reality*, for Daniel Lerner's (ed) *Evidence and Inference*, and for Ernest Nagel's *Sovereign Reason*; to Prentice-Hall, Inc. for R. M. Chisholm's *Theory of Knowledge* and Philip Frank's *Philosophy of Science*; to The University of Chicago Press for Jerrold J. Katz's

The Problem of Induction and Its Solution and Alan Pasch's *Experience and the Analytic*; to Yale University Press for J. B. Conant's *Science and Common Sense* and James G. Taylor's *The Behavioral Basis of Perception*; to Barnes & Noble, Inc. for Gilbert Ryle's *The Concept of Mind*; and to the *Journal of Philosophy* for the quotation from Donald C. Williams.

CONTENTS

"The true method of philosophical construction is to frame a scheme of ideas, the best that one can, and unflinchingly to explore the interpretation of experience in terms of that scheme."

A. N. WHITEHEAD

CHAPTER I

Introduction

Epistemology may be approached from either of two directions: from the analysis of a complex system of knowledge such as may be found in mathematics, in natural science, or even in the organized common sense of ordinary language; or from the investigation of the process of gaining knowledge both in simple and in complex situations. The first approach, in seeking to lay bare the structure of knowledge, encounters two dangers: the structure found, being composed of the invariants that go to make up a systematic scheme, is almost sure to be static. And if one concentrates on the conditions necessary to complex situations, one may overlook those operative in simple beginnings. For example, it may seem clear that there is a subject-object relationship in knowledge so that "*S* knows that *h* is true" or "*m* knows (or claims to know) such and such" can be taken as paradigm cases of what is being investigated.[1] The insight that there is a subject-object relationship in knowledge does not, however, explain the place of language in knowledge or the importance of learning a language to an infant beginning to acquire knowledge.

When one takes the paradigmatic approach illustrated

1. R. M. Chisholm, *Theory of Knowledge* (Englewood Cliffs, N.J.: Prentice-Hall, 1966) pp. 5–6; and A. C. Danto, *Analytical Philosophy of Knowledge* (Cambridge: at the University Press, 1968) 1ff.

above, one takes already formulated knowledge to be ultimate or logically primitive. Instead of being logically primitive, however, formulated knowledge is a complex product of an intricate activity. Everything that is known has been learned, and a theory that does not take learning into consideration is in danger of smuggling in assumptions concerning what it is that is to be called knowledge. The paradigm at issue makes assumptions of a Cartesian sort and assumptions concerning the nature of truth. The place of language in knowledge is overlooked. Knowledge depends on symbolism, and a child's earliest knowledge, perhaps even consciousness itself, rests on his developing the ability to use signs and symbols. Language is a complicated type of symbolism.

The second approach, investigating the process of gaining knowledge, is more apt than the first to be dynamic in character and by definition considers all cases, simple and complex. It may be found that the structure of systematic knowledge is a result of compounding and elaborating the basic principles that appear in the simple cases.

The present study adopts the second, the dynamic, approach and is frankly speculative in its method.[2] The structure of knowledge is the goal of the investigation, but the structure is clearly delineated only as it stands out in the processes of knowing and learning. The relation between structure and process is one of the things to be explicated, but no explication will be achieved by neglecting one of the terms of the relation. Explanatory principles, since they are speculative, are hypothetical. They are to be accepted or rejected only as they perform their explanatory function. The details of confirming or disconfirming the hypotheses must often be left to logic or to psychology, but the reasons for so doing and the criteria of confirmation are epistemological. Gathering the explanatory

2. I use 'speculative' as I understand Whitehead to explain it in pt. 1, chap. 1, sec. 1 of *Process and Reality* (New York: The Macmillan Co., 1929).

concepts into categories of the understanding also is a speculative undertaking, and thus it too is hypothetical, and the investigation of the hypothetical nature of knowledge is a further task of epistemology.

The prevailing tendency of the recent past has been for epistemology to approach its task in the first of the two ways mentioned above, that is, by analyzing fully formulated, relatively complex cases of adult knowledge. Prerequisite to such knowledge are both the mastery of language and the experience of a world full of things. Adults already have language and ordinarily experience things; consequently, it is assumed that things can be taken for granted as soon as knowledge of an external world to contain them has been established. Epistemologists who hold this sort of theory may admit that things are in process, but the things are there, and processes take place between and among them. Thus, much recent epistemology is the attempt to show how a ready-made mind can know a ready-made external world, and has assumed that this is a world of things, or to speak more technically, a world made up of discrete entities. The present study does not make this assumption. To the contrary, it assumes that the world is a world of process. The doctrine of process has been exploited in philosophy at intervals ever since it was first proposed by Heraclitus. The Platonic tradition, however, followed Parmenides in holding that the Way of Truth leads to permanence and the Way of Belief to change. This influence has been predominant in Western philosophy.

The world of the twentieth century is a world of process. Evolutionary thought has gradually penetrated all aspects of the world outlook. Within such a world, events are primary to things. In the course of attaining knowledge, things are abstracted from events; what happens is more fundamental than what is, because what happens gives rise to what is. Three important consequences, distinguishing the epistemological doctrines of the present study from more traditional ones, flow from replacing things by events: 1) time and continuity are taken seriously; 2) the epistemological dualism based on the Cartesian bifurcation of nature is rejected; 3) all knowledge is recognized to be hypothetical.

Emphasis on events rather than things gives time and continuity importance they do not have in much of classical epistemology. Events are selections from the continuous, ongoing flux of process, but things are static and discrete. To point out the continuity of time is to call to attention that there are no gaps, no preestablished limits or boundaries where one time stops and another starts. Ongoing process is a continuum, it is not a succession of discrete moments. It is true that time can be measured but only as it is conceptualized, and then only in terms of space and motion. *Conceptualized* time is a continuous frame or receptacle in which motion can take place, and in its own nature is empty. Space too is a continuum, and conceptualized space also is empty, but strange to say, it is a different sort of emptiness. This hardly makes sense. To suppose that time and space as they are grasped in concepts are data or possible data of direct experience is to commit the fallacy of vacuous actuality.[3]

It will be necessary to investigate the relation between the temporality of experience and its conceptualization. The concept of time is *derived* from the temporality of experience but it *is not* that temporality. The relation between the two boils down to the problem of relating the concrete experience of continuity to the conceptual grasp of a continuum. Contemporary epistemology has seldom dealt with this problem.[4] It is not solved by neglecting to notice it. Conscious experience within the limits of the so-called specious present (which I shall call 'the concrete present') is an ongoing process with no gaps, no separations, no preestablished boundaries either

---

3. *See* Whitehead, *Process and Reality,* p. 253.
4. An exception must be made for Stephan Körner's *Experience and Theory* (London, Routledge, 1966). Körner suggests a logic of inexact classes to deal with a continuum. His book is, however, closer to philosophy of science than to general epistemology.

internal or external. Temporality does not consist of moments that follow each other in empty succession.

Any philosophy must squarely face the problem of continuity. By 'the problem of continuity' I do not refer to the question whether a thing or a property persists over a period of time when it is not being observed or not producing an effect, but to the problem of what constitutes a continuum as against what is made up of discrete parts. The same whole cannot be continuous when the philosophical breeze blows from one side of the platform and discontinuous when it blows from the other. If continuity is not fundamental, discontinuity is, even if the philosophers fail to take note of it. Furthermore, unless there is only one continuity, discontinuity is fundamental, for if there are two continua that are not continuous with each other, only a part but not the whole is continuous. Continuity is then partial and subsidiary while the discontinuity between the parts is ultimate. Discontinuity breeds plurality whereas the continuous is one. This is an inescapable aspect of Plato's problem of the one and the many.

Both Plato's and Descartes' philosophies are examples of views in which discontinuity is ultimate. Plato's attempt to bridge the gap between the intelligible world and the sensible world with the doctrine of imitation or participation does not get beyond the pictorial metaphor, and the discontinuity remains unresolved. Descartes' attempt to bridge the gap between mind and matter with the activity of the pineal gland did not get beyond metaphorical physiology, and the discontinuity remains unresolved. The ensuing arguments about the impossibility of causal interaction between mind and matter rest on the assumption that there is continuity between cause and effect but no continuity between Descartes' mind and matter.

The philosophical problem of continuity concerns the relation between the concrete experience of continuity—the vaguely felt wholeness that contains no gaps or separations—and the conceptual grasp of a continuum. If the experience of continuity is to be understood, it must be analyzed and suitable concepts evolved and ordered into coherent theory. Concepts are discrete; thus, the theory of continuity will be elaborated in discrete terms. This does not give rise to paradox, however, for it is not the goal of the theory to recreate the experience. The goal is to yield understanding, and understanding is always conceptual. The understanding of continuity (but not the experience of continuity) requires an elaborate logical or mathematical theory of the structure of a continuous series as compared with various sorts of discontinuous series.

The logical relation between a continuous series and a discrete series was explicated by Dedekind and Cantor in the latter part of the nineteenth century in the theory of linear continuity and the relations between the series of real numbers and the series of rational numbers. The series of real numbers is a linear continuum and is composed of elements each of which is an infinite class, that is, each of which is a fundamental segment (or a fundamental sequence) having no last member but approaching a least upper bound as a limit. The least upper bound is determined by a Dedekind cut, a division of a set into two exhaustive parts such that every element in one part is less than every element in the other. The point of division may be made a member of either part at will.[5] A Dedekind cut may be made *anywhere* in a continuum. Philosophers from Plato to Whitehead have pointed out that the only way to grasp a continuous process is to stop it. We stop it conceptually, not actually. The Dedekind cut is the logical equivalent of stopping a process—stopping it conceptually—which is selective and abstractive. It puts limits to that part of

5. R. Dedekind, "Continuity and Irrational Numbers" *Essays on the Theory of Numbers,* tr. W. W. Beman, (La Salle, Ill.: Open Court Publishing Company, 1901) sec. IV. See also E. V. Huntington, *The Continuum and Other Types of Serial Order* (Cambridge, Mass.: Harvard University Press, sec. ed., 1917; New York: Dover Publications, 1955) chap. 5.

the continuum singled out for attention. But in order to make a cut and have both continuity and discontinuity, *one must start with continuity.*[6] One can then cut it into discrete parts. But one cannot start with discrete parts and jam them or glue them together into a continuity.

If one starts with process and continuity, the mind-body problem, in so far as it is relevant to epistemology, disappears. Cartesian dualism gave rise to the problem because it denied fundamental continuity by having two ultimately separate realities. The dualism furnished an ontological ground for the difference in knowledge between percepts and concepts: the sense-content of perception came from *res extensa,* whereas concepts were the result of the essential activity of *res cogitans.* The difficulty, however, was that the dualism could explain neither the relation between the two sources nor the way in which sense-percepts and concepts worked together to produce knowledge. The ensuing controversy between the empiricists and the rationalists grew out of attempts to resolve the problem of the source of knowledge. Yet it has no resolution within the confines of ontological dualism, for the discontinuity between mind and matter is fundamental to that doctrine. This might be a good reason for giving up the dualism—it produces an unbridgeable gap.

If epistemology starts with continuous process, it does not have a ready-made world and a ready-made mind at hand to furnish percepts and concepts. Rejection of Cartesian dualism does away with the separate sources of percept and concept. There is only one source, and that is the continuity of experienced process. But this does not deny that percepts and concepts can be analytically distinguished. They perform different tasks in gaining and articulating knowledge. There is a difference in the way they operate, but there is no occasion to hypostatize this into a difference of ontological status.

6. I have argued this more fully elsewhere. H. N. Lee, "Are Zeno's Paradoxes Based on a Mistake?" *Mind,* vol. 74 (1965).

The respect in which Plato followed Parmenides' Way of Truth has been pointed out. The epistemological assumption here is that knowledge is the apprehension of Reality, and this assumption ruled Western thought at least until the advent of the evolutionary world view. Under the influence of the evolutionary view, however, knowledge is not to be regarded as the apprehension of Reality. To the contrary, knowledge is an adaptive activity of an organism; it is a progressive adjustment of one part of the flux of process to other parts, and in the reaction the part reacted to becomes environment in relation to the part reacting.[7] A highly sensitive reaction is found only in organisms and is given the honorific title of knowledge only under special conditions. There is, however, no fixed boundary between what reacts and what is environment. Not only are the two relative to each other, but each partakes of the other; the physical organism is both part of what reacts and part of the environment. All parts are continuous with each other and relevant to each other in the flux of process, and all can have aspects or characters in common with others. Thus, knowledge does not indicate a bifurcation either into mind and a realm of Ideas or into mind and an external world. Rather, some parts of the flux react to other parts and often the reaction is acutely sensitive. Reaction at a distance, delayed reaction, and alternative possibilities of reaction ensue, but these adjustments involve new conditions, and chief among the new conditions are responses to stimuli which are not present. The organism reacts to something not actually in its environment, and at this point the organism becomes conscious, for consciousness consists in "seeing" in the present stimulus what is not there, in reacting to stimuli that are not present. The first dawning consciousness is a dim recognition of what has happened before. Reaction to the present stimulus takes place in the light of what *was* there but is *not presently*

7. I have explored these attitudes more fully in "Two Views of the Nature of Knowledge," *Tulane Studies in Philosophy* 18 (1969): 85–91.

there. This reaction is extended to the anticipation of what will be there, and consciousness is enriched.[8]

Reaction to stimuli which are not present can take place only through the mediation of symbols. Some present stimulus or some part of the reaction as it takes place becomes a surrogate for something not present; and when the symbolic process proliferates, reflection and self-consciousness appear. At this point but not before there is mind and knowledge. Repeated and continuing reaction and adjustment require that the environment, now extended by symbolism, be delineated and made definite. Past reaction and anticipation, in so far as they are relevant within the present response, become the *meaning* of the symbol, and concepts arise. By means of concepts, delineation and definition of the enivronment take place. Conceptualization is cognition, and there is knowledge. Concepts are mental not in the sense of being entities entertained by a mind but in the sense in which mind *is* conceptual activity, that is, response to more than what is actually present.

It follows that knowledge is not the mirroring or recording or apprehending of a wholly determinate and rigidly structured state of affairs. There is no returning to the position of Locke and Hume that the materials of knowledge come to the mind in ready-made units and are impressed as upon a *tabula rasa*. Kant's "revolution in philosophy" was well taken even if for the wrong explicit reasons and with the wrong details. The activity of knowing is constitutive in formulating even the materials of knowledge. One can agree with Kant on this point but reject the details of his architectonic, for the details are based on his acceptance of assumptions concerning the nature of mathematics and science that have been

---

8. The distinction between those parts of perception due to present stimuli and those parts due to past experience is not available to phenomenological investigation but is a conceptual distinction intended to be part of an explanatory scheme. *See* Alan Pasch, *Experience and the Analytic* (Chicago: University of Chicago Press, 1958) p. 133.

abandoned,[9] and on his working within the frame of Cartesian dualism: his scheme has a structured mind and a thing-in-itself as variants of *res cogitans* and *res extensa*.

It is true that knowledge arises within consciousness, and consciousness arises within experience, but consciousness and experience are not coextensive: experience is more inclusive than consciousness. Everything of which one is conscious is experienced, but much is experienced of which consciousness takes no note. In the broadest sense of the term, 'experience' refers to every way in which one part of process affects or is affected by other parts. Experience arises from participation in process but not the mind's participation, for there is no mind until consciousness has emerged. Experience is what happens when one part of the flux acts and interacts with other parts. Experience is essentially an act, and so also is the consciousness that arises within experience and the knowledge that arises within consciousness. Consciousness and knowledge are specialized modes of activity of an organism. Knowledge lies in reaction and response and in the possibilities of reaction and response. There is nothing in experience and thus nothing in knowledge to indicate either a rigidly structured reality or a preexistent mind. There is no warrant for assuming a mind either as an empty receptacle or as a supercamera apprehending what is the case in a rigidly structured world.

If a fundamental discontinuity is to be avoided, the conceptual element in knowledge cannot be imported from outside experience and then applied to it in the manner of Santayana's essences or Whitehead's eternal objects. To import the conceptual element from without is only to substitute a more subtle bifurcation for the Cartesian one. The conceptual element in knowledge must itself arise within the continuum of experience, but concepts are discrete, they are grasped by definition, and definition is limitation which puts boundaries. The

9. I have elaborated this point elsewhere. See "The Rigidity of Kant's Categories," *Tulane Studies in Philosophy* 3 (1954): 113–21.

experience within which knowledge arises is continuous and immediate, but knowledge is mediated by concepts which themselves are mediated by symbols, and the concepts and symbols are discrete. Thus, in so far as experience is known, due recognition must be given to both the continuous and the discrete, but the same thing cannot be both continuous and discontinuous at the same time. The cut of Dedekind theory is a way of obtaining discrete parts from a continuum;[10] and if it can be shown specifically how concepts can arise from the continuum of experience, a coherent theory of knowledge can be constructed without bifurcation.

Concepts can be shown to arise from the continuum of experience if process is taken seriously. The flux of process is ceaseless change, interaction; and action implicitly cuts the continuum into episodes, that is, into parts that act and react upon one another. There is no difference in kind, for every part both acts and is acted upon. Action, through symbolism, singles out characteristics in what is presently acted upon that are similar to what was acted upon before. If it did not, action would always be at random and no adaptation or adjustment would take place. An economy of action is demanded. This singling out, or selection, is a rudimentary sort of generalization in the sense that it is not a clear-cut generalization but can develop into one. The selection takes place when the organism responds to a new stimulus in the same or

10. *See Collected Papers of Charles Sanders Peirce,* vols. 1–6 Charles Hartshorne and Paul Weiss, eds. (Cambridge, Mass.: The Belknap Press, 1931–1935); vols. 7–8, Arthur W. Burks, ed. (Cambridge, Mass.: Harvard University Press, 1958), hereinafter cited C.P. with volume number, decimal point, and paragraph number within the volume. Present citation: 6.168. ". . . a continuum . . . contains no definite parts; . . . its parts are created in the act of defining them and the precise definition of them breaks the continuity," Peirce, of course, did not have Huntington's interpretation of the Dedekind-Cantor theory at hand. He did not always agree with Dedekind or Cantor, and often amended his views on continuity, not always for the better.

similar way that it responded to a previous one. The stimulus is different but the response is the same, and the similarity of response sets up a similarity in the stimuli. Thus, what is common to more than one instance of experience is established and an economy of response is achieved. No absolute identity of any characteristics in different stimuli is assumed—only the similarity to which the same sort of response can be made. The response is accomplished by means of a rudimentary symbolization, for some aspect of what is present refers in a dim way to what is not now present but was present before. I shall call this rudimentary and vague setting up of vague similarities and repetitions in the continuum by the economy of response 'proto-generalization'.

No reference to consciousness or to mind has been made in the foregoing account of proto-generalization. Proto-generalization is a specialization of process and is antecedent to consciousness. It is a mode of reaction, of response. Proto-generalization evolves from the continuum of experience, and consciousness evolves from proto-generalization. Both are specializations of the flux of process, but proto-generalization, through symbolism, furnishes the common elements in experience which elicit consciousness and to which consciousness is a further response. Thus, consciousness is the more highly developed of the two. Consciousness becomes reflective and knowledge arises. Knowledge is a further specialization within the flux of process and is not to be conceived on the analogy of receiving or recording or describing an already fully structured state of affairs.

There is nothing given to conscious experience in the sense in which 'the given' has often been used in epistemology. There is nothing presented to consciousness the intuition of which is either knowledge or a sure and unshakable foundation for knowledge. Conscious experience is already mediated by proto-generalization, a mode of activity. It is only through such mediation that consciousness itself arises. Thus, there can be no intuitive *knowledge* because pure intuition, pure immediacy, would be unconscious in the sense of being antecedent to the emergence of consciousness.

Although there is nothing given to consciousness, there is taking; that is, conscious perception involves an act of selecting from unconscious experience those elements mediated by proto-generalization—elements in which there is repetition and similarity. It is this taking that I understand Whitehead to mean by 'prehension'.[11] To be sure, the taking always may be a mis-taking, but at this stage, there would be no criterion of a mis-taking; a mis-taking could be only a taking that did not fit a wider, more comprehensive economy of response. It would be important as the source of error, but its full nature as error would depend on a wider context wherein the taking becomes interpretation of what is acted upon in relation to other takings.

Proto-generalization furnishes the ground for interpreting the presently taken episode of the flux of process in the light of past experience and the anticipation of future experience. This yields perception. Perception is the interpretation of a presently taken episode of the flux by means of proto-generalizations or the more precise concepts that develop from them. There is no conscious perception that does not involve interpretation in the light of at least rudimentary conceptualization and symbolization; that is, that does not involve some reference, be it ever so dim or vague, to what has gone on before. Percepts become clearer and more precise as the involved concepts become clearer and more precise.[12] There probably is no

11. This taking or selection is also the way in which the reaction partly determines the stimulus in a reflex arc. See John Dewey, "The Reflex Arc Concept in Psychology," *The Psychological Review,* vol. 3 (1896). Reprinted with slight changes in Dewey's *Philosophy and Civilization* (New York: Minton, Balch & Co., 1931) under the title "The Unit of Experience."

12. I do not say that percepts become more vivid and compelling as they become clearer and more precise. The determination of such a relation would be a task of experimental psychology.

HUNT LIBRARY
CARNEGIE-MELLON UNIVERSITY

clear-cut perception of persisting physical objects until language is learned, for such perception requires clear-cut conceptualization, and clear-cut conceptualization of this sort is socially inherited through the symbolism of language.

The sense in which the individual (the reacting organism) determines the world in which he lives is as profound as the sense in which the world determines him. The determination is itself an interaction. The world without regard to the acting individual is in flux, it is not fully determinate. In the absence of conceptual interpretation, it is not rigid in its structure. The individual cuts the continuum into discrete parts by means of his purposive acts of adjustment or adaptation. These acts put conceptual limits and boundaries into the flux by establishing similarities and repetitions through the economy of response.[13] Although the flux is not determinate, nevertheless it has character. At the place where it is cut it is just what it is, but the cut is not there apart from proto-generalization. The flux could have been cut anywhere, but if cut elsewhere, its character as realized would have been different. The individual does not create the world in which he lives, but he determines it to the extent of his selections and interpretations, and there is no evidence that it is subject to only one determination.

However, no one invents his own scheme of conceptual interpretation. It is handed down in language, and as a child learns language he learns the broad features of the more or less traditional interpretations of experience—interpretations that have stood the trials of history. Common nouns name concepts, not percepts. Only proper nouns name percepts, and the child's learning of language is not restricted to proper names. To the contrary, he learns common nouns first. It is

13. Stephen C. Pepper, in his Carus lectures, *Concept and Quality* (La Salle, Illinois: Open Court Publishing Co., 1967) takes the purposive act as the "root metaphor" for his whole theory; but the theory is cosmological, not primarily epistemological.

common nouns with their slightly later qualification by adjectives and a very few general verbs that establish for the child the habitual ways of cutting the flux. Hence, simple denotation cannot be the fundamental mode of meaning, for there is no object at which to point that does not involve at least a modicum of interpretation. Meaning begins with the proto-generalization of unreflective action and is influenced and molded very early in a child's life by his social inheritance of language.

It must not be supposed that a human being is first aware of an intuited content of perception which he next, in point of time, subsumes under a concept. To suppose this would be to return straightway to the discarded bifurcation. Perhaps a newborn infant only intuits, but as recurrent reactions are achieved, selective habits of response are set up, and these are the proto-generalizations that become mediating factors for dawning perception. As habits of reacting to stimuli which are not present and to different stimuli in the same way proliferate and give meaning to symbols, fully conscious perception is achieved, and the conditions for the emergence of mind obtain. The adult, having learned a language, lives in a world of ordinary perceptual objects which he directly perceives. What he perceives consists of *intuited data with their identifying interpretations adhering to them.* He perceives in habitual ways.

When an adult begins the pursuit of philosophy, he starts from the commonsense world of perceptual objects (commonsense to him). Santayana pointed out that the only place from which a person can start is where he is.[14] Since he is an adult, the world of perceptual objects is the world in which he lives, at least until he argues himself out of it. This solves the problem of some contemporary epistemologists who complain that there is nowhere to start. Such persons confuse the concrete

14. George Santayana, *Scepticism and Animal Faith* (New York: Charles Scribner's Sons, 1923) chap. 1.

beginning of the philosophic enterprise with the abstract, logical beginning of a deductive, explanatory system. The philosophic enterprise starts from what George Herbert Mead called "the world that is there";[15] while an explanatory system starts from abstract principles which can be obtained only by a critical analysis made by an adult—an analysis not only of what is there in conscious experience but also of logical possibilities.

Some philosophers demand a principle of absolute or indubitable certainty from which to start. The search for such a starting place may or may not have been warranted at Descartes' time, but what has been discovered in the past century about the nature of logic and mathematics robs it of any relevance today and makes it an anachronism. In the concrete case one starts from the perceptual world of events and objects, a world which yields no indubitable certainty. As Mead pointed out, there is nothing in "the world that is there" that cannot be put in doubt. The doubt is resolved by reflective, or consciously theoretic, knowledge.

Perception, perceptual knowledge, and theoretic knowledge will be examined at length in chapters III and IV. All perception does not yield perceptual knowledge, only veridical perception does. For most purposes theoretic knowledge may be contrasted to perceptual knowledge, but the contrast is never absolute and the distinction is not a dichotomy. There is a theoretic thread running through *all* knowledge, and it is to be found in perception even before that perception has been established to be veridical. 'What is theoretic' means 'what is general': it applies to more than one specific instance. The theoretic is the conceptual, the interpretative, the cognitive, and is present to a greater or less degree in all consciousness of objects. Cognition is the reaction to environment through the mediation of concepts. Concepts are meanings, and 'to

15. G. H. Mead, *The Philosophy of the Present,* Arthur B. Murphy, ed. (Chicago: Open Court Publishing Company, 1932) p. 5.

interpret' means to 'endow with meaning.' Highly theoretic cognition, when articulated, becomes a conceptual, logical scheme but such schemes, although they have come a long distance, have evolved from the proto-generalizations of rudimentary responses.

A conceptual scheme is summed up in a set of categories. Categories are the master concepts by means of which all others are organized. Concepts are related to each other in terms of inclusion and exclusion. They are made explicit in definitions, and the definitions are statements of inclusion or exclusion of meanings. Thus, the task of theoretic understanding is to evolve a set of categories which deals reflectively with the world that is there unreflectively. Theoretic knowledge in its highly developed form is the systematic elaboration of conceptual schemes and their application to the manifold of perception. They can be applied because perception itself contains a theoretic component. Generalities can be related to observation of facts through induction. Facts can in principle be perceived, hence can be subsumed under generalities because the perception of fact is based on proto-generalizations. When generalities are made precise, are articulated, and are systematized, they yield logically developed theory, but what is a fact is not independent of theory because of the conceptual element involved in fact itself.

Generality is always hypothetical in import; it is based on selection and symbolization, and its validation lies in its applicability to future situations. Thus, as generality is to some degree involved in all knowledge, for all knowledge is hypothetical in some sense or other. Exactly in what sense each kind of knowledge is hypothetical must be determined. Each kind will be found to be characterized by a particular interplay between percepts and concepts. For example, in perceptual knowledge the conceptual factor is at a minimum and a hypothesis of perceptual knowledge is verified mainly by practical action. The natural sciences, although still bound to perceptual observations, are highly elaborate theoretic structures and the role of induction and hypothesis within them is well known. In those sciences which deal with their subject matters quantitatively, mathematics plays an important part, and the nature of their hypotheses is complicated by the special way in which mathematics is related to experience. History, although its subject matter deals primarily with facts, is in a peculiar position because the facts of the past are not open to observation. This consideration influences the form and the method of verification of historical hypotheses.

The various fields of philosophy are often held to yield knowledge that is not hypothetical. The present study finds no support for such a view other than the yearning of many philosophers for acceptance of their conclusions as certain. There is no warrant for calling these yearnings knowledge. If all knowledge is hypothetical, and if the enterprise of philosophy issues in knowledge, then philosophy too is hypothetical in its own special sense, and dogmatic finality is not attained.

In all of this it is assumed that there is knowledge. No ground for skepticism is to be found in the lack of dogmatic finality. There is meaning in the use of the term 'knowledge' in human affairs, and it is the business of epistemology to find out exactly what that meaning is, how it is systematically elaborated and where it may be legitimately applied. The final aim of epistemology is to achieve an understanding of understanding, and this requires a categorial scheme for the knowledge process itself. Epistemology must issue in a theory of the nature of theoretic knowledge, for there is no knowledge to which theory is either irrelevant or unnecessary.

The following chapters will elaborate the view of the nature of theoretic knowledge summarily sketched in the present chapter. Chapters II through VII will give the essentials of the theory, Chapters VIII through XII will show how it can be applied to specific areas within which it is germane. It is not the intention of the author to develop a theory of induction or a philosophy of science or a philosophy of history in the latter chapters. To attempt such a task would go beyond a theory of the nature of knowledge. Yet such a theory must be applicable to those fields, and the attempt will be made to show that the present theory is so applicable.

No more dogmatic finality is claimed for this theory than it allows to other knowledge, and it allows none to other knowledge. There are more ways than one of cutting the continuum of experience. This theory is offered as an hypothesis concerning the nature of theoretic knowledge and is subject to the same criteria that it finds must be applied to other speculative hypotheses.

CHAPTER II

Intuition

The distinction between percepts and concepts is well taken and defensible, but it would be difficult and perhaps impossible to find an instance of perceptual knowledge free from all concepts or an instance of conceptual knowledge free from all percepts.[1] Concepts seem to depend on percepts, at least in elementary cases, for simple concepts refer to empirical classes composed of perceptible members. The classes themselves, however, are not perceptible. If one could get all the dogs together into one yelping pack, one would not have the class of dogs, for the class subsumes all the dogs that have died and all those yet to be born. Furthermore, the class is not identical with its extension. It is determined not by the perceptible dogs but by what it is to be a dog, and this, the intension of the class, is not perceptible.

Although sense-perception seems to characterize the empirical element in knowledge while concepts characterize the rational element, the questions immediately arise: What is the fundamental meaning of 'empirical'? To what does the term refer? What is the criterion of its application? Both ordinary language and philosophy assume that it is meaningful, but the meaning in ordinary language is vague, a vagueness that

1. I shall use the term 'perception' (and its cognates) throughout to refer only to sense-perception.

often carries over into philosophy. For example, to say that *experience* is the criterion of what is empirical is not precise, for experience may be either conscious or unconscious, and when conscious, may be either loosely or highly organized. The term 'rational', however, refers to order and organization. Thus, if 'empirical' is to be contrasted with 'rational', *conscious* experience cannot be the criterion, for all conscious experience has some degree of organization.

It will help to analyze experience into content and form. This is not to suppose that experience is a stratified affair, having a foundation and a superstructure,[2] for content is not to be found without form be it ever so rudimentary, and form is not to be found without content be it ever so tenuous. They are variables obtained by analyzing concrete experience and can be distinguished because they vary independently of each other. Conscious experience is a function of the two variables, content and form. Content consists of the felt qualities of experience while form consists of relations. Form is the way that the parts of a thing go together no matter what the parts are. Content is what is present in experience at a unique time; at a different time the content is different. Form is independent of temporal location. The content of experience is unique and specific while the form is general and abstract. Since form is general, to deal with it requires symbolization, for that which is general refers to content not actually present. This is the reason that *conscious* experience always involves form, structure. Response to what is not actually present is a condition of consciousness.

To say that empirical knowledge depends on perception is correct but does not furnish the criterion of 'empirical' because perception yields more than what is sheerly empirical. It yields knowledge of facts, and facts have form, have structure. One must abstract the content from the form before one has what

2. *See* G. J. Warnock, *The Philosophy of Perception* (London: Oxford University Press, 1967) p. 1.

is sheerly empirical. Even such a simple observation as 'that is a pig' is an interpretation of the present by reference to past action and future possibilities of action in other instances. Of course the analyst of ordinary language can, upon proper occasion, feel an unshakeable confidence in his observation,[3] and he should, for he is an adult with habits of perception and use of language fully formed and presumably adequate. But it still remains that the analyst perceives according to kinds, and kinds refer to more than what is immediately present.

There is always at least a modicum of interpretation involved in perception. The interpretation, referring to different instances, is general, formal, and conceptual or incipiently conceptual. Being interpretative, perception involves at least an incipient reference to concepts, to form. To get to the sheer content of experience, it is necessary to discard all interpretation and get down to that which is interpreted. The ultimate content is what is there—or equally well, what there is—to be interpreted.[4] This sheer content is the ultimate reference of the term 'empirical'.

I shall call the content of perception (that is, the content furnishing the final reference of 'empirical') the *flux of perceptual intuition,* or the *intuitive flux.* The sheer content of experience is intuited. Experience is participation in process: a part of the flux interacting with other parts. Intuition is *immediate* participation in process: the immediate presence of the interacting parts to each other. 'Experience' is a general term referring to mediated conditions as well as to those immediate. On the other hand, I shall use 'intuition' as a technical term of strict application always and only to immediacy.

3. *See* J. L. Austin, *Sense and Sensibilia* (Oxford: At the Clarendon Press, 1962) pp. 114–15.

4. 'Interpret' at this point in the exposition means no more than 'endow with meaning', and the meaning may be the most rudimentary sort of symbolic reference. That one should be able to formulate the meaning in an articulated manner is not required.

Much even of perceptual experience is mediated by symbols and hence is not intuitive. Sheer content is immediately present, it is intuited, but one is *not* conscious of it *only* as it is intuited.

When I speak of the *flux of process,* I make an ontological assumption, but it is a most general one—simply that something is going on and that it is continuous. The flux is posited to give a context for experience—parts of the flux interact, affect each other, and the interaction is the experience of each part. When I speak of the *intuitive flux,* however, I refer to experience specifically with reference to the part that is undergoing it. The intuitive flux, or the flux of perceptual intuition, is what is going on or what happens to a particular center of activity in the flux of process. Reference to the center of activity is part of the meaning of the term.

In saying that the sheer content of experience is the flux of perceptual intuition, 'perceptual' is emphasized because the content sought is to be found only in the context of perception. This serves to distinguish the immediate presence of content from other things that in other contexts by other persons have been called intuition. The content is called 'flux' because it is ceaseless change. It is temporal, ongoing passage. It is continuous and contains within itself no fixed or rigid distinctions, separations or boundaries; but it is not homogeneous, or a smooth characterless sameness. Being ceaseless change, it is perpetual difference. The intuitive flux is ultimate for empirical knowledge since it yields immediacy and continuity— the *content* of conscious experience. It must be emphasized, however, that there is *no* immediate awareness of content as such. 'Immediate awareness' is a contradiction in terms; as has been pointed out above, awareness involves reference to that which is not present, and thus is mediated.

The intuitive flux is continuous but is subject to being cut into episodes or events. It is undivided passage, and as such is a whole, but not an absolute whole (if that expression has any meaning). The most general meaning of the term 'whole' is what can be divided into parts; and 'parts' means what can constitute a whole.[5] A whole is relative to parts and parts are relative to a whole. A part is a selection from a whole. The flux may be divided into parts but these parts do not exist separately or in distinction. No separations are given in a continuum. For example, the spectrum of hues is a continuum and there is no separation in it between red and orange and yellow; yet it is intelligible and correct to speak of red or orange or yellow. These terms name selections from the continuum, but there are no absolute boundaries between the selected elements. There is no place in the continuum of hues where red stops and orange begins.

Selections arise within the flux because the flux puts no limits to its own process and change. If the continuum is a dead-level sameness, it does not change and is not flux; but if there is no dead-level sameness, there are parts of greater or less activity and sensitivity in it. However, there can be no absolute distinction or separation among them. They are parts in that they are selections from the whole, but there is no whole that cannot have parts. Action and sensitivity are no more than one part affecting and being affected by other parts. A polar distinction appears between what acts and what is acted upon, and the one becomes agent (the center of activity) and the other environment, but agent and environment are continuous with each other. Activity cuts the flux but activity is process and is of the nature of the flux itself. The selections it makes are not imposed from without. To assume that they were would be to posit something not of the continuum, and

5. ". . . it is of the first importance to point out that until a thing is presented as having parts, it cannot be said to be a whole." W. E. Johnson, *Logic* pt. 1 (New York: Dover Publishing Co., 1964) p. 110. It is unnecessary for present purposes to distinguish between special meanings of 'whole'. See Ernest Nagel, *The Structure of Science* (New York and Burlingame: Harcourt, Brace & World, Inc., 1961) pp. 381–83.

would make fundamental discontinuity with its insurmountable bifurcation.

The selections cut from the flux by action, since they are parts of a continuum and are immediate participation in process, are themselves continuous and intuitive. I shall call such cuts *the data of intuition,* or *intuitive data.* No separate data are given, but selections are made and the selections yield intuitive data. Intuitive data are to the flux of perceptual intuition as a particularly observed red or orange or yellow is to the particularly observed spectrum of hues. Intuitive data are parts of experience, being a manner in which parts of the flux affect and are affected by other parts. Experience becomes differentiated in the selection of intuitive data.

Intuitive data are not to be defined by reference to consciousness; rather, consciousness arises within intuitive data— within the activity of selecting and reacting to them.[6] Conscious experience requires more than intuitive data actually present to the center of activity at a given moment. (I shall call the center of activity 'the reacting organism'.) In conscious reaction there is response to stimuli not actually present at the time of the reaction. (I shall call that to which the organism responds 'stimuli'.) Consciousness involves response to repetition and similarity of stimuli; there is no repetition or similarity without reference to what has gone on before and eventually to what can go on again. Something in the present becomes surrogate for what has happened in the past and may happen in the future. Clear-cut past or future as separate times are in the present only symbolically. The necessary condition of consciousness is symbolic reference of intuitive data to past or future occasions. Consciousness arises within experience and is a proper part of experience. Highly complex conditions of sensitivity and irritability, animal organisms, evolve as epi-

6. Compare James G. Taylor, *The Behavioral Basis of Perception* (New Haven: Yale University Press, 1962) who maintains that "all *conscious* experience is a function of learned behavior." (Preface, vii, my italics). Hereinafter cited as BBP.

sodes in the flux, and with them come delayed action, response at a distance, reflective action, choice of alternative action, adjustment to anticipated outcome, and similar responses.[7] All these complications of reaction involve response to stimuli not actually present but present only by symbolization. This use and control of intuitive data is what is called consciousness, an activity too highly specialized to be the source of the more elementary data. Nothing is given to consciousness but something is taken, and that which is taken, the intuitive data, becomes the content of consciousness. Although there is no immediate awareness of content or of anything intuitive by itself, nevertheless, intuitive data as they are component in consciousness when consciousness arises are what is empirical in empirical knowledge.

Experience has been defined as participation in process, and intuition as immediate participation in process. Consciousness arises within experience and is a specialization of experience, having intuitive data as its content. Consciousness is a process of doing something with intuitive data—of reacting to them and assimilating them into a past and a future. Thus, there is no consciousness of intuitive data except as they are assimilated, and the assimilation is an interpretative process, a process wherein the data acquire meaning in a rudimentary sense of the term 'meaning'.

One must exercise care at this point not to confuse *having* experience, even conscious experience, with *explaining* experience. The experience one has is not a concept but it is explained in terms of concepts. When one starts to philosophize, 'experience' (the word) names a commonsense concept for what concretely happens. It is in the sense of what con-

---

7. *See* G. H. Mead's concepts of the conversation of gestures, the vocal gesture, and the significant symbol in his *Mind, Self and Society* (Chicago: University of Chicago Press, 1934) pt. II, sec. 7, 8 and 9. Hereinafter cited as MSS.

cretely happens that one *has* experience, and one does not need to be a philospher to have it; indeed, one must have it before one can be a philosopher. On the other hand, when it is said that experience is participation in the flux, or is the continuity of intuitive data, an abstract concept is being defined as part of an explanatory scheme. If the explanation does what an explanation is supposed to do, however, the concrete experience and the conceptual scheme can be fitted to each other, or as a mathematician would say, can be mapped one upon the other. Thus it is not necessary to exhibit or even to be aware of the intuitive element in experience in pristine purity in order to have experience. It may nevertheless be enlightening in *explaining* experience to analyze experience by means of the concepts of content and interpretation, where the content is defined to be intuitive and the interpretation is defined to be a formal, relational factor.

To take an illustration from the subject matter at hand: one does not need to know or even be aware of the difference between stimuli that are present and those that are not present in order consciously to perceive. To the contrary, the distinction is a conceptual one made only upon analysis of perception and as part of an explanatory scheme. The study of the conditions and processes of perception are subject matter for psychological science.

When intuitive data are referred to classes, as when one says "This is a stone" or "This is water" or "This is shrill" or "This is cold," the data are interpreted in terms of concepts. What it is to be a stone or water or shrill or cold is not intuited. Other episodes in the flux may be stones, water, shrill or cold. These terms symbolize generalities, and generalities are not intuited, they are grasped through mediation of symbols. In observation and perception, intuitive data are interpreted in general terms. Observations and percepts are interpretations of selected data in the infinite variety of the flux. In them intuited data are not only taken, they are taken *to be* something in reference to other data.

The strict and literal sense in which I use the term 'intuition' to mean only 'immediacy' is of such importance in what follows that it may be well to emphasize it at the risk of repetition, and to point out some of the ways in which the word will not be used. I shall *not* use 'intuition' in the vague and metaphorical sense of ordinary speech or in some of the more specialized senses in which it has been used in philosophy. The immediacy of intuition means only that it is not mediated in time or by concepts or by symbols or in any other way. If intuition is not mediated in time, it cannot be discursive, or go through steps; neither can it be general, for generalities refer to more than is immediately present, they go beyond immediacy. If intuition is not mediated by concepts or symbols, it cannot be true or false, for truth and falsity are semantic properties.

In illustration of one of the ways in which I shall *not* use the term 'intuition', let me quote the opening words of Benedetto Croce's *Aesthetic:* "Knowledge has two forms: it is either intuitive knowledge or logical knowledge." The present study holds that there is no intuitive knowledge. There is intuition, yes, but it is not knowledge, it yields the raw materials out of which knowledge is made. Intuition is immediate participation in process. Knowledge is discursive and mediate. If there is any factor in experience that is nondiscursive and immediate, then there is intuition, but it is not to be considered knowledge. Nondiscursive and immediate knowledge, even if there could be any such thing, would be indistiguishable from feeling and action.

In ordinary speech, the feeling of certainty about the truth of some conclusion which one reaches without seeming to go through a train of reasoning to get it is often called intuition. This is a bogus intuition. It is discursive and mediated by symbols even though the steps of the reasoning are suppressed and no attention is given to the symbols as symbols. It yields conclusions that are supposed to be true or false. The sense of immediacy is spurious, it is the kind that means 'all of a sudden'. In so far as this so-called intuition yields satisfactory conclusions that are true it is better called insight. When one displays insight the reasoning processes are vague or implicit, but if the conclusion has been reached as a result of thorough acquaintance or profound thought about a topic, it may be of great cognitive value.

Descartes' doctrine of intuition will be rejected here not only because what he called intuition is better called insight when it is cognitively warranted but also because it is based on Descartes' acceptance of self-evidence and of reason as an innate faculty of a substantial mind. He says in the third of his *Rules For The Direction Of The Mind* that intuition is one of "those mental operations by which we are able, wholly without fear of illusion, to arrive at the knowledge of things." "Intuition is the undoubting conception of an unclouded and attentive mind, and springs from the light of reason alone." If there is no substantial mind outside the flux there can be no such intuition; and I shall argue further on in Chapter VI that the concept of self-evidence is self-contradictory.

Mathematicians sometimes use 'intuition' where they mean 'insight' and sometimes where they mean an imaginative construction or reference to concrete experience.[8] They seldom attempt to define it when they use it in any of these ways, and the usage remains vague. They also have a special use for 'intuitionism' to mean the doctrine that no mathematical statement or theorem has meaning unless its construction can be displayed in a finite number of steps. This use of the word can be left to the mathematicians since it has technical use within their field but not within epistemology.

The mystic vision *is* intuition in the strictest sense of the word if there is a mystic vision. Whether there is or is not is not to say for one who has not had it, but in either case it is not *perceptual* intuition, and it is of no help in explaining theoretic knowledge. It is neither knowledge nor the raw

8. *See* Philipp Frank, *Philosophy of Science* (Englewood Cliffs, N.J.: Prentice-Hall, Inc., 1957) pp. 88–89.

materials out of which knowledge is made. The term 'intuition' in the present work does not connote mysticism. It has been said that philosophy should lead to the mystic vision, but in that case the goal of philosophy is to lose itself. The goal here envisaged is not so self-effacing.[9]

Finally, I shall not use 'intuition' as Santayana does in *Scepticism and Animal Faith*.[10] Santayana's intuition is of essence, and although the essences of his doctrine partake of quality, they are definite, discrete, and universal. Intuition for him is the name of a conscious process which contemplates essences as its objects. In the present study 'intuition' is not used as the name of a conscious process and it does not yield objects. Intuition is immediate participation in the flux, which is indefinite and undefined, is continuous, and is unique. In intuition there is no difference between subject and object. The subject–object distinction is not intuited but is known; it develops out of the intuitive flux as the flux is interpreted in perception. Intuition is that out of which subjects and objects emerge. In perceptual intuition there is only flux with merging parts of which one acts and the other is acted upon, and the action is immediate, continuous, and unique.[11]

It is difficult verbally to denote intuitive data because to say anything about them is more than to intuit them. Even to call them the data of perceptual intuition is more than to intuit them; it is to subsume them as instances under a generalization. To be *aware* of them is more than to intuit them; it is to give them some measure of recognition or identifiability,

9. Bergson uses 'intuition' not only to mean knowledge but a preintellectual, nondistorting type of knowledge that leads to mysticism. This view is also rejected here although Bergson's emphasis on duration and continuity has had manifest influence on the present theory.

10. *See* especially pp. 74, 117, and 128.

11. After examining the different varieties of what has been called intuition, Mario Bunge, in *Intuition and Science* (Englewood Cliffs, N.J.: Prentice-Hall, Inc., 1962) concludes that intuition is not reliable knowledge, at least unless it is carefully qualified. *See* especially p. 120.

and to do so they must be to some degree definite and must refer to more than what they presently are. If one talks about them one interprets them, and although one uses terms that can be defined, one does not and cannot define what is only intuitive.

Language is not constructed in such a way as to allow one to talk about intuitive data without at the same time talking about something else in addition to them. Language is unavoidably permeated by concepts. Common nouns do not denote what is unique, they denote classes. The only way to refer by language to what is unique is to use a demonstrative (usually accompanied by a gesture) such as 'this' or 'that' or to use a proper name. Whenever a locution involving a common noun or a verb is used, a concept is indicated. A language consisting of demonstratives and proper names alone could not be constructed. As Abelard pointed out to the nominalists of the Middle Ages, to make a predication involves the use of universals. Anything said about perceptual intuition requires the use of locutions that indicate some degree of generality, and generalities are not intuited, they require mediation by symbols.

Even if an artificial language composed only of demonstratives and proper names could be constructed, it could not be applied directly to the flux, for the flux is a continuum of passage, that is, it is not composed of a series of discrete particulars which keep their discreteness unchanged over an interval of time. Every event in its full concreteness is unique, and every word in the proposed language would refer only to a specific event in the flux. Hence, no word could be used twice, for the *same* event does not occur twice, and the so-called language would be an unending succession of new words. "If we cannot speak of the same thing twice," Whitehead remarked, "knowledge vanishes taking philosophy with it."[12]

12. A. N. Whitehead, *Adventures of Ideas* (New York: The Macmillan Co., 1933) p. 288.

But there *is* knowledge and there *is* philosophy and one *can* speak of the same thing twice.[13] The reason one can is that one speaks of intuitive data interpreted as instances of kinds.

Most of the words of speech refer not to unique events but to generalities, and generalities have more than one instance. Generality is what is common to more than one event. In its simple manifestations it is a relation of similarity between different events. It depends on abstraction of aspects or characters of the events,[14] and thus, being an abstract relation, is grasped only by the mediation of symbols. This is a conceptual process since it involves meanings. Meaning is the mode of reference between a symbol and what is symbolized, requiring definition, limitation; but there is no indication that only one set of meanings can be applied to the flux, even to the same portion of the flux.

The flux can be grasped only by stopping it not actually but conceptually, and the grasp is interpretation by reference to meanings even when the meanings are not reflectively explicit but are only implicit in action. Grasp of the flux, even enough grasp to allow anything to be said about it or even to allow awareness of it, involves interpretation. Distinctions are analytic and concepts are discrete, but discreteness is not intuited. Language refers to interpretations of the flux. No language refers to the flux as only intuited.

Although it is impossible to say anything about intuitive data except in terms that go beyond intuition, it is necessary nevertheless to fit them into the theoretic structure of knowledge because they are the final reference of the term 'empirical.' Fortunately, and in spite of the famous last words of Witt-

13. "The mind can always intend, and know when it intends, to think of the Same. This sense of sameness is the very keel and backbone of our thinking." William James, *The Principles of Psychology* (New York: Henry Holt & Co., 1890. Reprint, Dover Publications, 1950, 1:459). James' italics omitted.

14. More complex generalities and abstractions will be considered in Chapter VIII.

genstein's *Tractatus*,[15] enough to serve the purpose can be said: one can use circumlocutions that mutually supplement each other; and one can explicitly call to attention that the conceptual elements in what one says are not what one is talking about, but that what one is talking about is that to which the concepts are applied. For example, even to call intuitive data the content of concrete perception is to use the concept 'content' (among others), but I have emphasized that it is not the generality but the specific instances which fall under the generality that are indicated by the term 'intuitive data'. Something can be said about the manifold of intuition by interpreting it in various ways and then pointing out that the manifold is not the interpretations but is what is being interpreted in each case. I have done this in some measure by saying that the intuitive element in perception is that which is interpreted as a stone or water or shrill or cold when instances of them are observed. 'Stone', 'water', 'shrill', 'cold' can be defined but the intuitive element in perception is that which, *as intuitive,* eludes definition; it is what all definition is about.

If it be granted that intuitive data are the content of actual perceptual processes, then generalizations can be made about them and they can be fitted into knowledge. The intuitive data are not generalities, nor are generalities intuited; neither are the intuitive data knowledge, nor is knowledge intuited. The intuitive data are known, but they are not in their own nature knowledge. They are known by being interpreted and by entering into generalizations. Knowledge depends on interpretation, and interpretation is effected through the mediation of concepts and symbolism. Generalizations are made about intuitive data, and thus these data enter into knowledge.

15. Ludwig Wittgenstein, *Tractatus Logico-Philosophicus* New York: Harcourt, Brace & Company, Inc., 1922) 7. "Whereof one cannot speak, thereof one must be silent."

Intuitive data are the ultimate constituents of what is empirical in knowledge.

Ultimacy of this sort, however, is analytic and is reached at the end of a reflective process; it is not to be found in simple awareness. 'Ultimate' means 'as far as one goes', and here it means as far as one goes in analysis. It does not necessarily mean an absolute terminus. Human beings have usually turned out to be wrong when they have supposed that they have reached an absolute terminus of analysis. Intuitive data are the ultimate content of experience in the sense that this is as far as the analysis goes. It may stop here because no one sees how to go any farther. To say, then, that intuitive data are the ultimate content of experience is an analytic statement, for whatever I find to be ultimate content is what I call intuitive.

The concept 'intuitive data' occupies a place in the present conceptual scheme somewhat similar to that occupied in much contemporary epistemology by the concept 'given in experience', but there are important differences. The given in experience is often sought as a reliable starting place for the explanation of knowledge: reliable because it is simple, indubitable, and the mind contributes nothing to it but only passively receives or registers it.[16] In contrast, intuitive data are not here assumed to be simple or indubitable or passively received by a mind. As remarked above, there is no given in experience, there is only a taking, and it is not necessarily a mind that does the taking. A center of activity in the flux is an organism before it is a mind.

It is true that intuitive data are here regarded as the ultimate content of perception, but there is no reason to suppose that what is ultimate is simple. To the contrary, intuitive data are held to be selections from a continuum, and continuity can be cut in indefinitely many ways. There is no evidence that

16. *See* H. H. Price, *Perception* (London: Methuen & Co. Ltd., 1932) repr. 1954, p. 15.

analysis ever reaches anything absolutely simple, that is, not containing parts. The epistemology that starts from atomic propositions or from atomic facts that are known in atomic propositions overlooks the consideration that whatever is a proposition or a fact is structured and has parts, and whatever is structured and has parts is not simple. Thus, such epistemology uses 'atomic' in a Pickwickian sense or else clearly misuses it.

Intuitive data are neither indubitable nor dubitable, neither true nor false, neither certain nor uncertain. Not being propositional, they cannot have propositional characteristics. Of course, propositions can be made about them, and any such proposition may be in error, for the proposition is interpretative, and interpretation, being conceptual and asserting relations based on abstraction, may be in error. Doubt, certainty or uncertainty, and truth or falsehood are reflective and arise with consciousness and mind.

Furthermore, there is no assumption that mind, when it has emerged, passively receives or records anything. Mind is a process, not a substance or an empty receptacle. It is part of the flux and selects its data by acting on other parts of the flux. Mind can intuit the flux because it is immediately present with the flux, being wholly immersed in it and being of it; and intuition has been defined as immediate participation in the flux. Mind delineates and defines its own environment by its action. In selecting its data, it does something with them: it assimilates and interprets them.

Epistemologists have often appealed to the given in experience to supply noninferential premises for inferences and judgments. All knowledge, according to such a view, is divided into inferential and noninferential. This is a false dichotomy. Procedures other than inference are important in knowledge. Three major ones have already been pointed out: selection, interpretation, and analysis. None of these is strictly inference as logic uses the term, and an imprecise or metaphorical use of the term 'inference' will not yield a dichotomy.

It is supposed by those who search for a noninferential foundation for inferential knowledge that such a foundation somehow guarantees the validity and certainty of the inferential conclusions based on it; that the inescapability and indubitability of the noninferential premises pass over into the conclusions if only the rules of inference have been properly carried out. Thus, grounds for the certainty of empirical knowledge have been assured. The search for such assurance is somewhat quixotic, however. If empirical knowledge were worthless unless it were certain, then perhaps the search for some ground of certainty would be reasonable. The natural science of the twentieth century, however, has shown that such an ideal for empirical knowledge is unwarranted. To continue to search for a ground of certainty is to revert to an earlier concept of the nature of empirical knowledge and to rush to the defense of what is no longer there.

The search for a noninferential source for empirical inference has given rise to the distinction between knowledge by acquaintance and knowledge by description. Russell explains knowledge by acquaintance as immediate awareness: "I am *acquainted* with an object . . . when I am directly aware of the object itself." Knowledge by acquaintance "brings the object itself before the mind. We have acquaintance with sense-data, with many universals, and possibly with ourselves, but not with physical objects or other minds. We have *descriptive* knowledge of an object when we know that it is *the* object having some property or properties with which we are acquainted."[17] In short, what one knows by acquaintance is what is present in immediate awareness.

The distinction between knowledge by acquaintance and

17. *See* Bertrand Russell, *Mysticism and Logic.* (Garden City, N.Y.: Doubleday & Co. Inc., Doubleday Anchor Books, n.d.) pp. 202, 223; Italics are Russell's. For a shorter (and more confused) account, see chap. 5 of his *Problems of Philosophy* (New York: Henry Holt & Company, n.d. This is in the Home University Library series).

knowledge by description has a naive appeal to common sense but it will not stand up under criticism. I shall lay aside the present argument that immediate, conscious experience is a contradiction in terms. Russell's distinction as it stands assumes that the world is made up of discrete things which one finds out about much as one who is taking an inventory looks at his shelves and sees what is there. This is knowledge by acquaintance. He also records it so that later he can refer to his list and describe what is there without again coming into its presence. This is knowledge by description.

If the distinction were clear and precise, Russell (or anybody else) would know without hesitation whether or not he had acquaintance with his own mind. All he would have to do would be to "look" and see. He could either "bring the object itself before the mind" or he could not, for there is no technique involved in acquaintance except putting one's self in the presence of that with which one wants to be acquainted. But Russell is not sure about the status of knowledge of his own mind, and the hesitation indicates obscurity in the concept of acquaintance. Russell *is* sure that he does not find other minds when he takes his inventory: he knows other minds only by description. This means that they function in knowledge as logical constructs composed of items of acquaintance. His doctrine asserts that *"Every proposition which we can understand must be composed wholly of constituents with which we are acquainted."*[18] One can understand propositions about other minds, but what are the constituents with which *one mind* is acquainted that constitute *other* minds?

Russell's knowledge by description is an application of his logical theory of definite descriptions, but this theory serves only the logical purpose of showing how a specific individual can be referred to in terms of logical variables. Its epistemo-

---

18. *Op. cit.* Quotation may be found about half-way through "Knowledge by Acquaintance and Knowledge by Description," in his *Mysticism and Logic*. Italics are Russell's.

logical import is dubious, and it has no connection with the problem of acquaintance unless one grants Russell's rather irrelevant position in *Principia Mathematica* that the primitive variables of the logical system must refer to elementary propositions the constituents of which are cases of what he calls knowledge by acquaintance.[19] This interpretation of the logic of *Principia Mathematica* is not widely held by logicians.

The search for a noninferential source for empirical inference has also given rise to the Sense-datum Theory with its proliferation of existents, its *ad hoc* hypotheses to account for dreams and hallucinations, and, in some of its variations, its paradoxical unsensed sensa.[20] Sense-data are posited in order to make possible a direct account of immediate experience. Such an account must be in terms that name existents and that are definite and definable. The sense-datum is taken to be the one indubitable thing in what one takes oneself to perceive. It is that which is directly apprehended, and therefore that about which one cannot be mistaken.

Within the framework of the present conceptual scheme there is and can be no direct account of immediacy. There is immediacy—here called perceptual intuition—and there is immediate experience, but it is unconscious. Until there is mediation there is no consciousness, for consciousness involves reference to what is not immediately present, and such reference is symbolic. Any account of immediacy, then, is indirect and circumlocutory and is expressed in conceptual terms. It is necessarily incomplete and indefinite, and nothing can be

19. Whitehead and Russell, *Principia Mathematica*, sec. ed. (Cambridge: at the University Press, 1925) 1:91. For my adverse criticism of this position, *see* H. N. Lee, *Symbolic Logic* (New York: Random House, 1961; London: Routledge & Kegan Paul, 1962) chap. 22.

20. The Sense-datum Theory is too complex for summarization here. It is not the purpose of the present work to expound different types of epistemology. One of the best sources is Price, *Perception*. Or *see* the summary in R. J. Hirst, *The Problems of Perception* (London: George Allen and Unwin, Ltd., 1959) chap. 2.

inferred from it. Sense-data, being conceptually definable, are discrete whereas the intuitive flux is continuous. This marks the greatest error of the Sense-datum Theory: it holds the ultimate content of experience to be a series of discrete existences. Thus it holds no place for continuity except the vacuous continuity of empty space and time. This is the source of many of the difficulties of the theory, as, for example, those arising from the relativity of sense-data: how long is the duration of any sense-datum; and how many sense-data are involved in a concrete act of perception. (How many speckles has a speckled hen?) If the ultimate content of perception is continuous, and if concrete percepts involve selections from the continuum, these difficulties do not arise.

Occam's razor leaves short shrift for the Sense-datum Theory. Not only does that theory multiply existents unnecessarily, but in doing so is seeking to accomplish an unnecessary task—a task that would have been in harmony with the mid-nineteenth century ideal of the certainty of scientific knowledge, an ideal that has now been given up.[21]

Psychological theories of perception often assume that the content of perception is given in sensation. And yet, after studying the question, Hamlyn concludes, "an explicit distinction between sensation and perception has only rarely been made."[22] Sensation carefully defined in physiological or psychological terms as the conscious response to the stimulation of a sense organ or receptor cannot be used to explain the content of perception without begging the question, for such a sensation is the causal result of an occurrence in a highly structured, external, physical world. There is no point in attempting to distinguish between sensation and perception except by referring to the actual stimulation of receptors. This is part of an external world, knowledge of which is obtained through

21. *See* Alan Pasch, *Experience* . . . , p. 74.
22. D. W. Hamlyn, *Sensation and Perception,* (New York: The Humanities Press, 1961) p. 186.

perception. If intuitive data are identified with sensations, the whole structure of a complex, external world is smuggled in; and if mind or consciousness is emphasized, Cartesian dualism is smuggled in. There may be an external world, and Cartesian dualism may be metaphysically tenable, but smuggling is not a respectable occupation.[23]

If the term 'sensation' is used, it is contrasted with 'dream', 'hallucination', 'illusion', 'sense imagery'. All of these experiences have the same kind of intuitive content, but sensations are assumed uncritically to be veridical in reference to an external world while the other experiences are not. The criteria that distinguish veridical perception will be considered in Chapter III, but they are to be found in judgment, not in intuition. The point to be noted here is that the distinction between the veracity of sensations on the one hand and the lack of veracity of dreams, hallucinations, and imagery on the other is not an intuitive distinction. Anyone who says that he intuits the difference between dreams and so-called veridical experience uses the term 'intuition' in the sense repudiated on page 29. Sometimes the conceptual interpretation involved in dreams, hallucinations, and imagery is slighter than in actual sensations, but if it were completely absent, the experience could not be remembered. Those who hold sensation to be the content or raw material out of which perceptions are made usually are doing no more than giving the name 'sensation' to low-grade, simple perceptions assumed uncritically to be veridical.

I do not have any practical doubt but that in most cases a quite satisfactory distinction can be set up between veridical

23. Until I read Taylor's BBP (see note 6, p. 26), I was of the opinion that 'sensation' was only a source of confusion in epistemology and should be left to the psychologist. But in Taylor's formal derivation of the variable identified as perception, there is no variable identified as sensation. *See* section 3.4, pp. 39–41. He thinks there is no point in talking about sensations. *See* p. 284, p. 293, p. 300. He leaves the term to the philosopher.

and nonveridical perception,[24] but the distinction is known, not intuited. As far as perceptual intuition goes, the intuitive data in dreams, hallucinations, sense imagery, and illusions are on exactly the same level as the intuitive data in veridical perception.

Perhaps the closest that one can come to identifying in consciousness an intuitive datum is to point to the felt quality, that is, the quale, which is a component of all consciousness.[25] The quale is that to which 'crimson' refers when one points to a crimson patch, or 'cold' when he touches a piece of ice (whether the seeing or the touching is judged to be in veridical perception, in a dream or in a hallucination is beside the point). Even to call the intuitive datum 'quale' is not strictly accurate, however, for 'quale' is the name for the generalization of all specific qualia. 'Crimson' or 'cold' may be used to help point out a specific quale, but they too are generalities. It must be emphasized that the intuitive datum, as intuitive, happens only once. Hence, when one says that intuition yields qualia, one means each time a specific and unique instance of a quale. The intuitive datum indicated by 'crimson' or 'cold' is the single case to which one points when one says "there is crimson" or "there is cold" but the statement is not to be understood as making the predication of crimson or cold to an object. Neither is the crimson or the cold an object. If the felt quale of the experience is generalized so that it applies to other experiences or is predicated of an object, it goes beyond intuition.

Even so it must be remembered that it is not specific qualia that are intuited, it is the flux of qualia. The intuitive flux is a flux of temporally changing quality. If one cuts the flux into

24. The excepted cases are those of schizophrenia, further mentioned in Chapter III.

25. It is interesting to note that S. C. Pepper in his Carus lectures takes actuality to be presently felt quality, even though his problem is not primarily epistemological. *Cf. Concept and Quality*, p. 59.

different qualia, one has made selections and has grasped these selections by means of some concept even though it be rudimentary. It is only at this point that one can speak of consciousness. Intuition yields the content of perception but there is no consciousness of content until there is perception, and perception is grasp. Definite selections could not be made without grasp by means of a concept, for the concept is the principle of definition. But if one identifies the flux with discrete qualia, one has compromised the continuum. The ongoingness of the flux is not a mere succession of states but is process, passage. The basis for the consciousness of time is to be found in passage, and passage is continuous. Empty passage is not a datum of perceptual intuition. If there were no qualitative change, there would be no passage. Felt passage is felt change, process.[26]

The use here of the words 'quale' and 'qualia' indicate the indebtedness of the present theory to that of C. I. Lewis in *Mind and the World Order*.[27] Lewis talks in terms of 'the given in experience' whereas I have rejected that expression, but the difference is largely terminological or at most marks a difference in emphasis. I wish to emphasize continuity and selection and to avoid suggesting that there is a mind which merely receives anything. Furthermore, neither continuity nor the selective process is to be defined in terms of mind or consciousness; it is the other way around. Lewis' qualia are com-

26. *Cf.* Whitehead's adverse crticism of Hume's treatment of time as pure succession. *Symbolism, Its Meaning and Effect* (New York: The Macmillan Co., 1927) pp. 34–35.

27. C. I. Lewis, (New York: Charles Scribner's Sons, 1929) hereinafter referred to as MWO. I consider his later work, *Analysis of Knowledge and Valuation* (LaSalle, Ill.: Open Court Publishing Company, 1946), to be an elaboration and application of the epistomological program set forth in MWO, not a rejection or even essential modification of it. The term 'quale', however, is to be found earlier in the writings of Peirce, Dewey, and Mead.

patible with the present theory on these points,[28] but the emphasis on the given tends to obscure the compatibility.

There are two important respects, however, in which the intuitive data in the present theory differ from Lewis' qualia. Lewis calls qualia a sort of universal, although he distinguishes them from universal concepts.[29] By calling them a sort of universal, he is referring to their repeatability in different contexts.[30] Of course they are repeatable, but *this is not part of their nature as intuited*. The repeatability refers beyond the immediacy of the present intuition to other intuitions. Different intuitive data may have aspects in common. 'Common' in this context means that reactions to these data do not distinguish between them in respect to the response that occurs. The reactions are similar although the data in their concrete wholeness are different. The commonness lies not in the data themselves but in the interaction between the data and the response. The repeatability is a function of this commonness and is a rudimentary sort of generalization. All that I am saying is that a quale can be a specific selection from the intuitive flux, and that it can also be generalized into a concept to refer in addition to other specific cases where the reaction is similar. These two meanings of the term should not be confused. It should also be remarked that this is not a strange use of language. I think it is what Lewis means by calling qualia a *sort* of universal and distinguishing this sort from universal concepts. When one explains the content of experience by reference to qualia, one conceptualizes the experience. The concept 'quale' is to some degree general. Hence, qualia *as conceptualized* may be universal. Each experience that is subsumed under the concept is not universal, however, but is unique.

The second respect in which Lewis' qualia differ from intui-

28. MWO, pp. 64–66.
29. MWO, p. 61, 121.
30. MWO, p. 60.

tive data is that the qualia are said to be subjective.[31] Perceptual intuition in its nature as intuition cannot be subjective, for 'subjective' connotes a great deal that goes beyond intuition. The intuitive flux is neither subjective nor objective, or it may be said equally well that it is both. The distinction is not in the flux; rather, knowledge applies it to the flux. All empirical distinctions that knowledge makes stem from the flux, but they are not intuited, they are known. If the intuitive flux is not the ground of all that is objective in experience, then nothing is objective. Hence, it is apt to be misleading to call qualia subjective. The distinction between subjective and objective refers to a world that is to some degree ordered and organized, and such a world is not intuited but is known.

If intuited data were subjective, the ultimate content of experience would be subjective and there would be nowhere from which to get anything objective. Such a position has often and rightly been held to lead to solipsism. I shall lay aside solipsism, however, for I am not a solipsist, and therefore cannot consistently hold that anyone is genuinely a solipsist. If there is another who thinks himself to be a solipsist, I must hold that he is necessarily wrong, for he is another, but solipsism says that there is no other. In the present case there are at least two of us. All this is merely to say that one who is not a solipsist cannot consistently entertain solipsism to be a viable doctrine. Thus, to argue against solipsism is pointless. Intuitive data are the source both of what is objective and what is subjective in experience when the distinction becomes relevant. The distinction, however, is known, it is not intuited.

In spite of the consideration that the grounds of what is objective, when any grounds are needed, are in the flux, it is not strictly accurate to speak of the intuition *of* the flux, for such a manner of speaking, if taken literally, makes the flux objective and intuition subjective. It is more nearly accurate

31. MWO, p. 121.

to say that there *is* intuitive flux. It means that there is flux in which there is immediate participation. An intuitive content can be analyzed and prescinded from all concrete perception, from dreams, from hallucinations, from imagery, from anything that can be talked about in the context of empirical knowledge, but any definition or characterization of it involves conceptual interpretation. If there is no intuition, there is nothing to interpret, and the last words of Wittgenstein's *Tractatus* could not be said.

Intuitive data are not knowledge, they are the raw material of knowledge. They are not a certainty from which knowledge can be inferred. Nothing can be inferred from intuitive data as they are merely intuited. If there is any such thing as pure intuition,[32] only a new-born infant has it and a new-born infant does not know. The data of intuition are in no way conceptual, but knowledge and cognition always involve a conceptual element even though it be only rudimentary. Although the data of intuition are not knowledge, they are not unknowable. They are the content of all empirical knowledge when they are taken up into perception. Thus, in the last analysis, far from being unknowable, they are what all empirical knowledge is about.

---

32. By 'pure intuition' I do not mean Kant's *reine Anschauung,* which in Kant's meaning would be a contradiction in terms within the present context. I mean immediate (unmediated) participation in process *unaccompanied by anything else.*

CHAPTER III

Perception

In pursuing the task of epistemology it is of first-ranking importance to make and keep clearly in mind a distinction between the realm of experience and the realm of discourse. The distinction is not a dichotomy, for discourse is a proper part of experience—a highly specialized part, consisting of symbols, primarily symbols formulative of concepts and relations. Discourse has meaning when applied to experience; hence, it has meaning when applied to itself. The distinction was noted before in Chapter II by emphasizing that having experience must not be confused with explaining experience. The term 'concrete experience' will refer to that portion of experience outside the realm of discourse. Concrete experience is what takes place, what is undergone. 'Concrete' refers to the wholeness of direct experience before anything has been taken from it by abstraction. Concepts, on the other hand, always involve some measure of abstraction and generalization, and discourse is conceptual. Concepts are meanings, and meanings are general, for they apply to more than one instance. Discourse involves relations, and in being formulated, relations are abstracted from a context.

Explanation is conceptual and thus falls within the realm of discourse. Philosophical explanation consists in the construction of a conceptual scheme (I shall alternatively call it a categorial scheme or a logical model) by means of which concrete experience can be ordered and thus understood. Concepts introduce definition and discreteness, therefore clarity, into the flow of experience. They can be built into articulated structures by putting them into logical relations with each other. Logical relations belong to the realm of discourse, hence do not hold directly between items of concrete experience but only between concepts. If the concepts apply to concrete experience, however, it is possible for the whole experience to be fitted within the logical structure and thus indirectly to become articulated, logically ordered, and in this way explained.

The concepts of commonsense discourse will not serve for the construction of a logical model: they are too vague and imprecise. They must be sharpened and refined before they can be built into a consistent system: this requires analysis and critical definition. Thus, a commonsense concept is not explanatory but serves merely to indicate what is to be explained when one undertakes the philosophical enterprise.

In the present conceptual scheme, the commonsense concept 'experience' has been analyzed into *content* and *form* with the purpose of sharpening the meaning so that it may become part of an explanatory scheme. Content has been identified as what happens when episodes in the intuitive flux affect and are affected by each other. The very concept of episodes involves a cutting of the flux, but the cuts do not represent absolute separations or distinctions. The flux is activity which may be analyzed into actor and acted upon, but actor and acted upon are continuous with each other.

The other term of the analysis of the commonsense concept 'experience' is form, order, organization. Form is the way that the parts of content go together without respect to what the parts may be. For example, the ongoingness of process is content. Only the actual, concrete process is ongoing; but regular, measurable, conceptualized *time* is formal, it is an abstracted order of succession. Again, the spreadoutness or contemporaneity of intuitive data is a character of the data, hence content; but geometric space is formal. Even here, however, the ongoingness and the spreadoutness in their actuality are not found separate from each other or separate from changing quality.[1]

The concrete experience with which the philosophical enterprise begins is ordinary perception, but the ordinary, commonsense concept of this experience, 'perception', is too vague to serve a purpose in an explanatory conceptual scheme. It must be refined by analysis and by relating it to other concepts of the scheme. The present chapter endeavors to accomplish this task of clarification. A clear-cut concept, 'perception', must be critically fitted into the whole explanatory scheme.

The *explanation* of knowledge begins with the concept of perceptual intuition, but *knowledge itself* begins with the concrete act of perceiving. The commonsense concept of this act when analyzed into content and form yields results similar to those reached by the analysis of the commonsense concept 'experience', for perception is the basic conscious experience. The content of perception is intuitive data, and the form of perception is the rudimentary generalizations by means of which the data are grasped and assimilated into an accumulating body of experience, that is, the way in which the data are related to other data.

One perceives red, for example, or hard or cold or shrill. Perception grasps them as instances of a kind, and the clearer the perception, the more definite the kind. I am not talking about words such as 'red', 'hard', 'cold', 'shrill', for there are percepts before there are words to symbolize them. I am talk-

1. Alan Pasch, in *Experience* . . . , holds the formal-nonformal distinction to be important but wants to know whether "the distinction arises at some relatively sophisticated stage of experience or whether it is present from the very beginning." (p. 91.) From the present point of view, the question is slightly mis-put. The distinction belongs to discourse: it is a conceptual distinction that *applies* to all conscious experience but is not an aspect of concrete experience.

ing about a unique instance of what is symbolized by each English word, an instance of a recognizable and identifiable qualitative kind. The recognition or identification may be ever so dim and vague, but if there is *nothing* identifiable, there is nothing of which to be aware. Concrete perception is the awareness of intuitive data interpreted as being, at least dimly and vaguely, of a kind. In perception intuitive data are not only taken, they are taken to be something in reference to other data. For example, they may be taken to be like or different from other data.

The taking of intuitive data in perception to refer to other data is low-grade symbolization. Present data refer to data not now present, but there is no occasion to assume that the reference takes place in a preexistent consciousness; it takes place first of all in active response, or behavior. Consciousness itself is a reaction to data not present: present data are taken to be surrogate for data not present. This is low-grade symbolization and establishes a vaguely apprehended common factor in the data; it is a rudimentary act of generalization. In my introduction I have called it 'proto-generalization' to emphasize its rudimentary character and to contrast it to the full-blown generalization of reflective thought.

Proto-generalization is not intuitive, for it involves reference to what is *not* immediately present. Neither is it introduced into the flux as a separate principle from without. It is a mode of action that arises within the flux itself. The flux is continuous change, and as such gives rise to continous difference. This is the ground of its cutting itself into parts, or events, each of which I call an episode. But there is no boundary of which it can be said "Here one episode stops and another begins." Episodes in reacting to each other are not discretely separate from each other. Episodes themselves are activities, and since there is no dead-level sameness, some are more active and sensitive than others. Sensitivity is the degree to which one episode responds to that within which it is immersed, that is, to its environment. But again it must be remembered that there is no absolute boundary between episode and environment. Experience is the result of participation, or being a part of the flux. Hence, those episodes that are more active and sensitive constitute a richer, more varied experience than those that are less active and sensitive.[2]

An episode's experience comprises what that episode *is:* it is merely a portion of the flux acting and being acted upon, responding and being responded to. Its responses are not disconnected from previous responses, and they come to include a reference to previous responses, thus setting up a low-grade symbolism. In the continuity of the flux, past responses are relevant to present responses; thus *ways* of responding are set up. The flux is infinite diversity, but the ways of responding are limited by the selections to which the responses are made. Similarity of response establishes, through selection, similarity in the environmental situation to which the act is a response.[3] Aspects of the present environment are not distinguished from those of a previous one for the purposes of this act. A manageable economy of action sets up a manageable selection of similar aspects in the infinite variety of the flux. These selections are not episodes for they are not durations, or temporal intervals. They are rudimentary abstractions— rudimentary because they are not established reflectively or even consciously but only implicitly in action.

2. In concrete, illustrative terms the stone in the meadow is a relatively inactive episode in the flux; the blade of grass is more active and sensitive; the animal that feeds on the grass is still more so, while the man who domesticates the animal is the most. But these illustrations are hardly appropriate at this stage of development of the conceptual scheme. They will become more appropriate as the scheme develops.

3. J. Piaget points out in *Judgment and Reasoning in the Child* (Paterson, N.J.: Littlefield, Adams & Company, 1959) p. 144, that the awareness of resemblance in objects is "the product . . . of the identity of our reaction to those objects."

There is no assumption here of any absolute identity in different portions of the flux. There could be no evidence in concrete experience for any such identity even if it were assumed, and it is gratuitous to assume it. Similarities are established, but similarity is not identity. Similarities can be established because a center of activity can respond to different intuitive data in the same way; thus, similarity is the result of achieving an economy of response. When no economy of response is achieved, the center of activity is soon dissipated and no knowledge ensues to be explained. Similarities in intuitive data are taken as common factors in the data, but here too it must be noted that 'common' does not connote 'identical'.

When unreflective response establishes common factors in intuitive data, the response is a rudimentary act of generalizing. Generalizing is reacting to what is common to different situations, but the generalization under discussion is rudimentary because the common factors are not explicitly or reflectively noted and they are not critically assessed. They are only implicit in action. It is this rudimentary establishing of common factors in intuitive data which I call 'proto-generalization'. Proto-generalization is response to present intuitive data, but response which is determined in part by previous response to previous data. Something similar has happened before, possibly many times. Previous responses have left traces in the continuity of action and response. Present data implicitly refer, in action, to data not now present, and an act of low-grade symbolization has been performed. This is the first step in all conceptualization. Proto-generalization is a mode of action, but is the ground of the reflective repeatability of common factors in experience.[4] It is not necessarily conscious; rather it is a condition of perceptual consciousness. Proto-generalization is the necessary and sufficient condition

4. For example, qualia are repeatable in the mode of proto-generalization, but not as sheer intuitive data. *See* p. 44.

of the first dawning awareness of that toward which reaction takes place.[5]

The simplest case of actual perception is awareness of intuitive data *as they are interpreted by proto-generalizations.* Proto-generalizations are the interpretative factors in all direct perception. They are a rudimentary conceptual factor in perception. Involving low-grade symbolism, they introduce dim meanings into intuitive data. Percepts must, in order to be percepts, have at least a modicum of meaning. The meaning may be ever so vague, but when critical reflection ensues, it is made precise and definite in an explicit concept. Experimental psychology has long known that all concrete perception contains a reference to past experience and that perception occurs in habitual patterns. This reference to past experience, whether explicit or not, is a type of symbolization and establishes a meaning relation. It introduces a conceptual element into perception; without this element there is no reference to kind and therefore no perception.

Plato saw that to explain perceptual knowledge one must note the conceptual element in it, but he held that the conceptual element could not arise from the flux. Thus, he pointed out in the *Theaetetus* that, on the hypothesis of the flux alone, there can be no knowledge (179c–183c). His only explanation for the *source* of concepts was some sort of intuition. As he saw that there is no conceptual intuition in this world, he held that there must have been a direct envisioning of the Ideas at a previous time when the soul was unencumbered by a body, and the Myth of Recollection was offered to explain the source of concepts. To show how concepts can be applied to the flux, he required the metaphor of "imitation" or "par-

5. As long ago as 1923, C. A. Strong insisted that learned muscular response is an indispensable part of perception. *See A Theory of Knowledge* (New York: the Macmillan Co., 1923) pp. 1–5. He held that the word 'awareness' should not be used for the element of immediate experience in perception. (p. 11.) Strong was not friendly to behaviorism, pp. 77–78.

ticipation." Thus, Plato's epistemology requires an elaborate and detailed cosmological foundation.

Under other historical conditions, Descartes held that the conceptual factor in knowledge came from a substantial mind whose proper object is concepts. In this case, epistemology was based on a metaphysical dualism. Neither Plato's cosmology nor metaphysical dualism is required, however, if the conceptual factor in perception can be shown to arise from the intuitive flux. No metaphysical assumption is necessary beyond the assumption that the flux is a continuum of ever changing quality in which some parts affect and are affected with different degrees of activity and sensitivity by other parts.

Those episodes in the flux that react with a high degree of activity or irritability are the bases for the development of minds. The episodes to which they react are the environment. Mind, then, is a process in the flux. It is a process characterized by ways of reacting in which selections from its environment are taken to be low-grade symbols of previous experience. The resultant proto-generalizations become a factor in the reaction, and simple, direct perception occurs. Fully developed minds require more complex conditions such as the more abstract and clear-cut symbols of language, and the acts of communication dependent upon language, with conscious memory and anticipation; but these conditions can be laid aside here as being not necessary to direct perception.[6]

It must be repeatedly emphasized that the perceiving mind is not first (in point of time) aware of intuitive data which it then deliberately subsumes under a concept. There is no concept empty of content which receives content when applied to intuitive data. A concept depends on a symbol, and an empty concept would require a symbol that does not symbolize. It was pointed out in Chapter II that there is no consciousness of purely intuitive data. Consciousness arises only as the data

---

6. G. H. Mead held that a *self-conscious* mind is a product of social interaction. *See* MSS, pp. 163–73.

are interpreted. The description of a mind that is aware of content without interpretation and of interpretations without content and then puts them together would be strange indeed. Perhaps it would make sense on the dualistic hypothesis where mind is a substantial entity by itself, but it would make no sense on the hypothesis that mind is a process in the flux. Mind is aware and perceives only what it can assimilate, and it assimilates in the light of what has happened before. Both mind and what it perceives are parts of the continuity of the flux.

It is misleading to speak of perception as a *fusion*[7] of intuitive and conceptual factors if the use of this expression reinforces the misunderstanding remarked in the foregoing paragraph to the effect that the mind has separate concepts and separate intuitive data and then melts them together. Intuitive data are not to be confused with the sensations or sense impressions of a dualistic psychology to which mind or consciousness as an agent adds specific acts of objectification and apperception to achieve perception.[8] There is no mind or consciousness to start with to be an agent; and intuitive data are neither attributes of mind nor presented to mind. To the contrary, mind is a complex emergent from perception. There are concrete percepts, which in the critical task of epistemology can be analyzed into intuitive and conceptual aspects. The percept is a concrete whole, and if it is to be described in terms of its analysis, it must be said that perception is awareness of intuitive data *with interpretations adhering to them*. The distinction between the data and the interpretations is analytic and discursive.

The concept of perception as it fits within the present scheme must not be restricted to adult human perception.

7. I take the term from R. J. Hirst, *The Problems of Perception*, p. 244.

8. *See* the discussion of Husserl's theory of perception in Aron Gurwitsch's *The Field of Consciousness* (Pittsburgh: Duquesne University Press, 1964) pp. 266–69.

Newborn infants, both human and animal, soon begin to respond to sounds, light, warmth, tastes.[9] Human infants develop what seem to be acute perceptual responses in their prelanguage period. Animals often display complex activities into the control of which enter both past responses and reference to possible future responses.[10] The explanation of perception must apply equally to simple and to complex cases, and to cases uninfluenced as well as those influenced by language. Language is primarily conceptual, hence the conceptual factor in postlanguage perceptions is more predominant than it is in prelanguage perceptions. For example, the conceptual factor in prelanguage perception is probably limited to proto-generalizations, whereas, after language has been learned, the better defined concepts carried in its symbolism enable one to perceive enduring physical objects with another side and an inside.

There are two covert references to the adult human situation even in the preceding paragraph, however, and they cannot be avoided without tedious and pedantic circumlocution. There "sounds, light, warmth, tastes" were spoken of. First, these terms ordinarily name sensations. Next, they refer to sense departments. Both references must be eliminated from the concept of primary, direct perception as it is fitted within the present conceptual scheme, for both suggest considerations that apply only to the sophisticated world of ordered adult experience.[11]

9. James G. Taylor begins his investigation of visual perception with a newborn infant. BBP, p. 14.

10. *See* G. H. Mead's example of the "conversation of gestures" in a dog fight. MSS, pp. 14, 63.

11. By 'direct perception' I mean the simple cases of perception of quality that seem immediate even though the immediacy is specious. Examples are a blow on the head, a flash of light, a pure tone, the blue I see when I look straight up on a clear day. These are mediated by unconscious proto-generalizations, but all perceptions so mediated are ordinarily taken unreflectively to be immediate, and it is these I am calling 'direct'.

The term 'sensation' is either a commonsense term in which case it is not explanatory, or it is a term of psychological theory, in which case its definition requires the previous definitions of nervous systems, sense-organs, stimuli, and complex physiological and psychological processes. Its use in epistemology has tended to be vague.[12] Sometimes it has indicated what in the present study has been called intuitive data, but with the false assumption that they are "in consciousness" in their purely intuitive nature. Sometimes it has been used to indicate simple, direct percepts such as a patch of color or a tone or a pain. Sometimes it has been used to indicate the conscious response to the stimulation of a sense-organ. Ryle thinks that the ordinary usages of 'sensation' refer either to feelings of pain or discomfort or else to "reporting something found out by tactual or kinaesthetic observation."[13] H. M. Chapman is quite sure that there are no such things as sensations "in the traditional sense of modern epistemology," and that the assumption that there are has led modern philosophy astray.[14] I suppose that there are such things as sensations in the commonsense usage; that is, what the term refers to can be roughly identified as an item of ordinary experience. Nevertheless, the concept refined for technical use in epistemology is quite superfluous. It is only a source of confusion and ambiguity and should be abandoned.[15]

So far as the sense departments, sight, hearing, taste, smell, and various kinds of touch go, perceptions do not come sorted

12. In *The Philosophy of Symbolic Forms* (New Haven: Yale University Press, 1957) vol. 3, p. 32, Ernst Cassirer calls an isolated sensation "a mere abstraction."

13. Gilbert Ryle, *The Concept of Mind* (New York: Barnes & Noble, 1949) p. 241.

14. H. M. Chapman, *Sensation and Phenomenology* (Bloomington: Indiana University Press, 1966) pp. vii, 154.

15. Note Merleau-Ponty's long recital of the difficulties engendered by the psychological theory of sensations. *Phenomenology of Perception* (London: Routledge & Kegan Paul, 1962) chap. 1.

out except to a developed mind with formed habits (including language habits). Only as the results of experience accumulate does the sorting-out process begin. Without the concept of sense-organs there can be no separate sense departments. They are part of an articulated external world, but there is no articulated external world in the present conceptual scheme until veridical has been distinguished from nonveridical perception.

There is no distinction between subject and object in the flux of process, but when perception emerges the distinction emerges with it. The sensitivity that begins to perceive, that begins to interpret intuitive data in the light of proto-generalizations, is a rudimentary mind, and what it perceives is environment. The one is subject, the other is object. But mind is a process, it is neither a "thing" nor a "place." It is a process reacting to other processes, and there is no sharp dividing line between them. Whatever is subjective may be, under other conditions, objective, and vice-versa. It is most difficult to apply the definitional distinction between subject and object to concrete experience in such a way as to draw a sharp line of division that applies in every case. It is also unnecessary to draw such a line, for the distinction is a relative one when applied to the continuity of the intuitive flux. Between subject and object there is only a difference of degree of acting and being acted upon, but with the emergence of consciousness and concepts the action becomes cognitive, and there is a distinction between subject and object.

The distinction between subject and object is primarily epistemological, not ontological. It is coextensive with perception but has no application outside the context of consciousness. Metaphysical dualism in the seventeenth and eighteenth centuries, by a mental sleight-of-hand, passed from the epistemological distinction to the ontological one. The budding natural science of the period needed to separate the fields in which exact measurement could be applied from those in which it could not. The primary qualities could be measured and were clearly objective in the perceptual relation, hence were referred to an external substance, matter, defined in terms of extension and mass. Secondary qualities, on the other hand, could not at that time be measured, and science got rid of them by holding them to be subjective in the perceptual relation. They were referred to a different substance, mind, defined in terms of consciousness. The distinction between what could and what could not be measured was made absolute and the metaphysical dualism was accepted because it filled a methodological need.

The legitimate epistemological distinction between subjective and objective has been greatly obfuscated recently by philosophers who have called that which is subjective 'private' and that which is objective 'public'. This is a bad metaphor based on a most extraordinary use of ordinary language. In ordinary usage, 'private' means 'available to inspection or use only to the owner or whomever he designates'; and 'public' means 'available to inspection or use by anyone'. The view under discussion holds that whatever is subjective is necessarily private because it is open to inspection only to the mind that "has" it. If an individual mind is a separate entity which "has" conscious experience, then it is substantial. This substantial mind takes the theory back to metaphysical dualism and the result is that not only are some experiences private, all are private. The *objects* of experience may be public, but now the difficulty is to get from the experience to the objects, which in being *substantially* different from experience are independent of it and cannot be established on the basis of experience alone. The spectre of solipsism raises its ugly head.

Difficulties such as these are gratuitous and will be laid aside here not only because they lead to solipsism but because experience is here defined as a process, and mind as a refinement within that process. Experience does not take place within a mind; rather, mind arises within experience. Mind is subject, but experience is not subjective. The materials of knowledge are to be found in experience, and in this sense knowledge begins with experience, but no one except a highly sophisticated philosopher supposes that it begins with what is subjective.[16] The philosopher who assumes that knowledge begins with what is subjective has stewed too long in his own juice.

The world of experience is not a private or an internal or a subjective world. To suppose that it is, is to suppose that all experience is conscious by definition. But if experience is wider than consciousness, the problem is not how an internal or private world somehow gets external or public. Rather, the pressing question is: how does the world of experience, which is the world of reaction and interaction, give rise to consciousness?

What those who use the terms 'private' and 'public' instead of 'subjective' and 'objective' seem to be trying to get at is communicability. That which is private in experience is uncommunicated but need not be. If I keep my thoughts to myself, they are uncommunicated though not necessarily incommunicable, but as long as I keep them to myself, they are private. They are private because I keep them to myself, not because they are incommunicable. There is no point in calling anything private unless under other conditions it can be public.[17] Communication is possible because there are common elements in knowledge. It not irrelevant that 'communication' and 'common' are words of related etymology. That which is communicable is that which is formulated in concepts; concepts are generalizations, and generalizations refer to what is common. That which is common is found in different instances, and generalization refers to what is common to different instances.[18]

16. For illustrative detail, *see* J. Piaget, *The Child's Conception of The World* (Paterson, N.J.: Littlefield, Adams & Co., 1960) pp. 124–31.

17. *See* L. Wittgenstein, *Philosophical Investigations* (Oxford: Blackwell, 1958) 398. *See also* Philip P. Hallie, "The Privacy of Experience," *Journal of Philosophy* 58, (1961): 337–46.

18. In order to avoid misunderstanding, it may be well to point out that by *common* I do not mean *ordinary;* and by *general* (or *generally*) I do not mean *usual* (or *usually*). When I mean *ordinary* or *usual*, I shall say *ordinary* or *usual*.

No perceptual experience is inherently incommunicable. Perception depends on the grasp of common factors in intuitive data. In order to communicate about a percept, an explicit concept must be formulated. The concept may refer to relatively simple common factors such as red or cold or hard or shrill; or it may refer to more complex constellations of common factors such as ship or shoe or sealing-wax. But if nothing were common or repeatable, there would not only be no communicability, there would be no perception. It must be remembered, however, that what is common in perception does not indicate any absolute identity, but is the result of proto-generalization. One is aware of intuitive data only as they are content of perception, and one can communicate only in so far as common factors are established and recognized in perception. Common factors are results of selective reactions to intuitive data, and no selections exhaust the concreteness of perception. Other responses and other selections can be made, but even innumerable responses and selections will not exhaust a continuum. There is always something left over, but what is left over is what is not rendered by a concept. Perhaps this is what the confused term 'private in experience' tries to get at. But it is not ineluctably incommunicable. What is left over at one time may be formulated and communicated under other conditions, but then something else is left over.

Concepts are meanings and meanings are symbolic reference. The simplest sort of meaning is the proto-generalization in which present intuitive data become low-grade symbols of rough similarities in response. Intuitive data are assimilated into an implicit schema of action[19] and in the assimilation, consciousness and perception arise. More complex meanings require explicit definition in terms of critically assessed generalizations, but in any case consciousness depends on some

19. Note how this principle can be illustrated in genetic psychology. *See* J. Piaget, *The Child's Conception of Physical Causality* (Paterson, N.J.: Littlefield, Adams & Co., 1960) pp. 282–84.

degree of structuring or organizing experience. Whether one uses the word 'concept' or 'meaning' or 'generalization' to denote the organizing principle in any given context depends on where one wants the emphasis to lie: with 'concept' it lies on cognitive grasp, with 'meaning' it lies on symbolic reference; with 'generalization' it lies on how the reference is related to concrete experience. All perception requires some degree of meaning even if it is only the meaning embodied in the symbolic reference to ways of reacting which I have called 'proto-generalization'.

A concept is not a proposition or a judgment although it may be defined or explicated in propositional form. By 'proposition' I mean what can be proposed for assertion or denial. A proposition can be entertained without making the assertion or denial.[20] A judgment makes the assertion or denial, and propositions are usually expressed in judgments. A judgment attributes truth or falsity to a proposition. Concepts are necessary to propositions and propositions are necessary to judgments, but judgments are not necessary to propositions nor are propositions necessary to concepts. Hence, although perception involves concepts, it does not necessarily involve either propositions or judgments, and the perceptual interpretation of intuitive data is not to be understood as a discursive or inferential act. Perception falls within the realm of concrete experience, not the realm of discourse.

Perception has specious immediacy in point of time. Not being discursive, it does not run through mediating factors of which we are conscious.[21] It is the taking of intuitive data to be something identifiable as a kind. This taking is interpretation because it endows the data with meaning. It is an act of direct and simple awareness, not an act of inference or deliberate choice between possible classifications under which to

20. See C. I. Lewis, An Analysis . . . , p. 49.

21. When discussing the apparent immediacy of direct perception, Taylor says "All that immediacy means, then, is that the mediating processes are not conscious events." BBP, p. 351.

subsume intuitive data of which one was previously aware. If doubt or challenge arises, one *does* deliberately classify, but what one classifies in this case is intuitive data *already interpreted* in perception. Deliberate classification or predication or relation or inference is not a necessary condition of perceiving. Any one of these acts requires judgments, and the judgments supervene on perception.

In inference there is always ground and consequent. In simple acts of perceiving there is no awareness of a difference or relation between ground and consequent. Perceiving is an act consciously performed, and that of which one is not conscious is not perceived, although the focus of awareness, that is, attention, is not equally distributed in all parts of the field of perception. One sees a flash or hears a click or feels a blow, and in these perceptions there is no movement from ground to consequent. To suppose that there is, is to revert to the view that one is first aware of pure intuitive data to which one then applies a concept that was empty before application.

To say, as many Idealists are wont to say, that the interpretation in perception is unconscious inference is to use the word 'inference' in a loose way that comes from their loose and imprecise use of 'logic'. Although there is no actual movement from a recognized ground to a recognized consequent, the Idealist holds that he may supply a ground and a consequent, and he prefers his rational reconstruction to what the evidence indicates. His assumption that Reality is logical turns the trick for him and perception is inference even if it does not appear to be. He confuses the percept with the judgment that supervenes on it when it is taken to be veridical. Such confusion is the result of too exclusive a concern with adult human perception. Not all perception is of this degree of complexity. Give the old horse the reins and he will find his way home without help.

Although perception is not inference or any sort of logical or discursive process, *veridical* perception is a different story. Veridical cannot be distinguished from nonveridical perception except by logic and inference. Direct perception does not make the distinction until after new complex, cognitive habits of response have given rise to new proto-generalizations, and even then, what is habitually perceived as veridical is often in error. The error can itself be discovered only logically. The first step in distinguishing between veridical and nonveridical perception consists in formulating the percept in a proposition. Then it can be related to other percepts formulated in other propositions. For example, a child about four years old sees a streetcar on the street in front of his home. He may begin to be puzzled by having seen a streetcar on Audubon Street whereas he sees under other conditions that there can be none, for he sees no tracks or trolley wires. He vaguely apprehends an inconsistency between 'that there is a streetcar on Audubon Street' and 'that there are no tracks or trolley wires there'. Within a year or so, with the help of adults, each proposition is placed within a context in his total experience such that he knows what it means to say that he dreamed he saw a streetcar.

I do not say that the child states explicit verbal propositions and recognizes explicit contradictions. No one but a philosopher or a psychologist does so, but the distinction between veridical and nonveridical perception must be made and applied with some semblance of consistency before it can become a problem for the philosopher or psychologist. Before the distinction can be made, logical processes must develop, and before it can be established on a firm theoretical basis, they must become explicit and articulate.

By the time a child is about five years old, he is roughly successful in practice in categorizing some of his percepts as dreams and paying little attention to them in the course of his practical behavior. It usually takes somewhat longer successfully to categorize his "day dreams," that is, his imaginative percepts; but by the time that adulthood is reached he has various categorial wastebaskets labelled 'dream', 'hallucination', 'illusion', 'fancy' into which he discards those percepts which he cannot fit into his practical experience. Of course, the discarding is not beyond the possibility of error, and one sometimes finds it desirable to retrieve what one has discarded. If one is sane and well-adjusted, one uses the wastebaskets freely and is not bothered by what one discards. This is part of what is meant by calling a person sane and well-adjusted. Those persons who are not successful in using their wastebaskets—that is, not successful from the point of view of the large majority of those in their social environment—are apt to be called schizophrenic. There is little epistemological justification for the ordinary attitude toward some types of schizophrenia except from the more inclusive point of view of the socially accepted categories. The socially accepted categories cannot be disregarded however, since sociality is essential to the development of language and of mind.[22]

The critical basis of the distinction between veridical and nonveridical perception is not to be found in the circumstance that the nonveridical variety (especially dreams) cannot be authenticated by the testimony of other persons. If this were the criterion, the hunter who, when alone, shot at and missed the deer or the fisherman from whom the big one got away could have had no veridical percepts of the deer or the fish. Perhaps his absent companions did not believe that he did, especially since he is a known liar, but what if he did see a deer or hook a fish? The testimony of other persons is irrelevant except in so far as it is a part of the larger experience into which the percept must fit in order to be socially accepted as veridical.

It may be suggested that the criterion of the difference between veridical and nonveridical perception is that the object of the veridical is real in the external world whereas there is

22. *See* Mead, MSS, pt. 2.

no such reality to be the object in a dream or hallucination.[23] Such a suggestion is not well made, for there is no knowledge of what constitutes the external world until veridical perception has been established and its object identified at least in action if not in logical detail. The criterion seems to operate in the way opposite to that suggested: one of the most compelling reasons for believing in the external world is that a clear-cut category of veridical perception can be established both in action and theoretically.

The recognition of perceptual error illustrates that the distinction between veridical and nonveridical perception involves judgments. One may see a man in a dim light but on approaching closer or in a clearer light what one took to be a man turns out to be a bush. A traveler in one of the Western states may see a small lake in the distance, but be told by someone acquainted with the region that it is a level field of blue camas flowers. When there is no doubt or question and no challenge, the man or the lake is what is perceived. The perceptions are part of what Mead called "the world that is there."[24] They are there unreflectively, but anything in "the world that is there" may be put in doubt, and when it is, reflection is called for and the judgment resolves the doubt. As soon as there is any question of the man or the lake, they are not what is perceived but what is proposed as a reflective identification of what is now perceived—a dark spot or a blue patch. The direct perception is what is not questioned at the time, although under other circumstances it may be questioned, and then what is perceived is something else. Each percept bears its own identification on its own face even

23. *See* the analysis of the argument about "there being no object" of a hallucination in Dallas Willard, "A Crucial Error in Epistemology," *Mind*, 76, No. 304 (Oct. 1967): 517.

24. G. H. Mead, *The Philosophy of the Act* (Chicago: The University of Chicago Press, 1938), ed. by Charles W. Morris with the help of John M. Brewster, Albert M. Dunham, and David L. Miller, p. 64, p. 96.

though it may wear a false face. The traveler may perceive a lake in the distance[25] although later and under other conditions he may perceive something else such as a blue patch, and judge his first perception to have been in error. Within the ordered whole of his experience, lakes do not suddenly change into fields of dry-land flowers. To a child of four, however, there is nothing strange or incoherent in lakes changing into fields of flowers. He does not genuinely judge (that is, except in adult language the use of which in this context he does not clearly understand) the perception of a lake to have been in error.

Perception makes a naive knowledge-claim, naive because it is uncriticised and unassessed. When one acts consciously, one does so on the implicit assumption that perception yields knowledge, but the assumption can be recognized and investigated only reflectively. Reflection gives rise to judgment which deals with percepts theoretically, that is, by relating them to concepts of a degree of generality higher than the proto-generalizations of the direct act of perceiving. It is only by so doing that veridical percepts—those whose knowledge claim is warranted—can be distinguished from those not veridical.

Perceptual knowledge, then, goes beyond direct perception to veridical perception. Veridical perception yields knowledge of fact, and knowledge of fact is not theoretic in the ordinary sense of 'theoretic'. Nevertheless, knowledge of fact depends for its content ultimately on direct perception. Even if ordinary language does not acknowledge it, there is a theoretic thread woven into all direct perception: it is the proto-generalization, the interpretative factor in all direct perception. The theoretic factor is at a minimum, but it is there, and affords the continuity running through direct perception, perceptual knowledge and more highly generalized theoretic

25. Other proto-generalizations, such as 'seeing perspective', go into the perception (not the judgment) of distance.

knowledge. The difference between perceptual and highly theoretic knowledge is not an absolute difference.

No attempt has been made in the present chapter to present a complete theory of perception. Such a theory would in part be psychological and would have to draw heavily on natural science, the concept of which has yet to be placed within the present conceptual scheme. The purpose of this chapter has been to formulate a concept of perception belonging to a categorial scheme of epistemology—a scheme that applies to evolutionary as well as to static conditions, to simple as well as to complex situations, and to infant or even animal as well as to adult situations. The concept is primarily analytic, but one that provides for genetic and evolutionary applications.

CHAPTER IV

Fact

I walk past my neighbor's garden where a red, ripe tomato is hanging on a vine. I see the tomato. I see the vine and the garden. I do not see colored patches which then, with a discursive movement of thought either explicit or implicit, I take to be a tomato, a vine and a garden. My perceptions are of the tomato, the vine and the garden. I am familiar with these sorts of things, and on this occasion, not being engaged in philosophical reflection, I am directly aware of them. If I were suddenly asked what colored patches were present to me, it would require a discursive movement of thought to identify them.

Some time later, I meet my neighbor and say: "You have a fine tomato in your garden." He is a sense-datum philosopher, and answers "I wondered if I could fool you. You saw a red, round patch which you took to be a tomato. Actually, it is a skillfully wrought piece of wax which I hung on the vine to find out whether you would take it to be a tomato." We go back to look and sure enough, now there is a colored shape which I take to be a piece of wax hanging on the vine. (I probably still see the vine, however, since my perception of it has not been brought into question.)

My perception of a tomato was in error, but so was my neighbor's conclusion as to what I saw. When I first walked past, I saw a tomato. I did not see a red, round patch which I

69

took to be a tomato. But there was no tomato there, so how could I see one?[1] Upon returning with the knowledge that there was no tomato but only a piece of wax, I would find it difficult to see a tomato again, but perhaps not impossible. If I continued to see a tomato in the face of knowledge that there was no tomato, the percept could be classified as illusory, but it was not an illusion that I saw a tomato when I first walked by. It was a mistake, and I often find myself and others making perceptual mistakes. The error involved a misinterpretation of intuitive data, but the interpretation was direct and not reflective until challenged. The interpretative factors were proto-generalizations that were misapplied, but misapplication here means only the application of proto-generalizations that are incongruous or inconsistent with a larger context of reactions and responses to intuitive data of the same kind. Such a context goes far beyond present intuitive data, hence, misapplications can be discovered only in reflective judgment occasioned by questioning or challenging the perception.

In attempting to solve the problem posed by my illustration, I note that the language in which I stated it is a veritable nest of equivocation. 'Tomato' sometimes referred to a percept and sometimes to a physical object in an external world. The same is true of 'a piece of wax'. 'Red, round patch' usually referred to a percept, or perhaps to a sensation, though if the latter, it is not clear whether in the commonsense or the psychological meaning. Since my neighbor is a philosopher, I suspect a flavor of the psychological meaning. At any rate, the red, round patch was placed in a physical context, for we

---

1. This question lies at the heart of the "argument from illusion," so appealing to the sense-datum theorists. The classical treatment is to be found in H. H. Price, *Perception,* chap. 2. A shorter version may be found in A. J. Ayer, *Foundations of Empirical Knowledge* (London: Macmillan and Company, 1940) pp. 5–11. Or *see* the summary in D. W. Hamlyn, *Sensation and Perception,* pp. 175–76.

walked back to look at it, and the walking and looking were physical events in an external world.

The word 'see' in the illustration was used usually with the meaning 'perceive', or more specifically 'visually perceive'; but when my neighbor first said that I saw a red, round patch, he probably meant, at least obscurely, 'sensed'; at any rate, he was asserting his doctrine that sense-data are the raw materials out of which are made the percepts of physical objects such as tomatoes. When I went back to look, I perceived a red, round patch: it had been called to my attention; but I saw that it was a piece of wax in the sense of 'judged'. When the tomato (physical object) was brought into question, I saw (judged) that the proposition that it was a piece of wax was correct. This was a reflective act, and I then perceived a piece of wax.

The illustration, threadbare as it is, points out how propositions and judgments supervene on percepts when the meaning or interpretative element in perception is brought into question. Strictly speaking, only propositions or judgments can be true or false, and when one calls a percept erroneous, it means that the supervening judgment asserting the interpretative element in the percept is false. Literally, the percept by itself is neither true nor false. The interpretative element is a part of it, and it can be called into question only in relation to other percepts. When it is so challenged, it is asserted in a judgment that may be false. When I speak of errors of perception, this is what I mean. I think that it is reasonable to hold that it is what other persons mean too when they make their meaning critically explicit.

I unreflectively perceived a tomato in the illustration but there was no physical object tomato present in an external world at that time and place. On reflection, I judged that the physical object present was a piece of wax. The judgment supervened on the percept, and in the light of the judgment, the percept changed. As was pointed out in the previous chapter, a percept refers to more than what is intuitively present at the time of the perception. The accretion is conceptual and therefore might be expected to be influenced or changed when judgments, supervening on perception, supply new or different interpretative concepts. My percept of what was hanging on the vine was changed by a judgment about a piece of wax.

I originally perceived the tomato as roughly spherical, as having a back side and an inside, and the inside was succulent. A psychologist would tell me that these characteristics were not sensed since there were no physical stimuli for them.[2] It requires no psychological investigation to show that no one ever visually senses the other side of any physical object, however, for the other side is, by definition, the side that one is not looking at. The piece of wax had another side and an inside, but the inside was not succulent. This is an important difference between a piece of wax and a tomato no matter whether each is considered as a percept or as a physical object. If one is familiar enough with a physical object, those characteristics essential to it but not present in sensation (that is, for which the psychologist can find no physical stimulus) are supplied in perception by imagery. But there is no intuitive difference between sensation and sense imagery: the difference has to be learned. Both are present and an account of their difference by reference to the mode of their excitation lies within an elaborate theory of an external world and the place of mind in it. No such theory can be made explicit without establishing or assuming the distinction between veridical and nonveridical perception.

When one talks about stimuli for sensation and about physical objects, one is assuming that there is an external world and that it is made up of facts (such as that there is a tomato one can pick and eat or a piece of wax one cannot).

---

2. If Taylor is anywhere near correct (see page 41, note 23), this sentence is superfluous, since he holds that the physical stimulus is *never* sufficient to account for perception. Drives and conditioning are necessary conditions. *See* BBP, p. 41, (3.4.20), (3.4.28), (3.4.29). *See also* pp. 247, 262, and 268.

The evidence for such a world and for the facts that it contains is to be found in perception, but first veridical must be distinguished from nonveridical perception. The act of perceiving (without respect to its veracity) makes an implicit knowledge-claim which posits a fact as its object,[3] but when perceptual error is acknowledged the claim is explicity recognized and rejected. What purports to be perception of fact is rejected because the fact is *judged* to be not there. When percepts are in error, they are *judged* to be in error because the purported fact is not compatible with the knowledge-claims of other percepts which are judged to be more reliable in their claims. But the knowledge-claim made by any percept stands until something calls it into question. If the claim is brought into question, either directly or indirectly, it must be established, and it is established or disestablished in reflective judgments that supervene on perception.

A knowledge-claim is established or disestablished on the basis of the logical use of evidence. In critical knowledge of fact there are both percepts and judgments supervening on the percepts. Thus, there are two kinds of evidence for the knowledge of fact—perceptual and logical. Logical evidence establishes or disestablishes the perceptual evidence by fitting it to a larger theoretic structure wherein the relations between this perceived fact and other facts and generalizations are cognitively, that is, conceptually examined. A further study of evidence will be the topic of Chapter VI after logic has been considered in Chapter V.

Firmly established language habits prohibit the use of the term 'knowledge' for something incorrect or untrue. It sounds strange to speak of knowledge of a tomato when there is no tomato. Nevertheless, one cannot call all knowledge fallible

3. This is the "intentionality" of perception, of which phenomenologists make so much, but sometimes they forget that the intentionality in dreams and delusions is the same as that in veridical perception, so intentionality does not help distinguish veridical from nonveridical perception.

and at the same time pick some instance of knowledge and say "This *cannot* be false." To avoid the language difficulty involved it is better to talk initially of knowledge-claims. There is purported knowledge and the purport stands until it is reflectively questioned or put in doubt. The percept is what is simply and directly present in awareness, and as such it is the way things are taken to be unless or until some reason arises for taking them otherwise. If there is any such reason, it arises in the context of judgment, and the claim must be established in the context of judgment: If the claim is disestablished, it is dropped and one no longer speaks of knowledge.[4] In direct perception, the claim is not separately or discursively made. There is no occasion for its establishment or disestablishment in judgment until it is relevantly brought into question. This is what I take to be the meaning of Mead's doctrine that all knowledge is engendered by a problem.[5]

If I see a dark shape in a fog, I may wonder whether it is a bush or a man. I may judge it to be a man. In this case I have not perceived a man. I have perceived a dark patch which I tentatively subsume under the concept 'man'. If the fog thins or I come closer, I may find that my tentative classification was correct: I perceive a man. The percept in this case is veridical. There has been doubt, the doubt has been resolved by evidence and reflective concepts this time have entered into the interpretation of intuitive data. In the first case, when I perceived a dark patch, intuitive data were identified only on the interpretation afforded by proto-generalization, and the result was unreflective perception, neither veridical nor nonveridical. In the second case, when I perceived a man, richer and more detailed intuitive data were interpreted by proto-generalizations that referred to a greater accumulation of experience, but

4. As Gilbert Ryle says, 'know' is a "got it" verb, a verb of achievement. *The Concept of Mind,* p. 152.
5. G. H. Mead, *The Philosophy of the Act,* Essay II, "The Limits of the Problematic," pp. 26–44.

that was not all. The doubt concerning the further identification of the dark patch brought reflective concepts to bear on
the interpretation of the data. I looked for evidence and my
reflective concept of what it is to be a man was applied to the
problem. The reflective concept was not irrelevant to my subsequent perception. The perception of the man was formed
with reflective tools and was veridical. It was a fact that a
man was there.

A fact is the object of veridical perception. Perceptual
knowledge is knowledge of fact. A fact is an episode in the
flux with definite limits in time and space; therefore, a fact is
whatever has a locus in time and space, but time and space
are not new principles introduced in addition to the intuitive
flux. The flux does not occur within separately given time and
space. The concepts of time and space are generalizations
obtained from the flux. There is ongoingness in the flux—the
flux is process. There are also from any single point of reference contemporaneous differences in the flux. Before a question of fact can be raised, these differences are apprehended
by a mind which itself is an episode in the flux, reacting to
other episodes. The episodes are not discrete, for there is no
absolute dividing line in acting and being acted upon. The
concepts of physical time and space are abstractions refined
from the proto-generalizations of ongoingness and spreadoutness, or voluminousness. When percepts become ordered in a
developing mind, they are located by reference to each other
in this physical time and space, and the act of locating further
contributes to the clarification of the *concepts* of time and
space. Ongoingness and voluminousness are already dim characteristics of perception. As the percepts become more precise
and definite through mediation by more reflective concepts,
they partake of more highly conceptualized time and space, as
will be shown in later chapters. Judgments of time and space
can and do supervene on perception, and it is as the concepts
of ordered time and space become part of the mind's concep-

tual apparatus that percepts can become veridical, that is, perception of fact.

The knowledge–claim of perception is the unreflective taking of the object of perception to be a fact, that is, to have a locus in time and space. The claim can be reflectively established only if there are facts, and there can be facts only within a system of facts within the conceptual organization of time and space. There can be no isolated fact, for the very existence of fact depends on selecting and prescinding from the flux. A fact is differentiated by its temporal and spatial relations to other facts and is known in veridical perception, which requires a conceptual apparatus of generalizations referring beyond itself.

Fact and the knowledge of fact must not be confused, for the fact is the object abstracted from the knowledge relation. By this very token fact is not independent of knowledge, for selections must be made before there are any facts. Without selections and prescissions[6] there would be only flux. Selections and prescissions are not arbitrary, however, for the flux accommodates some and does not accommodate others. The flux has character, it is qualitative difference, but the character is fluid, and by 'fluid character' I mean that there are no fixed internal divisions, but that some selections and prescissions can be applied to the flux while others cannot. When the flux is cut, a definite character emerges at the place of the cut, but if it were cut differently, a different character would emerge. Nothing can be prescinded that is not a character at some selection or place where the flux is cut.

A particular fact may be perceived, but the system of facts without which there would be no particular fact can be established only reflectively in judgment. Thus, judgment is a necessary condition of fact; the criterion of knowing a fact to be

6. Peirce needed a noun cognate of the verb 'prescind' and after trying several spellings settled on 'prescission,' perhaps on the analogy of 'rescind' and 'rescission'. See CP, 4.235.

a fact depends on judgment, for we know that the purported fact is such only by relating it coherently to other purported facts. This consideration does not make a fact a judgment, however. A fact is not constituted by its criterion. Rather, it is a result of a process of differentiation in the flux.

Yet a fact is more than a selection from the flux, for its temporal and spatial locus goes beyond both present intuitive data and proto-generalizations. Higher degrees of abstraction and generalization are necessary which require a more highly developed symbolism than the low-grade symbolism of proto-generalization. Thus, more precisely defined concepts go into the structure of facts. For example, a fact is not only what one sees and hears or even how what one sees and hears (or otherwise perceives) go together. A fact is also what it can do and what can be done to it. An automobile is what one sees and hears and the way they go together, but it is also what will bump one if one does not get out of the way, and what one can drive and use for transportation. All this and more, depending on how familar one is with automobiles, is what is perceived at a locus in time and space when one perceives an automobile.[7] Its locus is not rigidly bounded in time and space, however, for a fact, being in part conceptually determined, has meaning, and is to some extent wherever its meaning takes it, for meaning is symbolic reference. The fact spreads both in time and space from its perceptual locus as a center, for a fact is relative to other facts in a coherent system. Facts do not have simple location in Whitehead's sense of the term.[8]

Any or all of the parts that go to make up a fact may be called into question in judgment and may be critically estab-

7. This "thickness" and "richness" of concrete, adult perception based on fullness of past learning is what Merleau-Ponty exploits for the purpose of establishing his brand of existentialism in *The Phenomenology of Perception*, pp. 52–63, 143–47, 313–24 among other passages.

8. A. N. Whitehead, *Science and the Modern World* (New York: The Macmillan Co., 1925) p. 81; or *Adventures of Ideas*, pp. 201–2.

lished or disestablished according to how they are related to other percepts and other judgments. When I perceived a tomato, I unreflectively took it to be a fact that a tomato was there, but later, upon reflection, I found that I was in error. Even though it was not a fact that a tomato was there, it nevertheless remains a fact that I perceived a tomato, for the act of perceiving was an event with a locus in time and space. It had references to the past and repercussions on the future. When I discovered that the existing physical object was a piece of wax, I perceived the wax to be a fact. I judged that it had been a fact all the time but that I had not known it either in perception or in judgment. If I had perceived it as wax at first, my neighbor would not have fooled me and we would have had nothing to talk about—no problem would have arisen.

If the term 'fact' is to play a useful part in an explanatory conceptual scheme, it must have a precise meaning. Scientific methodology holds that observation, that is, perception under carefully controlled conditions, yields knowledge of fact, but that facts are not to be confused with the generalities under which they can be subsumed. Generalities are not observed for they cover instances that are not perceived as well as those that are. For example, the proposition 'that two and two make four' does not state a fact, it states a generality. Facts may instance a generality: when I add two more apples to the two which I have, there are four apples; but the proposition of arithmetic is not established by counting apples. If I add two pints of alcohol to the two pints of water I have in a container, I do not get four pints. This instance does not disprove the generality, it merely does not fall under the generality which is just another way of saying that generalities are not observed.

It is reasonable within the conceptual scheme to use 'fact' to mean whatever has a locus in time and space, for this usage points up the special place of observation in scientific methodology. 'Fact' is used idiomatically in the English language in such loose and imprecise ways as almost to rob it of meaning.

For example, the locution 'It is a fact that . . .' or 'As a matter of fact . . .' is often used for purposes of emphasis and without reference to specific fact. The expression filling the '. . .' is sometimes a generality of high degree. It may be that the person using the locution means that whatever he is talking about is a generality firmly based on facts, but if this is what he means it is a pity that he does not say so. If emphasis is desired, some way of obtaining it without an equivocal use of language should be devised.

Facts, then, are unique. Each is different from every other since each has its own locus in time and space, although the loci spread and intersect in their relations to each other. Facts are characteristically known in perception, that is, they are observed, but they are critically known only through judgments of relationship with other facts and other judgments. Perhaps there are facts that can be only inferred and not directly perceived, such as facts of past history, but the basis of knowledge of fact lies in perception.

Even though each fact is unique, there is a theoretic element in the perception of fact, for facts have structure, structure is formal, and form is grasped conceptually. The simple identification of what is objective in perception depends on proto-generalization, that is, on establishing aspects of the flux that are common to different instances and so are repeatable. Generality is not a fact, however, for it does not have a unique locus in time and space. It is what is common to different loci. It is known conceptually by means of symbolism. Generality is theoretic and theory is general.

Systematic theory is not necessarily involved in perception, however, for systematic theory is a highly organized and complex structure of abstract relationships. It may nevertheless influence perception in future cases by furnishing general schemata for the interpretation of intuitive data. For example, in making a diagnosis a physician is able to perceive faint or obscure evidence such as a faint shadow in an X-ray negative because he knows what to look for. On the other hand, a theoretic schema sometimes hinders a scientist working on the frontiers of knowledge by keeping him from seeing what he might see if he were not looking for something else. In this case the theoretic schema keeps him from making novel interpretations. No concept or theoretic schema can exhaust the flux, for concepts involve selection. The scientist impoverishes his subject matter when he treats a systematic concept as if it were an adequate or full picture of a concrete entity instead of an abstract principle of interpretation. Dealing with this context, the physicist Louis de Broglie has said "We could hold, contrary to Descartes, that nothing is more misleading than a clear and distinct idea."[9]

The word 'theory' is not always used in ordinary language with the meaning assigned to it in the present conceptual scheme, and it will be well to distinguish some of the usages from the one advocated here. The expression "This is only theory, it will not work" is ordinarily used to indicate some sort of vague contrast between theory and practice, and to be derogatory of theory. If this were all, it would hardly be worth remarking, but there are several senses in which the expression may be used that are more precise and critical. A mathematical system that has no known applications in concrete experience is highly theoretical and may be said "not to work" in the sense of having no practical application.

There are persons who hold as a reflective doctrine that theory is irrelevant to practice because theory is only "hot air." The expression did not originate in modern slang, for those medieval nominalists who said that universals (general terms) are *flatuus vocis* were expressing an exaggerated version of the doctrine that all theory is hot air. But if theoretic knowledge is general knowledge, this doctrine leads to ultimate skepticism, for all knowledge and even consciousness

9. Louis de Broglie, *The Revolution in Physics* (New York: The Noonday Press, 1953) p. 219.

itself involves at least some degree of generality. Empirical theory that is irrelevant to practice is only pseudo-theory. Although couched in general language, the generalizations indicated by the language do not adequately cover the facts they purport to cover.

Another ordinary use of 'theory' may be found in the expression "My theory is that the butler committed the crime." This is a commonsense use of the term which, if it is understood in its commonsense context, can do no harm. Its only connection with a precise epistemological use of 'theory' is that it indicates a conclusion based on theoretic reasoning and not on direct perception.

This study will lay aside the problems of normative theory as found, for example, in ethics, political philosophy or aesthetics. In these disciplines a theoretic construction of a future situation deemed better or more desirable than the actual situations of present or past experience may be offered. The term 'theory' can be used in such normative constructions in its epistemological sense, but whether or not the constructions are useful guides to practice depends on how reliable their predictions are as scientific predictions.

A special use of the word 'theory' is found in natural science where 'hypothesis', 'theory', and 'law' are contrasted in meaning. This will be discussed in context later, but for the present it can be said that the meaning of all three of these concepts is theoretical and all are hypothetical in import.

Let us return to the argument. I have pointed out that even to refer to intuitive data is to break up the continuity of the flux. No separate data are given, yet activity does not respond to the flux in its undifferentiated wholeness. It responds to parts selected from the infinite complexity of the continuum. In the first instance perception is controlled by the demands of action and identifies or recognizes its object according to common elements selected from the flux. The act of perceiving is what Angus Sinclair called 'selecting and grouping' portions of the flux.[10] The principle underlying the selecting and grouping is similarity or repetition—the principle of generality.

The continuum is ceaseless change and the continuum of perceptual intuition is ceaseless change of quality. There are no limits or absolute distinctions in it—no place of which it can be said "here one datum stops and another begins." But a continuum can be cut anywhere and a limit or boundary is set up by the cut. A distinction is imposed upon the continuum, and the character of the continuum will be different at each place where it is cut. An essential difference between a continuum and a discrete series is that in a discrete series, the boundaries of the units are absolute distinctions. Cuts in a discrete series are preestablished by the separate units whereas in a continuum the exact places of the cuts are not preestablished—they can be anywhere.[11]

An example of a continuum in which there are parts with character yet no separations is a series of simple water waves. Here there are differences and recurrences, but the way in which the recurrences are regarded is not rigidly determined. The waves may be regarded as a series of convexities, or as a series of concavities, or equally well as alternating convexities and concavities. To the question "But what *are* the waves, convexities or concavities?" it can be answered "Either, according to the way one cuts the continuum."

The illustration is oversimplified. A multitude of waves may move through the same medium and in doing so form

10. Angus Sinclair, *Conditions of Knowing* (New York: Harcourt, Brace & Company, 1951) p. 93. Sinclair does not use the term 'flux'.

11. I am using the analogy of the Dedekind cut in mathematics. One of the properties of a continuum (the Dedekind property) is that it can be divided into two parts such that every element belongs either to one part or to the other. The series of integers also has this property, but the division can be made only at one of the elements of the series. In a linear continuum, the division can be made anywhere because the elements are neither denumerable nor discrete. See E. V. Huntington, *The Continuum . . .* , chap. 5.

nodes—places where they mutually reinforce or cancel each other. In the infinite diversity of the flux there would be multitudes of these "thickenings" and "thinnings," places of high intensity or low intensity, marking repetitions in diversity, or patternings. There are, however, no discrete units in such a model. No node has precise boundaries, but the nodes are there and can be distinguished.

Cuts made in the continuum are the source of the conceptual factor in knowledge. The cuts are the proto-generalizations of selective response. As the responses become more complex, they become a conscious mind, selecting, grouping, and relating aspects of the flux which become identifiable and recognizable—that is, definite. The more definite they are, the more definable they become until clear concepts are reached, for concepts are grasped in definitions. The activity of the organism, in reacting, becomes a mind, and the product of this activity is concepts. The conceptual factor is the interpretative factor. There is no knowledge or even awareness without at least a modicum of interpretation.

Concepts are grasped in definition and definition is limitation. A definition puts boundaries and if the definition is precise, the boundaries are exact and clear. Thus, concepts are essentially discrete. All discreteness in experience is conceptual, and thus the product of mind.

Yet the formation of concepts is not arbitrary. The exigencies of action demand that the cuts in the continuum respond to the continuum. Cuts made at the places of high or low intensity that I have likened to nodes can be said to "cut reality at the joints." The precise places of the cuts are not preestablished, for nodes have no precise boundaries, but one set of cuts is better than another in so far as it yields conceptual interpretations that better serve the demands of action. Perceptions arising from such interpretations yield perceptual knowledge. Those percepts that do not serve the demands of action or of understanding are discarded by an adult, sane mind as dreams or hallucinations or some other kind of nonveridical perception.

Concepts are further subject to logical criticism. Meanings may be inclusive or exclusive of each other since some are more general than others. This topic will be pursued later.

There is not one and only one way of "cutting reality at the joints." There are many more nodes than those which practical action or logical attention singles out at one time. In addition, the nodes are not discrete. There is no absolute boundary to a node and therefore the precise nature of the cut even when it is a cut at a node is not predetermined.

The metaphor of 'node' may be carried even farther. The *fact* in the perception of fact is based on a node in the continuum. My neighbor fooled me and I perceived a tomato where there was no tomato. I took to be a fact what was no fact. I later judged my first perception to have been in error. The conceptual or interpretative factor in the percept was misapplied. The intuitive data were mis-taken, and I say, idiomatically, "I made a mistake." All perception is fallible in that it may involve misapplication of the conceptual factor, but such misapplication can be discovered only in the wider context of supervening judgments. All perception is corrigible (unless it has sudden fatal results) but it is corrigible also only in the wider context.

Facts are not absolute, and there is no conclusive evidence that the flux can be interpreted in one and only one set of facts. There is no a priori reason that it cannot be interpreted by means of alternative "compossible" sets of facts (to borrow a concept from Leibniz). Given one basic schema of interpretation, all the facts indicated within it are determined, but with another schema a different set of facts is determined. This situation finds an analogy within contemporary physics. Time and space are relative to the frame of reference within which observations of fact are made. What may be simultaneous or a straight line or in motion or at rest within one frame of reference may be nonsimultaneous or a curved line or in different motion or not at rest within another. Fact is whatever has a locus in time and space, but time and space are not absolute. Thus contemporary physics seems to indicate that facts are relative to the frame of reference in which they are taken. Within one frame these and no others are the facts, but within another frame the facts will be different. There is a systematic shift of the interpretations upon which the perception of facts is based.

Of the possible alternative perceptions of fact some will be better than others. Those percepts which enable one to deal with the flux more adequately both in action and in understanding are the better ones. If they do not enable one to deal with the flux at all, they are in error. This is what 'in error' means. If I had picked and bitten into the tomato of my illustration, the error would have been apparent. I did not, but my further experience with my neighbor showed the perception to have been in error.

If the interpretative schema is too rigid, the probability of its misapplication to the flux is increased through overemphasis. It is possible that some of the systematic delusions of paranoia are illustrative of a too rigid schema of interpretation. Successful application of the interpretative factor (successful from the adult, social point of view as well as from the individual point of view) requires some latitude in interpretation or, in some cases, complete reinterpretation. Further illustrations can be found in psychological studies of the testimony of eye witnesses who, in court, give different honest accounts of what is presumed to have been the same event.

Not only is there legitimate latitude in the perception of fact, there is some give and take in the fact itself, for facts are not discrete. Facts are events the precise boundaries of which are set by the conceptual activities of the mind. In so far as the fact is based on a pronounced or emphatic node, less latitude is permissible in setting its boundaries. The application of alternative interpretations successfully acted upon is restricted. Facts are there in time and space, although they are not there in absolute definition or precision or in simple location, but it must be remembered that *conceptualized* time and space are themselves ordering principles of the mind. Facts are temporally and spatially ordered intuitive data, and intuitive data are not subjective, hence facts are not subjective. The character of the flux at the place where it is cut is the stubbornness of stubborn fact. The perception of fact is responsible to the continuum, and if the shipwreck victim sees help coming when there is no help, he is suffering from hallucination. There are no intuitive data at that time and place that can be veridically interpreted as approaching rescue.

It is possible for criticism of perception to establish so-called practical certainty. The veracity of perception can never be established with absolute certainty, however, for it depends on the application and applicability of interpretation to the flux; the facts themselves are not absolutely precise and definite in their own nature. Nevertheless, practical certainty can often be reached if by 'practical certainty' is meant as high a degree of approximation toward theoretic certainty as is needed or could even be used for the purposes of action.

It is possible even for perception that has become so habitual as to preclude conscious reflection to attain practical certainty. A skilled motorist traveling at high speed has many percepts during the day to which he responds with split-second reaction that makes the difference between life and death. As long as he continues to live and drive, his perceptual knowledge is shown to have practical certainty. When an urchin threw a mud-ball at Zeno of Elea's head, it is to be presumed that Zeno ducked if he saw it coming, in spite of the lack of theoretic certainty of his perceptual knowledge.

If there is any cogency in the considerations set forth in this and the preceding chapter, reality (or "what is the case" as the Wittgenstein of the *Tractatus* would have it) is not composed of atomic facts. In the first place, there is no ready-made reality such as Wittgenstein and the Russell of the same period envisaged.[12] There is no ultimate reality which is fixed and rigid and of which knowledge is a logical picture. The intuitive flux is not Reality; it is the matrix—the all-encompassing, unwrought source—of whatever is real. Anything that is apprehended in perception or grasped in understanding is real in some category or other. Concrete experiences are real, concepts are real, facts are real. An experience that cannot be grasped according to the category 'fact' may nevertheless be grasped and fitted into an orderly whole of experience by categorizing it as 'dream', 'illusion', 'hallucination' or in some other way. There are real dreams, real illusions, and real hallucinations. If one pretends to have an hallucination when one does not, there is nevertheless a real pretense or prevarication. This usage would make 'real' practically synonymous with 'genuine' and is probably what the word ordinarily means except in the language of metaphysicians. Of course this meaning will not do for 'Reality'. A meaning for 'matrix-reality' will be discussed in Chapter XII.

If there were a Reality made up of atomic facts, there could be no continuity. But process and duration are continuous, time (until stopped conceptually, in abstraction) is continuous, change is continuous, motion is continuous. Atomic facts would be discrete, otherwise they would not be genuinely atomic. A philosophy that bases its explanatory scheme on atomic facts, even when it finds them only by analysis, can have no genuine continuity. Facts are there, but they are not atomic, they are cut from the continuity of the flux by the

12. *See* Bertrand Russell's series of articles "Philosophy of Logical Atomism," *The Monist,* vol. 28–29 (1918–19); republished, collected, by the Department of Philosophy of the University of Minnesota (n.d.).

conceptual activity of mind, and perceptual knowledge is knowledge of fact.[13]

13. In a publication of some years ago, I contrasted perceptual intuition with perception of fact. I had not at that time come to the conclusion that intuition unqualified by any meaning (that is, not involving any symbolic reference) would be unconscious. In consequence, the concept 'perceptual intuition' was there somewhat vague. What I called perceptual intuition was minimally interpretative and corresponds to what is here called direct perception. What I called perception of fact is here called veridical perception. See H. N. Lee, *Perception and Aesthetic Value,* (New York: Prentice-Hall, 1938; reissued, New York: Johnson Reprint Corporation, 1967) pp. 28–31.

CHAPTER V

Logic

Veridical perception can be distinguished from nonveridical only by the application of logical criteria, and perception of fact can be established or disestablished only by logical processes. There are two senses in which 'logical' can be used here: one refers to pure logic and the other to applied logic. In Chapters III and IV, the term was used in the sense of applied logic, but the precise meaning of this concept depends on that of pure logic, for it must be made clear what it is that is applied. It could not have been made clear before the development of symbolic logic in the past hundred years.

Previous to the development of symbolic logic, logic had been defined with reference to verbal reasoning. Leibniz, in the late seventeenth century, saw that verbal reasoning is not definitive of logic, for mathematics is rigorously logical and the deductive processes involved in it are not primarily verbal. His insight went unnoticed and unimplemented at the time, but in the latter half of the nineteenth century, mathematicians and logicians developed the concept of pure logic from the study of the foundations of mathematics. Logic can now be defined as the science of abstract form or the study of types of order. (The two definitions are roughly synonymous, differing mostly in emphasis.) Order is considered in abstraction from that which is ordered.[1] The understanding of what it is to understand lies in the relation between the principles of order and that which is ordered.

The present study has emphasized that there is no knowledge of content without form. How, then, can there be knowledge of form without content? The answer is to be found in the technique of using the mathematical variable. There is no concrete experience of form without content, but there are forms which are the same no matter what the content. The use of the variable is a technique for representing whatever content there is without specifying what it is. By its use a high level of abstraction and generalization can be obtained. The symbolism furnishes a token content without regard to its specificity in terms of experience, and the form or structure is abstracted from whatever content can assume that form or structure.

Pure logic, then, is defined as the science of abstract form which in this context means form without regard to content. Of course such form can be grasped only conceptually. The point is that when the technique of abstracting and generalizing is mastered, it can be carried to a high degree until finally all considerations of empirical content are disregarded. This is possible because concepts are grasped by means of symbolism. The technique of manipulating symbols without regard to empirical meaning has been developed to a high degree of precision.[2] Form cannot be displayed except in relation to some symbolic content, but when it is stipulated, as it is in the use of the variable, that the actual content is irrelevant

---

1. A short sketch of the development of symbolic logic may be found in the author's *Symbolic Logic,* 1961 and 1962, chap. 1. For a fuller account, see C. I. Lewis, *A Survey of Symbolic Logic* (Berkeley: University of California Press, 1918; New York: Dover Publications, reprint. 1960) chap. 1.

2. For example, a perfect symbol system for natural numbers (Arabic numerals) enables one to do with the symbols everything that can be done with the numbers.

because any other content would serve, then relations are displayed between whatever content there is without regard to what it is, with the relations comprising form or structure. Form may be defined as the way the parts of a thing go together regardless of what the thing is or what its parts are. Logical form, then, is known only in abstraction. Form consists in relationships. Relations order the terms that are related, and simple relations may themselves be ordered into more complex relations until a highly systematic development of logic ensues. Ordered relations display structure. 'Organization', 'pattern', 'structure' are synonyms of 'form'.

Pure logic is elaborated in theorems rigorously proved from a small set of initial assumptions called postulates or axioms or primitive propositions by means of a small number of precisely stated rules of procedure. There is no one necessary set of postulates. Different sets that produce equivalent logical systems have been elaborated. Sets can also be devised that produce different logical systems, roughly analogous to the different sets in geometry that produce the alternative systems of Euclidean, Lobachevskian, and Riemannian geometry. Choice is always possible in the selection of postulates and the only limiting requirement is that the postulates be consistent with each other. Mathematics and logic have given up the notion of self-evident principles or even of any rigid starting place, and if 'axiom' is used to name the initial assumptions, it is wholly devoid of its older meaning of self-evidence. There is no warrant for holding that there is only one system of "true" logic.

In pure logic the proof of theorems consists of putting uninterpreted variables together in patterns following from the postulates according to the stated rules of procedure. The variables have no meaning or reference to anything in ordinary experience. The rules of procedure have no meaning except in terms of the variables. The variables take on meaning as soon as they are put together in various patterns according to the rules, but it is a purely logical, abstract, intrasystematic meaning, not an empirical meaning. Except in relation to each other in the structure of the system, variables are only characteristically shaped marks that may or may not recur in a given structure, but which can easily be identified as recurring when they do so. Roman or Greek letters are ordinarily used for no better reason than that they are easily recognized and already have names. Their meaning as letters in a phonetic alphabet is irrelevant and disregarded. Thus, the structure of a system of pure logic is independent of its possible interpretations in experience, but all its parts are rigorously inter-dependent: the rules, postulates, and definitions set up necessary relations between the parts of the structure *no matter what the parts are*. The proofs find and display these relations.[3]

After adequate symbolism for dealing with highly abstract concepts and relations has been devised, and facility in its use has been achieved, it seems that further abstract concepts and relations can be formulated almost at will. Thus, the concepts and relations of logic, because they are highly abstract, appear to many persons to be arbitrary even though they are not. Freedom of construction can be exercised only within limits, for concepts must be consistent with each other and constitute a coherent and consistent system. Consistency is the controlling logical relation. Although one cannot always systematically prove consistency when one has it (the demand to be able to do so seems to be narrowly circular), one can recognize inconsistency. The presence of inconsistency in a logical structure enables one to prove both a proposition and its contradictory in the same system, and when one can do this one can prove anything and the system suffers self-destruction.[4] A so-called system in which anything can be proved is not a

3. *See* H. N. Lee, "On the Use and Interpretation of Logical Symbols," *Tulane Studies in Philosophy* 16, (1967): 111–22.
4. *See* Irving M. Copi, *Symbolic Logic*, sec. ed. (New York: The Macmillan Co., 1965) pp. 61–62.

type of order and cannot be used to order experience or knowledge.

Since pure logic is independent of ordinary experience, it is not surprising that many mathematical structures having no application to experience have been devised. For example, no application has yet been found for Lobachevskian geometry. Riemannian geometry has been applied: the theory of relativity uses it. Euclidean geometry is adequate for dealing with small triangles such as can be drawn on a piece of paper, but Riemannian geometry better handles the larger triangles of interstellar space. Does this mean that interstellar space is *really* Riemannian? The question is misput; it misinterprets the relation between geometry and perceptual experience and in so doing misinterprets the role of logic and logical models in the understanding of experience.

Geometry is an abstract logical system. It is not a description, even a highly generalized one, of ordinary spatial perception.[5] There is nothing in experience that corresponds exactly to the precise concepts and relations of geometry. This is as true of Euclidean as of Riemannian or Lobachevskian geometry. One does not perceive a point which is without length, breadth, and thickness, or a line which is without breadth and thickness. In consequence, one does not perceive a circle defined as all points equidistant from a given point, or a triangle defined as an area bounded by three straight lines; but geometry deals with what is defined, not with what is perceived. Nevertheless, geometry can be applied to perceptual experience when one can formulate empirical things and relations that can be taken as instances of the mathematical concepts within a tolerable degree of approximation. The fit

5. *See* Ernst Cassirer, *Substance and Function* (Chicago: The Open Court Publishing Company, 1923, reissued, New York: Dover Publications, 1953) pp. 93–94. Cassirer illustrates by reference to Hilbert's postulates for geometry. In some ways, Huntington's postulates offer an even better illustration. See my comparison of Hilbert's, Veblen's, and Huntington's postulates in *Symbolic Logic*, pp. 258–63.

is never perfect. If the degree of approximation lies within the error of observation, the application is highly satisfactory and cannot be improved in practice. Geometric theory is a logical model by means of which spatial perceptions can be interpreted and put in order.[6] Spatial relations are *understood* within the logical system. When the system can be applied to perceptual experience, the geometric aspects of perceptual experience are understood. The understanding of experience is the application to it of a logical model whereby it is ordered.

A logical model is a system of pure logic in which theorems are rigorously deduced from a stock of primitive (and it may be, uninterpreted) elements and relations according to explicitly stated rules, both descriptive and prescriptive; this system is used to delineate the structure of some portion of experience to which it may be applied. The model itself may not be absolutely perfect, yet the very case of geometry as it has been developed in postulate sets since (roughly) the beginning of the twentieth century[7] comes very close to the ideal if it does not reach it. Euclid's formalization is only a rough approximation but it laid the ground (and furnished problems) for later developments.

Two questions arise: how can logical models that have no necessary reference to experience be constructed; and is it not a miracle that such constructs, if independent of experience, can have applications such that the apparently necessary connections within the model are carried over into the connections of experience? Both questions are answered by the following considerations.

Although geometric theory is not a description of perceived space, psychologically the development of the theory started

6. An instructive discussion of the relation between geometry and perceptual experience may be found in G. A. Bliss, "Mathematical Interpretations of Geometrical and Physical Phenomena," *American Mathematical Monthly* 40:8 (Oct., 1933), pp. 472–480.

7. Hilbert's set was published in 1899; Veblen's in 1911; and Huntington's in 1913.

nevertheless from selected aspects of perceived space and generalized them. Percepts were used heuristically as the source of abstractions and generalizations. Thus, theoretic concepts were formulated. To take a simple example: in spite of not being able to perceive a point without length, breadth, and thickness, one can think of diminishing the dimensions of a visible dot to the limits of visibility, or of making a visible line thinner and thinner until it approximates length only.

In a similar fashion, the very concept of geometric space (for geometric space is highly conceptualized) is itself a derivation from the proto-generalization of voluminousness in direct perception. A vague consciousness of similarity of quality arises from the similarity of response to different intuitive data. The similarity of response in this case is adaptive muscular activity (including eye muscles). The quality is the awareness of the place of the data, that is, the muscular movement that brings the data under the control of the reacting organism. As experience accumulates and coordination of responses is effected, the different instances of vague voluminousness are related to each other and take on a fullness of meaning by the increase in symbolic reference. The qualities become instances of a class of delayed and inhibited responses, and the concept of space is achieved. With the fullness of meaning comes also definition (delineation) wherein the meaning of spaciality is separated (abstracted) from the meanings which it is not but with which it is always joined in perception. For example, visual extensions are always colored and colors are always extended, but the organism reacts differently to one than to the other, and in the increasing specificity of response the shape is prescinded[8] from the color, and a more or less reflective concept of space is achieved. Spatial relations can now be elucidated and defined in terms of each other without reference to perceptions except in so far as the perceptions are suggestive and guiding to the construction.

8. *See* CP, 1.549.

The construction can be carried on strictly according to rule, and the final result is a logical model articulated wholly according to rule. It is composed of what are often called "ideal" entities, such as geometric points or lines or, in physics, bodies not acted on by an external force or perfectly elastic bodies. These entities are systematically connected by "ideal" relations and the whole is a logical model.

Thus, using perceptual conditions heuristically, concepts of a high degree of abstraction are obtained—concepts which are defined in terms of other concepts to which they are related —and percepts (except the symbols of language or logic) are left behind. The interrelatedness of concepts is systematically elaborated in rules of structure and of procedure, and a logical model is obtained.[9]

It is no miracle that a model so obtained should find application to experience. It was constructed to allow for such application with an intended interpretation in view. Other models, obtained by free construction after the methods, rules, and procedures have been learned and the techniques mastered, sometimes do and sometimes do not apply to experience. That they do when they do is not surprising, for the analogies of experience are still at work even when not uppermost in mind; but that they should not apply is more to be expected in so far as experience has been deliberately disregarded in their construction.

A simple illustration of the application of a mathematical (logical) model to empirical things and processes may be found in the application of arithmetic to physical measurement by the early physicists of the Renaissance. Of course, arithmetic was not presented to them as an abstract model; the concept of an abstract model had not yet been formulated. Simple arithmetic had been developed heuristically at the

9. *See* Pasch on natural, artificial, and ideal languages; *Experience and . . .* , pp. 238–39.

dawn of history from the empirical process of counting, though some aspects of its theory, such as the recognition of zero as a number, awaited the development of an adequate symbol system. Nevertheless, it was the application of arithmetic to measurement that lay behind the successes of the early physicists.

Direct measurement depends on counting units and manipulating the sums according to the rules of arithmetic. Of course, since the model was not presented as an abstract system to the Renaissance physicists, the rules of application were not stated with the logical precision since attained, but Plato, long before, had recognized that number is not a thing of the perceptual world, and in Book VII of the *Republic* had clearly distinguished between the theoretic study of arithmetic and its uses in application to practical affairs.

Physical processes are not composed of ready-made units, but the physicists had at hand rough units of measurement already in use by artisans. Refining these they cut the continuum of distance or of motion into parts to which they could make accurate application of the concepts and operations of arithmetic. Units of distance traversed by balls rolling down an inclined plane were correlated with units of elapsed time; or the height of a column of mercury was correlated with pressure, measured in units of weight per area, exerted upon its free surface. Ratios were established between the arithmetical values so obtained. It was at this juncture that Descartes made his mathematical discoveries, defining what is still called a Cartesian function, and laid the foundations for the development of more powerful models to be applied to the understanding of nature.

The precise character of the knowledge process is clarified when the logical model in knowledge is formulated explicitly as an abstract system, and the uninterpreted symbols of the system are interpreted as symbols of empirical concepts by means of semantic rules. In this form, the logical structure can be made critically precise. The semantic rules should be clearly and explicitly stated, and the approximation of the fit of the empirical concepts must be high. Riemannian geometry had been developed as a pure mathematical system, and fifty years elapsed before the discovery of semantic interpretations that permitted its application to physical space. On the other hand, Euclidean geometry had been developed heuristically by means of generalizations and "idealizations" (higher level abstractions) of perceived space and spatial shapes. This method of constructing a logical model remains the more usual one.

When one starts with an empirical situation to be explained and with concepts that are empirical generalizations, one uses these familiar ingredients to be guided in making further abstractions and generalizations. If one is successful, they are built into a complex logical structure. The structure applies to experience because it was constructed to do so, but experience is not what makes the logical system logical. Empirical generalizations have been only heuristic throughout, even though the same words are used both for the elements of the structure and for the empirical generalizations. Because the same words are used, the illusion is created that the logical model is literally a generalized description of perceptual experience—that the generalizations are there as a part of the content of experience simply to be recognized by a keenly observant mind. It is often overlooked that the concepts in the model no longer have direct exemplifications in perception. It is not noted that perception furnishes instances of the highly abstract and precise concepts of logic only within a degree of approximation.

This illusion gives rise to what I shall call the blackberry bush fallacy—the assumption that generalities come on accumulations of fact like blackberries grow on blackberry bushes and are *there* ready to be picked by someone searching for them. Of course, there are difficulties, for the bush may be hard to locate, and the berries have a way of hiding beneath the factual foliage, and there are always thorns; but perseverance, a measure of luck, and sharp observation will find the berries. In the light of the present theory, this assumption—that generalities are *there* in accumulations of fact, ready to be discovered—is false, and there will be occasion later to say more about the blackberry bush fallacy. Generalities and logical relations are in perceptual experience as the mind puts them there in its capacity of bringing the experience into intelligible order.

It is not strange that the mind should be able to apply logical concepts and relations to perceptual experience, for the fundamental processes of generalization are present, though in slight degree and low abstraction, in awareness itself; and it is in the development and refinement of these processes that humans have learned how to construct logic. It was pointed out above that perception depends upon a primitive generalizing ability, proto-generalization. This is no more than the ability to react similarly to different episodes in the flux, for the awareness of similarity and therefore what is common (general) depends on the economy of response, of reacting to the infinite variety of the flux with a limited number of kinds of responses. The economy of response itself is a selecting and ordering principle, and common elements in the flux are the result of a primitive ordering of the flux, at least as much order as is found in adaptive response. Some degree of order and definition must be put into intuitive data before there is any apprehension of them. If for purposes of argument it were assumed that there is awareness of completely unordered data (if the expression has any meaning) there could be no memory of them, for there would be nothing with which to connect them or by means of which to assimilate them, and hence no means of recall. If there were no memory, could there be perception or knowledge? The assumption seems to be self-defeating.

With increasing adaptivity and complexity of response (this is what is meant, in large part, by increasing maturity of mind) the simple identifications or recognitions involved in perception become definite concepts. Conceptual activity carves individuals or particulars from the flux, and the concepts, by disregarding differences, associate the particulars into classes. Inclusion and exclusion of classes, then disjunction and conjunction (logical addition and multiplication) of classes are noted, and with increasing proficiency in abstracting, these become logical relations between concepts.[10] When the relations have become completely generalized and are grasped without necessary reliance on particular, perceptual experiences, the universality and necessity of logic is achieved. Thus, pure logic is made possible by an extension and development of the process of ordering that is implicit in all conscious experience.

The concepts which apply to intuitive data are not determined in an absolute or rigid way by the data, for the data are parts of a continuum and there are no limits or boundaries in a continuum until they are put there by selection. Thus, the application of logical concepts to intuitive data plays a part in determining the precise nature of the facts which the interpretations of the data constitute. The logical model helps to delineate the facts. The application of concepts to data is not arbitrary either, for the data are not characterless. The continuum, when cut, has character at the place of the cut; this means that some concepts will apply and others will not. There is some free play in the interpretation of intuitive data constituting fact, but the interpretative factor cannot be irrelevant to the data. The test of relevance is the success which the interpretation yields both in action and in understanding. The degree of strictness of interpretation is the measure of the "stubbornness" in stubborn fact. Facts that are very stubborn are facts in which the success of alternative interpretations is strictly limited.

Successful generalizations cannot be made where there is

10. *See* J. Piaget, *The Child's Conception of Number* (New York: The Humanities Press, 1952) pp. 155–57.

nothing in common; and where no similarity of response is possible, there is nothing in common. But even when something in common is found, it is not simply *found*. Common characteristics are not simply there in intuitive data in all their specificity. To suppose that they are is to commit the blackberry bush fallacy. Common characteristics in the flux are potentialities in the sense that they mark possible repetitive ways of reacting. Care must be exercised, however, not to hypostatize such potentialities into a sort of a shadow existence. A potentiality is nothing but a condition or constellation of conditions such that if a specifiable additional condition not present were present, a foreseeable state of affairs not in existence would be in existence. Common elements in the flux are potentialities in this sense of becoming possible objects of selections and distinctions that are increasingly definite and definitive as complex traces of former selections and distinctions accumulate. To assume that common characteristics in their full specificity are actually present in the flux before the flux is cut by an act or to suppose that they are actual identities in different parts of the flux is to leave nonveridical perception, errors of perception, and the possibility of reinterpretation unexplained.

The logical structure of experience is not independent of the mind. The precision and definiteness of experience arise from the way that action and mind cut the flux. Generalization is not a process rigidly fixed by the nature of intuitive data. Empirical generalities are not arbitrary, but neither are they precise and definite until instances are cut from the flux. The world that is known is a world to which knowledge and the definitive role of knowledge are not irrelevant. The parts of the world that are not known are the parts that are continually being found out about, and the nature of knowledge is not irrelevant to what is learned. This is the sense in which it can be said that the world is in some way and to some measure mind-dependent. The great question of modern metaphysics has been in what way and to what measure. Some of the answers that have been given claim to be derived from considerations of logic, but such claims rest on the confusion of pure with applied logic.

Pure logic tells nothing about the content of experience or of reality. It deals only with the structure or order of whatever content there may be. Thus, it deals not with actuality but with abstract possibility, and logical possibility means only what is free from internal inconsistency. It is only in pure logic that universality and necessity are to be found. A system of pure logic is a construction of the mind, and the principles of the system are not blackberries picked from a rigidly structured world.

Applied logic, on the other hand, tells nothing about the nature of order or structure. It merely illustrates order or structure as instances of it may be displayed in more or less concrete cases. If one equivocates rapidly and with sleight-of-hand ease between the concept of pure logic and that of applied logic, one can seem to produce concrete experience from logic in some cases; in others, one can seem to produce logic from concrete experience. The illusion is possible in either case because there is no *conscious* experience without some degree of order. Connectedness, similarity, relatedness of some sort, even if it is only of slight degree, is a necessary condition of awareness, but conscious percepts are not the ultimate content of experience, they are what the philosopher starts with in point of time when he undertakes the philosophic enterprise.

Metaphysical Idealism holds that Reality is mind-dependent, not upon individual but upon universal mind or Spirit. The Idealist purports to show that Reality is determined by logical principles and that logical principles are inherent in the structure of mind. He starts his investigation with judgment, that is, with asserted knowledge already propositionally formulated. Propositionally formulated knowledge has clear-cut subject and object, but the Idealist does not leave them in separate status. In judgment, subject and object are held together in a unity, and ultimately object depends on subject. As Empedocles remarked at the dawn of the philosophic investigation of knowledge, and as Plato further developed, "like knows like." There is a bond of unity, and the Idealist finds this bond in the rationality of what is known. Furthermore, only what is rational can be known, and since the principles of logic are the universal forms of rationality, the Idealist holds that they display the essential nature of Reality. Since, to him, the principles of logic are inherent in the structure of mind, Reality is mind-dependent. Perception is explained by the Idealist as implicit or telescoped judgment. The object of perception too depends on the principles of rationality, and thus is ultimately derived from the Universal Subject.

In the history of Idealism this argument appears in myriad variations, but through them all runs the theme of deriving the nature of Reality from the forms of rationality and from the universality of the logic by means of which Reality is known. This logic is, however, the applied logic of the ordering of the content of experience. A study of pure logic seems to indicate that logical principles are universal because they apply without exception to whatever content there may be. By this token the principles do not indicate any specific content. Hence, the nature of Reality cannot be discovered by investigating the nature of logical principles. A study of pure logic shows the principles to be rigorously abstracted from all considerations of semantic interpretation or application to anything in experience.

At the opposite extreme from the Idealists are those philosophers who hold that logic is the mind's grasp, or picture, of the structure of a fully ordered reality which is completely independent of the mind and whose order is likewise independent of the mind. The philosophy of logical atomism is such a doctrine. The present study has found no evidence for the existence of atomic facts. If there is any evidence, it is *not* to be found in logic. Pure logic does not use and has no need for propositions that are genuinely atomic. If its variables are interpreted as propositions (they need not be) the most that can be said is that some are unanalyzed, but even these may be given values under stipulated conditions in which analysis is displayed. For example, unanalyzed propositions may be given quantified values in quantification theory.[11]

If definitive order and therefore the principles of pure logic are to be discovered by observation in a fully structured external world wholly independent of mind, then the problem of epistemology is what many British and American philosophers of the late nineteenth-and early twentieth centuries held it to be, namely, to show how such a world can be known; until this problem is solved, there can be no logic.

Two major difficulties are encountered by such a view of the relation between logic and epistemology. First, the nature of a fully structured external world (even if there were any) could not be found by observation until veridical is distinguished from nonveridical perception. The problem of establishing this distinction is not solved by refusing to entertain it on the ground that most adult humans know the difference perfectly well; that is, in more exact language, they are usually successful in making the distinction in practice. Some theoretic grounds for the distinction must be found before it can be called a matter of knowledge. The grounds always include reference to some kind of coherence and order in the relations between perceptual experiences. Coherence and order are logical considerations. Thus, the knowledge of an external world depends on the ability to distinguish veridical from nonveridical perception which in turn depends on the application to experience of logical considerations. The philosopher-magician who now gets logic from a close observation of the external world, is simply getting out of the hat the rabbit he has put there.

11. For an explanation of quantification, see Copi, *Symbolic Logic,* chap. 4; or Lee, *Symbolic Logic,* chap. 13.

The second of the difficulties in the view that the principles of logic come from the structure of a fully structured world is that such a view is obtuse to the problem of continuity. Continuity cannot be fundamental in the doctrine, for the doctrine is dualistic. It has both an external world composed of ready-made facts known in perception and a mind doing the perceiving. Dualism cannot give priority to continuity. Even if mind is continuous on the one hand and the external world is continuous on the other, there is no fundamental continuity, for if there are two continua that are not continuous with each other, discreteness is fundamental.

The case is worse than this for the doctrine of a rigidly structured external world. If the world has a ready-made structure, all the parts and relations comprising it are precise and definite in their own natures. Thus, a structured world would be composed of discrete elements. In this case there could be no continuity, for a continuum cannot be obtained from a summation of discrete units, not even if there is an infinity of them.[12] Hence, the doctrine that the world is prestructured and that the principles of logic depend on this structure can have no genuine continuity in its system and cannot assimilate the continuity of process, qualitative change and motion. This result is satisfactory for a system of pure logic since that is abstract, but the continuity in concrete experience must be recognized.

It is not my present intention to pursue the study of pure logic; that is the province of the logician. But the epistemologist must not build his theory upon a palpably inadequate or confused conception of logic, and he must be able systematically to explain his meaning when he says that a consideration is logical or that evidence can be either perceptual or logical. Perception is not a logic-process, for perception is not the

12. The elements of a discrete series are denumerable, but the elements of a linear continuum are not denumerable. *See* E. V. Huntington, *The Continuum and . . . ,* §37, §58.

grasp of abstract relationships between concepts but is the interpretation of intuitive data. Systematic knowledge of an external world, however, involves both perception and logical activity, for knowledge of an external world requires judgment, relating concepts on relatively high levels of generality and abstraction. Chief among such judgments are those of consistency and coherence.

Judgments of consistency and coherence among perceptions are considerations of applied logic, but to be able to apply them requires the ability to grasp the relations between concepts that give them meaning, and this grasp depends on the development of high-grade symbolism. A young child is not bothered by considerations of consistency, for his ability to symbolize and abstract the necessary relations between concepts has not matured.[13]

The enterprise of gaining knowledge starts with percpetion, but perception itself is ordered to some degree. The more clear-cut and definite perception is, the more internal order it possesses and the more knowledge it displays. Conscious experience absolutely without any semblance or degree of order (that is, conscious experience of absolute chaos) is a contradiction in terms. Experience in becoming conscious has something that is identifiable, recognizable, and can be referred to other episodes in the flux. It is that with which one can do something.

The definitive and ordering factor in knowledge, the logical factor, is contributed by mind. It is not arbitrary, however, nor is the mind's activity in the knowledge process arbitrary in any legitimate sense of the word 'arbitrary'. The form or structure is applied to content, and the content is the intuitive

13. *See* J. Piaget, *Judgment and Reasoning in the Child.* " . . . until he reaches a certain age (7–8 at least) the child is insensible to contradiction" (p. 163). " . . . child thought is ignorant of the logic of relations, . . . addition and multiplication of logical classes are unknown to it" (p. 233).

flux. The flux is in no way a product of mind or beholden to the activity of mind. On the contrary, mind itself is an episode in the flux, and its activity is an activity of the flux. Mind is a part of nature, not nature a part of mind.

The flux is not a rigid structure, but it can be structured. It can be cut into parts, and when it is, structure emerges, for by virtue of its continuity there can be no parts that are not related to each other and to the whole. If there are definite parts, there is order. The order does not appear until the parts appear, but when parts *do* appear they cannot appear except in some order. Using a material metaphor, one might say that the mind leaves its imprint on what it grasps.

However, the flux is not to be conceived as disorderly. Instead, it has potential order. Concepts are derived from it and applied to it. Concepts are discrete and thus may be said to impose discreteness upon the continuum, but the discrete elements are a selection from the continuum, they do not transform the continuum into a discrete series any more than the selection of the positive integers from the continuum of real numbers transforms the real numbers into a discrete series. It is only by this process of selection and the generalization that grows out of it that the continuum is grasped, for the continuum is infinitely complex. The first relatively simple grasp, wherein the materials of the flux predominate and are compelling while the conceptual element is at a minimum, is direct perception. With increasing powers of symbolization, the mind grasps abstract relations and veridical perception is established. An orderly external world composed of facts is systematically organized by further application of logical principles, and veridical percepts are placed in relation to this more inclusive order. Finally, the principles of order themselves can be critically examined in a system of pure logic.

Some philosophers have held that stopping and breaking up the continuum into discrete parts yields a falsification and distortion of reality.[14] There is no warrant for such a view. Nothing is gained by using 'reality' as an honorific term and applying it only to a source while derogating what issues from the source by calling it a distortion. What issues from the source is a selection, but one is as real as the other. The significant question is whether the selection is true to its source, the relative whole, from which it was selected. A map of a geographic area may show only the streams and bodies of water in the area. Another map may show only the cities, towns, roads and railroads. Each may be a true selection from the concrete detail of the area. In the illustration at hand, nothing shown on the one would be shown on the other, yet both may be true maps. Neither one is complete, but incompleteness is not to be confused with distortion. There can be no map that is complete, for nothing but the area itself can show the concrete whole.

A map is a true map if every detail on it and every relation between every detail can be put into one-to-one correspondence with a *selection* of elements and relations of the original. This is the only meaning of 'correspondence' indicated in a theory of truth. No literal "picture" correspondence or mirroring could be established even if it were proposed. A conceptual model or conceptual scheme for understanding experience is a logical map of experience, and is true if it has the required correspondence, and useful if it is complete enough to enable one to find one's way around in experience. Thus, alternative models or alternative theories may both (or all) be true about the manifold of intuition. A theoretic model is true to experience if it fits in application to experience. Here the only test of the fit is the success with which the application enables one

14. Henri Bergson is often interpreted as holding this view. I think that this is a misinterpretation of Bergson resting on an over-simplification of his philosophy; but I will admit that he often uses language that seems to justify the misinterpretation. See *Bergson and the Evolution of Physics*, P. A. Y. Gunter, ed. and tr., (Knoxville: The University of Tennessee Press, 1969).

to deal with experience both in action and in understanding. It is to be noted that the test contains both pragmatic consider- ations and logical considerations of consistency and coherence; and that the fit is defined in terms of correspondence—not "pic- ture" correspondence, but one-to-one correspondence between the relationships displayed in the logical model and a selection from the relationships displayed in concrete experience.[15]

The only falsification or distortion in such a conceptual scheme arises when the philosopher or the scientist who has made the selection thinks that the selection *is* the whole or that the whole can be reconstructed by putting the selected parts together. Selection, however, always leaves out some- thing. The understanding operates by forming concepts, and the formation of concepts requires abstraction. Abstraction takes something out of the context wherein it is found and dis- cards the rest of the context. Of course, putting abstractions together will not yield a concrete whole.

Bergson's insistence that the tools of the intellect, though adequate for natural science are not adequate for philosophy, arose from his reaction against the nineteenth-century view that the way to attain the philosophic goal is by analysis and synthesis: that a faithful knowledge of reality can be attained (if at all) by a synthesis of all the parts of knowledge. He accepted the goal that philosophy should lead to a knowledge of reality, but he saw that the activities of the intellect involve selection whereas reality is a continuum. Since no set of selec- tions can exhaust a continuum, knowledge of reality cannot be attained by the intellect. Bergson downgraded the intellect and held it to be unphilosophical. He kept the nineteenth century ideal of the task of philosophy but rejected the tools of the intellect.

The present theory, on the other hand, rejects the ideal and keeps the tools. The task of philosophy is not to take us into

15. For a fuller elaboration, *see* H. N. Lee, "A Fitting Theory of Truth," *Tulane Studies in Philosophy* 14, (1965): 93–110.

reality. We are already there. The task of philosophy is not to attain knowledge of reality if reality is conceived to be something other than appearances and if we can experience only appearances. The task of philosophy is to understand, and there is nothing to understand that is not either in experience or to be derived from what is in experience. The tools of the intellect are all that there is either to clarify experience or to use in the pursuit of understanding They can never exhaust the task but they have in many cases proved adequate to the understanding of special selected parts of the flux. The understanding deals only with selected parts by means of generalizations arising from reference to other parts. It is a perverse use of the terms 'falsification' and 'distortion' to say that the intellect falsifies and distorts that with which it deals. The intellect selects and generalizes, thus attaining the concept of order, which science and philosophy, through the application of logical models, can apply to the understanding of experience with considerable success.

CHAPTER VI

Evidence

The story is told that during a recent sharp earthquake an automobile mechanic in a town near the epicenter had an automobile on the rack for a grease-job. He inserted the grease-gun and the automobile winced—jumped away from the gun an inch or two. Wide-eyed, the mechanic raised the gun again, and again the automobile winced. This time he dropped the gun and ran, but by now everyone else was running too and yelling "earthquake."

What happened here? What were the experiences narrated in the illustration? Of what were these experiences evidence? Were they evidence of different things at different times of the story, although the whole span of the story covers only a few seconds? Was that of which the most direct experiences were evidence itself experienced? These questions cannot be answered except on the basis of an investigation of the nature of evidence and the relation between evidence and conclusion.

The most direct experiences narrated were commonsense percepts—for example, man, automobile, rack, grease-gun. The conceptual element here was at a minimum. In terms of the present analysis, the data of direct awareness were intuitive data with their interpretations in terms of the concepts man, automobile, rack, grease-gun adhering to them, but the mechanic was not a proponent of the present analysis. Neither was he a sense-datum philosopher, and his direct awareness was not of color patches. It is possible that he had not consciously noted the color of the car even if he could have told what it was afterward if asked. At any rate, the intuitive and the conceptual elements at this level of experience can be found only by philosophic analysis, and the mechanic was not a philosopher. He was doing a job with a grease-gun on an automobile standing on a rack. The intuitive and the conceptual elements were *parts* of the mechanic's experience as analyzed, but in the actual case he was not directly aware of either by itself.

As soon as the mechanic interpreted the strange movement of the automobile as wincing, the analysis of the experience shows that the conceptual element in the interpretation of the intuitive data became more pronounced. He may not have uttered the words either vocally or subvocally, but he unreflectively responded to the situation in terms of a child's reaction to a hypodermic needle. This obviously did not fit the situation and he "did not know what to think" so he dropped the gun and ran. The direct experience was not evidence for any conclusion he could accept and he got away from it as quickly as he could. When he heard the word 'earthquake', however, the direct experiences all snapped into place and the strange behavior of the automobile became evidence of an earthquake.

The behavior of the automobile was a fact: it had a locus in space and time. All of the perceptual evidence leading to the conclusion that there was an earthquake were perceptions of fact. The earthquake too was a fact, but there was no direct perception of it unless an earthquake is sufficiently defined as an aggregate of strange movements on the earth's surface. This is not what a seismologist says an earthquake is. He says that it is a series of shock waves emanating from a sudden slipping or breaking of a fault in the earth's crust. The strange movements of surface objects are effects of the shock waves. In this view, there is a causal relation between the earthquake and the perceived movements. The perceptions are evidence of the earthquake by virtue of this causal relation.

The conceptual element in the knowledge of an earthquake is relatively large if the seismologist is correct, which I assume he is; at any rate, his knowledge of earthquakes is the most adequate and reliable available. Ordinarily, earthquakes are not perceived, only evidence that there is (or was) an earthquake is perceived. The perceptual evidence by itself is not enough to establish the event; in addition there is theoretic evidence. The logical relations, both deductive and probability relations, between the perceptual and the theoretic evidence yield the conclusion. In the illustration at hand the theoretic evidence is embodied in the laws and hypotheses of an elaborate geological theory. Though most of the inhabitants of the United States are not acquainted with the details of that theory, the majority know something of it through informal education by means of mass communication or ordinary social intercourse. The mechanic of our illustration knew enough of this theory to come straightway to the conclusion that he had perceived evidence of an earthquake.

The point of the illustration is that evidence and conclusion are relative to each other. Evidence is evidence only if it yields a conclusion, and conclusions are conclusions only if they follow from evidence. Something happens and the question arises: what does it indicate? If knowledge is to be extended, what happens must be regarded as evidence and the conclusion it yields must be found. There is a movement from evidence to conclusion: an inference is made on the ground of the logical relations found in the evidence both perceptual and theoretic. Yet the distinction between evidence and conclusion is not absolute. What is conclusion in one circumstance may be evidence for another conclusion in a different circumstance, and vice versa. The distinction between evidence and conclusion lies in their relation to each other as ground and consequent in inference.

A problem arises here. In the process of gaining knowledge,

HUNT LIBRARY
CARNEGIE-MELLON UNIVERSITY

one does not have the conclusion to start with, it is what is sought. How can one speak of a relation between evidence and conclusion when there is no conclusion? This problem would be insoluble if there were an absolute difference between evidence and conclusion, but there is no such difference. A bond of relevance ties the two together and is a further mark of their relativity. The relevance consists in the conceptual content of the two: the concepts that go into making the conclusion are present in the evidence, and a tentative rearrangement of them may be asserted hypothetically. Evidence and conclusion must be relevant to each other. The relevance is a necessary condition of the relation between the two regardless of whether the conclusion has yet been reached.

Relevance between evidence and conclusion means that the two are held together by a set of concepts or generalizations that they have in common. Relevance in this context consists in the rule that the concepts or generalizations found in the evidential data are to be found also in the conclusion, and that no concepts or generalizations are found in the conclusion the grounds of which are not to be found in the evidence. The concepts in the conclusion are obtained from those in the evidence. In deductive inference the logical relation upon which the inference rests is usually implication, though not the so-called material implication of Whitehead and Russell's *Principia Mathematica*, since considerations of relevance do not appear in it. For example, the theorem that is usually described by saying "A true proposition is implied by any proposition"[1] can be given this application: "If sugar is sweet, then whales are mammals"; but here there are no concepts in common to the if-clause (the protasis) and the then-clause (the apodosis); they are irrelevant to each other and no empirical inference can be drawn. Because of possible lack of rele-

---

1. Whitehead and Russell, *Principia Mathematica*, vol. 1, *2.02.

vance, material implication alone is not sufficient ground for empirical inference from what purports to be evidence to what purports to be conclusion; but if by the analysis of concepts relevance can be established, implication and relevance together are sufficient ground.[2]

In inference the conclusion is obtained by analyzing the structure of evidence and rearranging the concepts in different relations. Some concepts include others, some exclude others, and some overlap others. The analysis and rearrangement is explicit in deductive inference and no increase in generality appears in the conclusion. In inductive inference, however, a higher degree of generality usually appears in the conclusion, as is apparent in the illustration of the earthquake; but the generality must be grounded in the evidence in such a way that when the greater generality is proposed as a hypothesis, the concepts contained in the evidence are seen to be instances of it.

Inductive inference is usually used in arriving at empirical conclusions, or, if the argument is complex, there is a combination of induction and deduction. The detailed structure of inductive inference has never been elaborated in as satisfactory a manner as has the structure of deduction; and furthermore, in actual inductions, some of the evidence may be implicitly assumed as for example the fragmentary geological theory and the knowledge of physical causation in the illustration of the earthquake. No sure-fire method of bringing home the

---

2. C. I. Lewis' strict implication may be sufficient ground for deductive inference in the theory of deduction, but doubt may be expressed that it is the ground of inference from empirical evidence to conclusion because conceptual relevance is still not completely accounted for as is shown by the so-called paradoxes of strict implication, especially theorem 19.75, which is usually interpreted "A necessary proposition is implied by any proposition." *See* Lewis and Langford, *Symbolic Logic,* sec. ed. (New York: Dover Publications, 1959) p. 174.

evidence or of producing conclusions has ever been achieved.[3]

The place of induction and scientific theory in theoretic knowledge will be topics of later chapters. For the present it may be pointed out that generalizations have been characterized in previous chapters as ordering principles in experience. Concepts are general. Hence, the suggestion of a concept that marshals and orders otherwise incoherent data may be enough to turn the data into evidence, as was the case with the mechanic of the illustration and the concept 'earthquake'. When such an ordering concept is achieved, there is inductive inference. The mechanic had evidence for the conclusion that there was an earthquake. As soon as there was evidence and conclusion, there was relevance; and as soon as there was relevance, there was evidence and conclusion.

In other cases, obtaining inductive conclusions from empirical evidence may be a slow process that advances step by step as relevance is achieved often making liberal use of the cut and try method. In physical science, for example, careful investigation of data plus a problem to be solved or a question to be answered may suggest a tentative conclusion (working hypothesis). Data are then sifted for relevant evidence and the tentative conclusion is modified. The modification leads to a further assessment of evidence and to a further modification of the conclusion, and so on until a full-blown hypothesis emerges. Amassing facts (data) with no hypothesis is not a fruitful scientific procedure, for a mere aggregate of facts is

3. See David Rynin, "Evidence" in *Synthese,* vol. 12 (1960) where he finds it necessary to substitute the concept 'as-good-as-true' (or 'invariably confirmed') for 'true' in characterizing scientific laws, and 'if P then probably Q' for 'if P then Q' in characterizing the relation warranting inductive inference. Since the 'probably Q' has weight depending on the degree to which the observed instance fits or is congruent with a systematic structure of general laws, it is an epistemic relation, not a purely logical one. *See also* G. H. von Wright, "The Concept of Entailment" in his *Logical Studies* (London: Routledge & Kegan Paul Ltd., 1957).

not evidence. Evidence is evidence and conclusion is conclusion only in relation to each other; but in actual situations, evidence and conclusion progressively suggest and correct each other in a process of mutual adjustment.

On the level of common sense the concepts are familiar. Conclusions may be suggested at once by perceptual data because one has reacted to similar data before, or has reacted to verbalization of the data and now draws similar conclusions from similar evidence. I step into the street, see an automobile approaching, and quickly step back to the curb. I do not reason "The perceptual data are adequate evidence that an automobile will hit me unless I move." The present study does not advocate any such suicidal reflective adjustment of evidence and conclusion in commonsense situations. I see an automobile coming and get out of the way. If I am asked why I stepped back, I might say "An automobile would have run me down if I had not." I have no warrant to say this or even to step back unless there is adequate evidence, but familiarity relates situation to conclusion in a flash of unreflective response.

In summary, evidence is evidence because of its relevance to a conclusion. The relevance consists in the relations between the concepts comprising the evidence and those comprising the conclusion. Concepts are generalizations, and generalizations comprise theory. Systematic theory consists of generalizations logically ordered by relations of inclusion, exclusion and overlapping. Relevance of evidence is determined by similarity of conceptual content between evidence and conclusion. Nothing is evidence unless it is relevant, and nothing is relevant except within a systematic context of meanings (concepts); concepts, in the last analysis, depend on reference of one part or aspect of the intuitive flux to other parts or aspects. The relevance of empirical evidence, then, goes back to the inclusion, exclusion and overlapping of generalizations involved in the perception of facts and to the relation between these generalizations and those of the conclusion. What is relevant and what is irrelevant depends on fitting into the context. The relevant belongs systematically to a context. Belonging systematically to a context is a matter of logical relationship. The relevance even of perceptual evidence depends, then, on theory.[4]

Victor F. Lenzen treats of the methods of scientific observation as a continuum in which the theoretic element (Lenzen calls it the hypothetical element) is least explicit in perception and becomes increasingly more explicit throughout the other methods of observation: counting, measuring length, measuring time, measuring weight, and similar methods.[5] According to the present analysis, perceptual evidence is that wherein conclusions are drawn from intuitive data with their conceptual interpretations adhering to them. The theoretic element is at a minimum. As the theoretic element in the evidence increases in comparison with the empirical content (interpreted intuitive data), the evidence becomes more logical until the logical evidence becomes predominant in the application of abstract mathematics and logic to empirical data. However both kinds are present in all empirical inference, and the difference is a difference of proportionate degree. At least some of the logical kind is necessary for perception to be perception of fact. Relevance demands that what is perceived be referred to a logical context if it is to be evidence. It also demands that what is logical be referred ultimately to perceptual data as long as there is any empirical content to knowledge. As Lenzen points out, there is a continuum of methods. The present theory holds that the continuity consists of the conceptual thread that runs throughout, from the proto-generalization of simple, direct awareness to the abstract relations of applied mathematics and logic. But logical evidence is evidence for

4. *See* Whitehead, *Adventures of Ideas,* p. 284. "A great deal of confused philosophical thought has its origin in obliviousness to the fact that the relevance of evidence is dictated by theory."

5. Victor F. Lenzen, "Procedures of Empirical Science," *International Encyclopedia of Unified Science* of the collected volume. (Chicago: University of Chicago Press, 1955) pt. 1, vol. 1, no. 5, p. 284ff.

empirical conclusions only when the logic is *applied logic*, that is, only when the data of experience are ordered by its means.

In cases before a lawcourt it is often difficult to distinguish "eyewitness" evidence from "opinion," that is, to distinguish evidence based on direct perception from evidence based on inferences made from perceptual data. For example, the witness may testify as to how fast the car was going or how tall the robber was. Did he directly perceive these? He is supposed to give only perceptual evidence unless he has qualified as an expert witness; but the distinction between perceptual and logical evidence may be difficult to ascertain because the actual situation is a continuum, and a continuum does not contain absolute lines of separation. The judge in a lawcourt may have to rule arbitrarily in specific cases, but the principle of the distinction between factual evidence and inference is clear: at one extreme the interpreted intuitive data, interpreted in terms of the commonsense concepts handed down in language, are predominant, while at the other extreme abstract relations are predominant.

It is customary to say that inductive inferences may be made directly from facts, but to say this is either an ellipsis of statement or an incomplete analysis. Empirical inferences are made from meanings. Inference is based on logical relations, and logical relations hold only between meanings. If facts seem to be logically related, the reason for it is that the facts themselves are in part logically constituted; and if facts seem to be evidence leading to conclusions, that is because facts have meanings. In the so-called unconscious inference of unreflective action, such as stepping out of the path of the automobile, the act is a direct response, not an inference although it is a result of habit formed on the basis of previous inferences. The inference in so-called unconscious inference is habit resulting from having made previous inferences.

Relevance between evidence and conclusion can be established only on the basis of conceptual analysis. Hence, for an inference to be explicitly drawn, or to be shown to be justified or to be warranted, the evidence and conclusion must be put into propositional form where the conceptual structure is exhibited and can be critically examined. A proposition is a proposed relationship between symbolized concepts or between a proper name and symbolized concepts. One holds some propositions to be true because of what one perceives; the proposition symbolizes relationships which are exemplified in interpreted intuitive data. Perceptual evidence consists of such propositions. One holds some propositions to be true because one already holds other propositions to be true. Logical evidence consists of such propositions. In actual empirical inferences varying degrees of the two are manifest. The structural relations of empirically true conclusions depend on the logical relations between the empirical meanings (generalizations) in the evidence.

Interpretation, as the term is here used, is not a process of inference. Perceiving is not inferring. Perceiving is interpreting intuitive data by proto-generalizations and generalizations. In the act of proto-generalization symbolism emerges. Some aspects of intuitive data refer to aspects of other intuitive data and become symbols of common elements. There is no rearrangement of concepts to form a conclusion as there is in inference. Perception is interpretative and not inferential when it is direct and no question of its veracity is raised; but if question is raised and veracity must be established in judgment, inference takes place. Even perception of fact is interpretative and not inferential when a percept is simply *taken* to be a fact as was the tomato in Chapter IV, but in this case the percept may be in error. If an unperceived fact is known, however, it is known by inference, as are the facts of past history or the earthquake in the illustration that opened the present chapter. A system of facts, such as the external world, contains multitudes of facts known only by inference. Of course, when a purported fact is challenged, it can be shown to be a fact only by inference, because its status as being known in *veridical* perception must be established. In interpretation, something is taken to be something else and becomes a symbol. In inference, relevant concepts already symbolized by some means, usually verbal if the concept is highly developed, are differently logically related in evidence and in conclusion.

At times in the history of thought perceptions or elements derived from the analysis of perceptions have appeared to some philosophers to be self-evident. At other times, logical principles have appeared to be self-evident. To the contrary, nothing is self-evident, and that anything should appear to be so is due to a faulty or inadequate analysis of the concept of evidence. Evidence leads to conclusion, but if anything is self-evident, the evidence and the conclusion are the same and no inference has taken place. Evidence must be relevant to the conclusion, but in self-evidence the relevance would be only to itself, and any proposition that is self-consistent could be self-evident. It has been pointed out that pure logic and pure mathematics find no self-evidence and need none.

In spite of the foregoing considerations an appeal to self-evidence is apparent in some philosophic writing today. The adherents to the latter-day cult of self-evidence usually avoid the term, but they appeal to the idea under some other locution, such as "it is an obvious truism" or "a familiar principle which is beyond doubt" or "which cannot be doubted" or "the contradictory is inconceivable." To the contrary, no proposition is beyond doubt except a logical tautology, and the tautlogy is beyond doubt only in the sense that it is a formula for asserting that whatever it says is true for all combinations of the truth or falsity of its constituents. All logical tautologies are materially equivalent, hence any one of them says nothing applicable specifically only to a part or detached fragment of experience. In addition, a tautology is beyond doubt only within the context of a two-valued logic, and a two-valued logic is not wholly adequate to a continuum, it is adequate only within a systematically conceptual context, and concepts are discrete. A two-valued logic deals only with selections from a continuum.

The essential characteristic of the latter-day cult of self-evidence is to be found in its doctrine that empirical knowledge (and therefore empirical science) rests on the firm authority of simple and direct observational statements of what it holds to be, in fact, the case.[6] If one grants, with the adherents of the doctrine, the firm truth of direct accounts of such observations, empirical sciences and philosophy that bases itself on empirical science can prove their conclusions in the strict sense of the word 'proof' provided that adequate language (natural or artificial) can be obtained.

The doctrine of the authority of direct observational statements is founded on an illusion. There is no such authority, for what appears to be simple and direct observational statements are interpretations involving conceptual elements (generalizations or proto-generalizations). If observational statements are about complex matters of fact, they involve more than simple conceptual elements; they involve some degree of logical structure among concepts, some degree of ordering the first data of awareness. The world of fact that one lives in and that natural science has for its object is made up of what is to some degree *orderly* experience. The order is conceptual, it involves generalization, and generalization depends upon an act of symbolizing.

The mistake of those philosophers who hold the doctrine of a self-authenticating direct observational report of the state of affairs in a ready-made factual world lies in their deriving the doctrine from investigating only adult, sophisticated, highly formulated knowledge based on fixed habits of thought. Empirical knowledge, however, is the result of a process and is *in process*. Its nature cannot be adequately ascertained by an investigation only of the later stages or the outcome of the

6. It is stylish today, with a strange perversion of ordinary language, to call statements of this kind 'incorrigible.'

process. Scientific knowledge has as its object an ordered world, but the origins of the order go back in evolution to a pre-language situation. This situation and its development is partially re-lived in each individual in the early months of infancy and in learning language. As a result, an ordered experience of commonsense fact is already at hand for the scientist and the philosopher to work on. If it were not, neither scientist nor philosopher would find any work to do. In spite of this some philosophers accept this ready-made world without critical inquiry into the question of how knowledge of it got to be what it is, thus mistaking an already developed experience to be an original experience.

No one can *prove* by recourse to theories of biological evolution or of genetic psychology the present view of the origins of knowledge. To attempt to do so would be to argue in a circle and to commit the very fault which is being adversely criticized. The philosophers who seek to deduce the possibility and nature of empirical knowledge from indubitable observations of fact together with adequate rules of language are following a will-o'-the-wisp. One would be equally misled, though in the opposite direction, if one were to attempt inductively to find the nature and possibility of empirical knowledge from the findings of biology and psychology.

On the other hand, it is quite legitimate to use evolutionary and genetic theories heuristically or in illustration of epistemological hypotheses or to suggest details of application. Such theories are useful also in the process of mutual adjustment of evidence to conclusion and of sifting data for relevance. The legitimate use of genetic psychological theories does not imply that the attempt to find an explanation of empirical knowledge must start with the study of a new-born infant. Whatever aid genetic psychology can offer lies within a highly organized context of theoretic, scientific knowledge. Epistemology must explain this context, among other things, and it cannot without begging the question both explain the context and prove the scheme of its explanation by appealing to the knowledge gained within the context. But a very young child is constantly gaining empirical knowledge, and an epistemological theory that ignores the process of gaining knowledge is not adequate. The task of epistemology is to construct a categorical scheme that will encompass all sorts of knowledge, not only the fully formulated, adult sort.

The doctrine of the present chapter that a conclusion merely rearranges the concepts of the evidence (with or without an increase in generality) runs counter to a tendency that has often been manifest in the history of philosophy, namely, that there are special logical structures which can be evidence for an existence stated in the conclusion that was not given in the evidence. This tendency has shown itself in arguments that run all the way from Anselm's ontological argument for the existence of God to arguments from particular structures involving the existential quantifier in symbolic logic. The point is different from that discussed in Chapter V concerning the relation between the principles of logic and reality. Here the point is that a particular existence is held to be proved by a specific logical argument. The only evidence for the *existence* of what is held to be proved in the conclusion is the structure of the argument itself.

All such arguments derive their apparent cogency from an equivocation or an incomplete analysis of the concept 'exist' or 'to be actual'. For example, Anselm, when he said "God exists," did not mean that God has a unique locus in time and space and is a possible object of (natural) perception; but his opponents, the nominalists, rejected his argument because it did not establish this. Anselm by 'exists' meant 'is real' in the context of the doctrine of realism of universals, but the nominalists, meaning something very different by 'exists', held his argument to be a non-sequitur.

For a contemporary example, let us take the existence indicated by the existential quantifier of modern logic. This quantifier is usually read "There exists an x such that . . ." or

"There is an x such that. . . ." Those persons who suppose that the use of this quantifier furnishes a proof for the existence of whatever value 'x' can take when thus quantified confuse two senses of the term 'exists'. In an uninterpreted logical system, the 'x' has only an intra-systematic existence, and this is a very special (and unfortunate) use of the term 'existence'. It is not existence in the sense of being actual in a spacetime context, and the logical structure does not endow its values with any such actuality.[7] The purely intra-systematic existence of logical entities means that there is something in the system (an undefined element, a defined element, a formula, a rule or some combination of these) such that the expression containing the existentially quantified varible is a legitimate construct of the system.

To take an example from Church:[8] "There is an x such that it is a number and is the sum of two cubes in more than one way." This is a theorem in arithmetic and if it can be proved, it offers evidence that at least one such number exists in some sense or other, but *as far as the theorem goes*, the sense of 'exists' is only that a number having this property is a legitimate part of the *system of arithmetic*. The theorem does not place the number in a realm of Platonic Ideas. Neither does it refer to any space-time actuality that can be counted by that number; for example, no storage capacity of exactly 1729 units is conjured into existence. Of course, neither Church nor Quine are under any illusion about this,[9] but there are persons

7. *See* Lewis and Langford, *Symbolic Logic,* p. 182, n. 10.

8. Alonzo Church, "Ontological Commitment," *Journal of Philosophy* 45 (1958): 1008–14.

9. *See* W. V. Quine, *From a Logical Point of View,* sec. ed. rev. (Cambridge, Mass.: Harvard University Press, 1961) p. 15, "We look to bound variables in connection with ontology not in order to know what there is, but in order to know what a given remark or doctrine, ours or someone else's, *says* there is." (Quine's italics.) *See also* p. 103, "What is under consideration is not the ontological state of affairs, but the ontological commitments of a discourse."

who do not follow the technicalities of the argument and are confused by the ambiguities of the word 'exists' who do think that some sort of Reality is indicated by the use of the logical quantifier. The only ontological commitment, however, is to a nonempty universe—if there is a system of logic, there is something—and the only existence indicated by a bound variable is that of an entity in a *universe of discourse*. Many kinds of universes of discourse can be defined none of which is Reality, for any one involves abstraction, and abstraction is a process performed by a mind using some sort of language. Clarity demands that the universe of discourse be defined and delineated in every case that calls for precise thought or understanding.

If an uninterpreted system of mathematics or logic is to be interpreted or applied, semantic rules stipulating the meaning of the logical symbols in terms of experience are necessary and govern the application.[10] In all cases where the structure of a logical argument seems to furnish evidence for the extra-logical existence of anything stated in the conclusion, it seems so because the semantic rules are not explicitly stated. If they were stated, it would be seen either that the extra-logical existence of whatever is concluded is asserted in them or else that there is some irrelevance in the conclusion and it is to that degree a *non sequitur*.

Evidence for existence in the sense in which facts exist arises only in the events and entities that emerge when the intuitive flux is cut. Concrete existence, or actuality, pertains to these events and entities. Whatever can be assimilated into the world of fact, whatever has a locus in space and time, is actual and it seems conducive to clarity of expression if the term 'existence' when unqualified would be used to apply only to actualities. Facts are entities within the universe of discourse of actuality. If logical classes or numbers are said to

---

10. *See* Rudolph Carnap, *Introduction to Symbolic Logic and its Applications* (New York: Dover Publications, 1958) pp. 1 and 101–2.

exist, their existence should be explicitly qualified as belonging to a logical or mathematical universe of discourse, and the locution 'logical existence' or 'mathematical existence' be used. In this way, fallacies of equivocation in argument and inference can be avoided.

When cuts are made in the flux, boundaries and definitions are introduced. Boundaries are definitive and mark off discrete units. An entity is a unit so marked, and some entities are concrete, or closer to the intuitive whole, while others are abstract, or more attenuated in their imposed separateness. To call anything an entity does not explain it, however, for 'entity' is not an explaining word except in a scheme where 'substance' is the fundamental category.

Particulars are concrete entities and universals are abstract entities, but there is no absolute dividing line between the two, for the theoretic activity of mind enters into the delineation and definition of particulars, while universals are abstractions and generalizations from concrete experience or from the meaning of symbols. Both particulars and universals are real. Cuts in the intuitive flux are real—when they are made, there they are. Proto-generalizations (primitive recognitions), ordinary generalizations (percepts of physical objects or events and limited classes of percepts), abstract generalizations (numbers, propositions, functions, infinite classes), are neither unreal nor more real to the degree that they are conceptual and theoretic. All are equally real each in its own category, and when we get each into its own category, we have put it into proper relation with whatever else that is real.[11]

---

11. The meaning of 'real' is primarily adjectival, but philosophers have been wont to hypostatize and take 'Reality' to mean the sum and substance of all that is real. Perhaps there is no such sum and substance.

CHAPTER VII

Belief and Knowledge

A persons's attitude toward his own conscious experience is ordinarily one of belief. The tendency to take this attitude is so strong that the having of experience has sometimes been held to be the paradigm of belief, but so to hold involves a double confusion. Experience is confused with conscious experience, and these are confused with an attitude of mind, an attitude of accepting conscious experience as a coherent part of a larger, orderly whole. It is true that some persons seem to be able to believe almost anything of which they are conscious. They have mouse-trap minds that snap closed at the slightest triggering and will not relinquish what has been seized. But if such a tendency were too prevalent among philosophers there would be no philosophy. Even if one has never had unbelievable experiences oneself, one should not deny the possibility of others having them.

I was once told by a woodsman in the northwest coastal region of the United States that he had had an experience he was not sure that he believed while he was having it. He was traveling on foot through heavily wooded, mountainous country and started up a strange animal. Its head, neck, forelegs and the front part of its body were those of a Canada lynx, but its hindquarters and hindlegs were those of a large and powerful jack-rabbit. It ran in jumps like a jack-rabbit, and made no attempt to climb a tree, although a lynx when pursued in such a situation invariably climbs. The woodsman was well acquainted with lynx and their habits. He pursued the animal, getting several glimpses of it. Twice he got a clear view, though the animal was in motion and the views were of short duration. Soon he lost the animal altogether, and though he returned to the place several times on later days, he never saw it again.

The woodsman was a high school graduate of high intelligence, who had studied elementary biology. He was not sure in any detail how much he believed of what he saw. The possibility that he was dreaming or having an illusion or even an hallucination occurred to him at the time, but the critical evidence was against these conclusions. He got glimpses of the animal over a period of about ten minutes and there was nothing strange or doubtful about contextual circumstances. The geographic relations between the place and other places of his acquaintance were clear. He had time to think about it while the experience was taking place. His belief of the contextual facts was unquestioned, but he was not sure what he believed about the animal or even about what he saw of the animal.

Exactly what was it that constituted his belief or his doubt in the situation? The question is not *what* did he believe and *what* did he doubt, or even *why* he believed or doubted in either case. The question is, what does it mean to say that he believed some aspects of the experience and doubted others?

The problem is further complicated by the question "Did I believe his story?" In what did my belief or disbelief consist? This question has a simple answer on a commonsense level, but the commonsense level uncritically assumes answers to the epistemological problems. I could find the place from his directions (I also was acquainted with the area). I was willing to grant that he actually had some such experience as that recounted. I knew him well and had worked and traveled with him sometimes under difficult conditions of terrain and weather. I knew that he sometimes loved to tell "tall stories," but I knew under what conditions he did so and what were the signs of his doing so when he did. The question remains, however, what did it mean for me to give credence to his story? Did it mean that if I had been there, I would have had the same sort of experiences that he did? But he was not sure that he believed his own experiences, so how could I believe them?

The question is still further complicated by the consideration that when I believed his story (including that he was not sure what he believed about seeing the animal), I was believing his memory of the event. Memory, presumably, was not in question in his original doubt, for he was not sure what he believed while the experience was taking place. Ever after, however, it was a question of his believing his own memory (including the memory of not being sure what he believed about seeing the animal). If remembered events are excluded, there is little left to be believed or doubted. Orderly and connected experience essentially includes memories and also includes relations between remembered events and present experience.

The present doctrine holds that there is no awareness of experience without proto-generalization. The vaguest recognition or identification involved in being aware of anything at all refers aspects of present intuitive data to data not now present. This implicit reference to data not now present is a necessary condition for the sense of memory. If there had been no past experience, there would be no present conscious experience. There is present conscious experience. Hence, according to the hypothesis, there has been past experience, and the reference to it in the proto-generalizations of simple, direct perception constitutes the initial credibility of memory.[1]

There is nothing to believe in present experience without the credibility of reference to the past. The point is not that this or that memory is credible in specific detail, but that without a reference to past occurrence in some cases and

1. *See* C. I. Lewis, *An Analysis . . .* , p. 334.

under some conditions there is nothing identifiable to be believed. Reference to past occurrences is the essence of memory, and the assimilation, or incorporation, of present data into this past and interpretation by means of it is the very form of believing reduced to its simplest epistemological terms. Whatever is assimilated to an orderly and connected experience is believed. If it cannot be assimilated, it is rejected or doubted.

Some epistemological theories assume that experience takes place in an absolute present, and that, arguing from the absolute present, it must somehow be proved that there has been a past and will be a future. Such a proof is impossible. If the present is absolute it contains no reference to a past or a future, and to attempt to get knowledge of past or future from it by inference would violate the rule of relevance of evidence. The doctrine of an absolute present would reduce experience to solipsism of the present moment, but the present moment, in its sheer presentness, has no experience to offer. Experience is what happens, but nothing would happen in an absolute present—an absolute present would be only being with no happening.

The present is "thick." It has an appearing edge and a disappearing edge, though neither one is sharp. Process takes place within the consciously experienced present, but there is no conscious experience that does not depend on a reference to the past and a possible future. There are no terms in which to reject or even to question the past that do not come from the past. It is not a delivery of experience that one is bound to the present and must somehow justify belief in the past and the future. On the contrary, it is only by an effort of analysis and abstraction that one can free oneself from reference to the past and anticipation of the future. The relevance of the past is part of present experience even though one be only dimly conscious of it or not conscious of it at all. Every concept is a precipitate of past experience and is also, in an important sense pointed out by Peirce, an anticipation of the future.[2] Since the definiteness and identifiability of percepts depend upon concepts, percepts likewise essentially refer to the past and the future.

To return to the illustration: the woodsman believed parts of the whole context of his experience. These were the parts that were assimilated to his orderly and connected experience, namely, the location, the trees, the rocks, the fallen logs, and even that there was some sort of an animal. But he was in doubt about what he saw of the animal, and he could not capture it for a closer investigation (not recommended in the case of a live wildcat) and he could not kill it for investigation, for he had no gun. He could not assimilate what he saw of the animal into his wider orderly and connected experience, including what he knew from his smattering of biological theory about the improbability of a hybrid cat-rabbit.

To say that one accepts or assents to or asserts what one believes is to give neither a definition nor an explanation of belief but is to give only synonyms. To say that belief is a disposition to act or to be ready to act in some specified way[3] is correct but is not definitive. It is correct, for an adult lives in a perceptual world where the percepts themselves are based upon the proto-generalizations of habitual action. The definiteness and order of this world emerge from the economy of response, and whatever is assimilated to this world is incorporated into the pattern of possible action. This assimilation is belief. The disposition to act is not definitive, however, for belief is a more fundamental attitude toward mental content than is implied by a specified way of acting. In addition, the disposition to act theory assumes that the world of orderly and connected experience is already there in all its specificity, ready-made to stimulate and receive reaction.

2. *See* CP, 5.402–3.

3. *See* R. B. Braithwaite, "The Nature of Believing" in A. Phillips Griffiths, ed., *Knowledge and Belief* (London: Oxford University Press, 1967) p. 30. "I have a disposition to act as if *p* were true."

Many philosophers define belief in terms of propositions[4] but to do so is unduly restrictive. Propositions can be believed but so also can direct percepts before they are embodied in propositions. It has been pointed out in Chapter IV that all direct perception makes a naive knowledge-claim. It is uncritical and unreflective, and of course does not establish any knowledge. Its relation to actual knowledge is only implicit. It might be said that on the unreflective level the naive knowledge-claim is simply the tendency to believe what is perceived. Seeing is believing on an unreflective level, and perceiving is uncritically assumed to be knowing on the same level. The question of explicit knowledge arises only when something challenges the naive claim. If a challenge arises from any source whatever, then the claim must be supported in the ways brought out in Chapters III and IV and is to be accepted as veridical or rejected as nonveridical according to its support. Percepts must be rendered propositionally, and reflective acceptance depends on establishing logical relations that show how the percept fits into the body of connected experience. If the perceptual data themselves are not sufficient or adequate to support the logical relations necessary to the fitting process, then a judicious person holds belief in abeyance or, if it is necessary to act, does so on the basis of belief held tentatively in such wise as to allow quick rejection or modification. The woodsman of the illustration was a judicious person.

Belief is an attitude. Knowledge is not to be defined as an

4. As does Braithwaite in the article cited above. *See also* H. H. Price's article in the same collection: "Some Considerations About Belief," where he gives the first element in belief as "the *entertaining* of a proposition" (p. 43). (Those persons who object to the word 'proposition' may substitute 'statement' in the present context and no great change in doctrine either adversely criticized or espoused will ensue.)

attitude: its differentia is evidence. Beliefs are not necessarily propositional, but knowledge is propositional. When belief is of propositions, *some* evidence is necessary for *justified* belief, but it may not be sufficient to establish knowledge. It follows, then, that there is no absolute dividing line between belief and knowledge. Braithwaite and Price in the articles cited define belief in terms of *entertaining* a proposition. On the other hand, it is only after beliefs are rendered propositional and distinguished from knowledge by adequacy of evidence that entertaining a proposition can be abstracted from the context. Entertaining a proposition is a more sophisticated procedure than either believing or knowing even though in some difficult cases of establishing knowledge it may be useful to entertain the proposition without commitment. It is only in reflective criticism that entertaining a proposition becomes disassociated from its assimilation. In entertaining one does not *consciously* incorporate the meaning of the proposition into a pattern of action.

Recent epistemologists such as Cook Wilson and H. A. Prichard emphatically reject the point of view expressed above that there is no absolute dividing line between belief and knowledge. Their position follows from their having taken their point of departure from Cartesian dualism and from their having accepted the Platonic distinction between belief and knowledge. Perhaps one of the reasons Plato contrasted belief (opinion) and knowledge is that knowledge is propositional whereas perceptual belief is immersed in the intuitive flux. Perhaps another reason is that the strictly cognitive character of knowledge can be contrasted with the volitional and emotional involvement characteristic of believing that is not knowing. Both of these contrasts hold, but they do not indicate a difference in kind between knowledge and belief. Some of what is believed is known; all of what is known is believed. If the knowledge-claim of belief is established, there is knowledge. Knowledge is a proper-part of belief.[5]

Knowledge is that portion of belief rationally founded on adequate evidence and progressively confirmed by new evidence. The knowledge is propositional; the evidence does not need to be propositional, but when it is, it itself must be known. Belief is the genus of knowledge but the crux of the definition of knowledge lies in the differentiae. Knowledge is cognitively superior to those beliefs that are not knowledge, and the superiority lies in the rational dependence on evidence. The rational dependence lies in the logical relationships between the concepts involved; what is evidence is determined by the relevance of concepts within a wide conceptual scheme. The differentiae of knowledge emphasize criteria other than volitional and emotional, for volitional and emotional factors are co-extensive with all belief, and in consequence will not serve to differentiate knowledge. Knowledge is not free from volitional and emotional characteristics, however, even though these are not differentiating, since all knowledge lies within the area of belief. For example, one can know that some forms of political organization are more conducive to human liberty than are others, and although one can have a passionate attachment to human liberty and therefore to those forms of government that foster it, it is not passionate attachment that constitutes knowledge in the sphere of politics.

The definition of knowledge given above is not circular as it might seem to be if put summarily "Knowledge is based on evidence, and the evidence itself must be knowledge."[6] This

5. I am using 'knowing' in the sense of Ryle's 'knowing that', not 'knowing how', precisely because 'knowing that' involves theoretic knowledge. I do not hold the Intellectualist Legend, however; I do not know of anyone who does. *See* Gilbert Ryle, *The Concept of Mind*, chap. 2, sec. 3. Of course, all knowledge is based on action manifested in proto-generalization, but this is not a consciously exercised skill.

6. Or, looked at in another way, it might appear to involve an infinite regress. *See* A. C. Danto, *Analytical Philosophy of Knowledge*, p. 27.

way of putting it is incorrect, for it does not recognize *direct* perception as evidence. It is when the evidence is propositional that it must be knowledge. Direct perception is not propositional even though, as has been pointed out before, propositions may supervene on it, that is, propositions may be made about it. When interpretations of intuitive data are successfully assimilated to orderly and connected experience, the percepts are unreflectively believed. The very success of assimilation makes the propositions supervening on direct perception, when they do so supervene, into perceptual knowledge which becomes evidence entering into the determination of further knowledge. A percept is interpreted intuitive data, but an empirical proposition about perception is a complex symbol, usually in terms of language having reference to a percept or percepts. The *knowledge* in perceptual knowledge is propositional, but it rests on mediating and symbolizing the content of perception. All empirical evidence goes back ultimately to the intuitive data that furnish the content of perception. Content may be regarded relatively instead of ultimately, however, and when so regarded, each step in the process of gaining perceptual knowledge furnishes the content for the succeeding step. Intuitive data, through interpretation, are the content of perception; percepts, through symbolic reference, are the content of perceptual propositions; and perceptual propositions are the content of perceptual judgments wherein what is proposed in the proposition is asserted to be a part of the orderly and connected experience making up the actual world.

Perceptual belief is the unreflective and uncritical assimilation of intepreted intuitive data into the body of orderly and connected experience. If such belief is challenged and surmounts the challenge, there is veridical perception. Perceptual knowledge results from putting perceptual beliefs into propositional form wherein the relations between the percept and the larger body of experience into which it is assimilated can be explicitly established. When it is judged that the relations actually hold and that the percept fits into the total context, the proposition is asserted in a perceptual judgment, and as long as the percept continues to fit, the judgment is held to be true.[7]

If the relations between the percept and the larger world of orderly and connected experience are disestablished, belief is held in abeyance or, more likely, rejected, and the percepts are assigned to some categorical wastebasket such as dream or illusion or erroneous memory image. As true perceptual judgments are taken up into wider and wider generalizations, and higher levels of abstraction are reached, the beliefs become more and more theoretic, and the knowledge-criteria become more and more predominantly logical, but the logic is always applied logic where empirical knowledge is concerned.

An essential part of the definition of knowledge is 'progressively confirmed by new evidence'. Reference to future experience is included within the nature of empirical knowledge. The generality of empirical concepts is not confined to the past and the present but extends also to the anticipation of future events. Since the future is always relevant, the evidence for empirical knowledge is never all in and the case is never closed. A scientific theory may attain a high degree of confirmation, and then new evidence may be found that requires its modification. For example, the discovery of radioactivity had a great impact on the atomic theory of the late nineteenth century. In the case of history, finding a long lost letter or document may cause what has been accepted as knowledge to be modified or abandoned. In all such cases the purported knowledge might have been warranted by the then available evidence and was correctly called knowledge; but knowledge that is not progressively confirmed by new evidence is to be challenged.

7. This is the *epistemological* import of the doctrine that the denotation, or extension, of a true empirical judgment is the actual world. *See* Lewis, *An Analysis . . .* , pp. 51–52. Lewis gives a *logical* reason for holding that the denotation of a proposition is the actual world.

New evidence itself may be based on perception or be more highly theoretic. Attempts to answer questions arising from the confirmation of purported theoretic knoweldge have led to the development of the scientific method with its formulation of theoretic knowledge claims in hypotheses and its criteria for the verification of hypotheses. These topics will be pursued in later chapters, but it must not be assumed at the outset that the only use of the scientific method of gaining and confirming theoretic knowledge is in the natural sciences. There are three fields in which the application and success of the scientific method of investigation must be considered: empirical sciences, rational sciences, and philosophic sciences. It may be summarily stated here that the method has attained its greatest success in the rational sciences, pure mathematics and pure logic, and its least success in the philosophic sciences. Varying degrees of success have been attained in different fields of the empirical sciences; physical sciences probably lead while social sciences are still in a rather insecure place. In any field, however, the scientific method is the most reliable way yet elaborated for determining those predominatly theoretic beliefs that are cognitively superior enough to warrant being called knowledge.

The application of the scientific method assumes, however, the validity of perceptual knowledge. Perceptual beliefs occur, that is, the human mind assimilates percepts into an accumulated experience. Some of these beliefs are fitted into an orderly and connected experience, which results in perceptual knowledge. The world so known is the world wherein the hypotheses of science arise and by recourse to which they are verified if they have empirical content. This is the world of fact in which human beings live. The facts, in one sense, are there; that is, in the sense that when the flux is cut, specific content is found. The content found is what the flux is *at the place of that cut*. If the cut had been elsewhere, the content found would have been to some degree different, namely what the flux was at the place of the different cut. The place of making the cut is not wholly arbitrary, either, for the exigencies of action demand that cuts be made at what were called, metaphorically, 'nodes' in Chapter IV. Yet the nodes have no absolute boundaries. Thus, in another sense, the facts are not there until they are carved out. The precise limits and definition of the facts are put by the mind in its conceptualizing activity. Mind contributes the delineation and meaning to the world which it inhabits.

Thus, perceptual knowledge is never to be assumed to be exactly the same for any two perceivers, though the demands of successful adaptive behavior and the possession of a common language will assure that all will cut at roughly the same nodes. The similarities are close enough so that differences can be disregarded and concepts can emerge in terms of which communication takes place. The social nature of language ensures that, as mind matures, one person's percepts will be more and more closely similar to those of others, at least of those who live in the same culture and speak the same language.

Higher-level abstractions and generalizations are built up on the basis of some sort of language, natural or artificial, and hence on the basis of communication. Nevertheless, different systems of abstraction and generalization are possible, and they will produce different bodies of theoretic knowledge, perhaps from similar factual bases. It is not to be assumed that one theoretic system is correct (true) and all others incorrect (false). If two theoretic formulations can be shown to be about the same facts, the choice between them is the choice between rival hypotheses. This topic will be pursued later, but it can be shown that the formulations are about the same facts only to a degree of probability depending on the means of communicating about factual experience, for each person is the center of his own ordered and connected experience. There is always room, then, for rival hypotheses in theoretic knowledge.

It follows from the view of the nature of knowledge here presented that all human knowledge is fallible. There is no absolutely certain knowledge. It also follows that all knowledge is in principle corrigible: errors can be corrected. Knowing is a self-correcting activity. Mankind is doomed to the possibility of error, but never to any inescapable particular error. Knowledge is subject to its own criteria. Man can not only believe that he knows, he can know that he knows. If the belief is well grounded in evidence and is progressively confirmed by new evidence, then this belief is itself knowledge. If, however, any piece of purported knowledge is shown not to be grounded or confirmed by the weight of evidence, it is no longer to be called knowledge. Unless the evidence is strongly against it, it may still be reasonably believed, but it is not knowledge.

As pointed out before there is no absolute dividing line between belief and knowledge. Knowledge is a focal point of cognitive clarity within belief, and it grades off without precise boundaries into beliefs that are not knowledge. Knowledge is continuous with belief; what is known is believed and what is reasonably believed is at least consistent with what is known. Perceptual belief is assimilation into orderly and connected experience, and knowledge depends on the logical articulation of the relations involved in the assimilation. The knowledge is theoretic to the degree that the relations are abstract and general.

The reason that belief cannot be coerced is that it is assimilation into a background of past experience. If the background for a different assimilation is not there, the different belief cannot be held. Belief is relative to the background of each individual. Persuasion is possible if the background for the different belief can be supplied, and in small matters it may be supplied briefly as in correcting the misbelief that Portland, Maine is farther north than Portland, Oregon by producing a map showing the latitude of each city (provided that the background is present for believing the map). Psychoanalytic techniques have shown that large changes in background can often be effected. Persuasion may be achieved also by showing relevancies between belief and background that were not apparent to the subject, or by pointing out something in the present situation that the subject had overlooked, thus affecting the assimilation.

Misbeliefs may be due to inadequate background. In this case, the belief is held to be reasonable from the point of view of him who holds it, but nevertheless may be incorrect from the point of view of him who has a larger or more comprehensive background. Examples of such misbeliefs may be found in the superstitions of ignorant persons. In other cases misbeliefs may be due to fragmented backgrounds, where different portions of past experience do not themselves make up a coherent whole. Extreme cases of such misbeliefs may be found in schizophrenia. Other sources of misbeliefs may be traced to an exaggerated dominance of some new concept or constellation of concepts, as when, shortly after the conquest of the air became a commonplace in the thought of many persons, there was a widespread belief in "flying saucers" and mysterious objects from outer space. It sometimes happens that incongruous mixtures of concepts form the background for the assimilation of experiences that are strange, and thus engender misbeliefs, as in the case of the belief in gremlins as willful personal agents of physical causation. Misbeliefs are often largely verbal. Because a verbal proposition is assimilated into a verbal background, a confused mind sometimes supposes that what it asserts is assimilated into the background of orderly and connected experience.

Whatever the proximate source of misbeliefs, they are all due to faulty assimilation of current experience into the body of past experience. Beliefs are reasonable to the degree that they are compatible with knowledge and approach it. Reasonable belief, when propositional, demands some evidence even though the evidence is not adequate to establish the belief as knowledge. If the belief is in conflict with knowledge, it is unreasonable. The volitional and emotional character of beliefs has been remarked before. When these characteristics are strongly involved or when there is a paucity of relevant knowledge (or worse, when there are both conditions), misbeliefs may be strongly held. To return to the illustration with which this chapter opened, some woodsmen whom I have known would have believed that they had seen in great detail a hybrid cat-rabbit.

It was stated several paragraphs back that one can know that one knows, but because the line of demarcation between belief and knowledge is not sharp in empirical matters there may always be borderline cases. The weight of evidence, either perceptual or logical, for any particular empirical judgment may be rather evenly balanced. A judicious person will not assert that he knows until he has more evidence. The ignorant person is one who either has no relevant knowledge or who does not coordinate his belief and action with this knowledge. The dogmatist makes the boundary between knowledge and belief sharp but too inclusive; he "knows" too easily and too much. The skeptic makes it sharp but too exclusive; he "knows" too little or not at all. The judicious person admits that there is a penumbral zone, but holds that it can be narrowed by new evidence. Even the clearest knowledge is subject to reevaluation in the light of new evidence, and the judicious person knows that no knowledge is certain.

In delineating the relation between knowledge and belief, the present doctrine has emphasized the explicit and articulated logical relations in the body of theoretic knowledge. Bodies of theoretic belief can be complex and logically articulated too, but this does not make them bodies of knowledge unless they are based on relevant evidence that is itself known. Complex political and religious beliefs illustrate the point. For example, a political theory may be built around a core of accepted value-judgments. The relations between the whole body of details and the underlying value-judgments may be logically structured, and the relations between the different details may also be logically structured. It is legitimate to call such a systematic set of beliefs a theory because of its structure and its claim to be a body of knowledge. Nevertheless, the claim is not to be granted unless the underlying value-judgments can themselves pass the test establishing them as knowledge. If their claim is based on volitional and emotional considerations to the exclusion of cognitive ones, they are not knowledge.

Presumably, the philosophic views at present widely prevalent that ethics and aesthetics are not to be considered bodies of knowledge are due to the foregoing considerations. It would take us far afield to argue whether or not ethics and aesthetics can be put upon a firm evidential foundation, but it is essential for the proponent of the view that they are bodies of knowledge to have a theory of the nature of knowledge and of evidence that would establish them.[8] At any rate, the status of politics, ethics, and aesthetics as bodies of knowledge is challenged if the basic value judgments are *merely* volitional or emotional or "intuitive" (using 'intuition' in a vague way rejected in the present study).

An organized and institutionalized religion yields perhaps the most characteristic example of a complex set of inter-related beliefs. In this case the set of beliefs can become the controlling factor in one's whole attitude toward the world—both the common world and the world of one's own experience. It can become controlling not only of action and emotion, but even of what the person who holds it is willing to call knowledge.[9] There may be very complex and highly general-

8. It is the opinion of the author that this has been done in various ways, for example by Lewis in *An Analysis . . . See also* S. C. Pepper, *The Sources of Value* (Berkeley and Los Angeles: University of California Press, 1958) especially chap. 1, sec. 3. A different approach is taken by R. M. Chisholm in *Perceiving* (Ithaca, N.Y.: Cornell University Press, 1957) where he elaborates a theory of perceptual knowledge on the analogy of the structure of the value experience.

9. Exemplified by William Jennings Bryan in the Scopes trial, testing the law against the teaching of biological evolution in the public schools, held at Dayton, Tennessee in 1925.

ized logical relations between the parts of such religious belief. When the belief is systematized in theological doctrine, it appears to be a body of knowledge. Systematic theologians characteristically refer to theology as a science, not a natural science, but a philosophic science, a body of knowledge.

The view of the nature of knowledge set forth in the present study requires that this claim to knowledge be challenged. In many respects systematic theology partakes of the characteristics of knowledge, especially in its logical articulation; but its use of evidence, both what it admits as evidence and the rules of inference between evidence and conclusion, is what is to be put into question. An element of faith underlies some of the crucial evidence in religious belief. Faith is primarily volitional and emotional. The present study holds that belief is anterior to the distinction between cognition, conation and affection. But when belief becomes knowledge, cognitive factors become predominant, and the other factors, although still present, do not differentiate that portion of belief to be called knowledge. Not so, however, in the deliverances of religious faith used as evidence. The volitional and emotional factors retain their status and become determinant as the body of religious belief is elaborated.

The sources of religious faith are largely, though not necessarily always, authoritative. Many persons adhere to their religious faith either as a result of having been molded in it from infancy, or as a result of the phenomenon of conversion, or as a result of accepting revelation other persons claim to have had. In the first case, the authority is that of parents and teachers. In the second, personal experience is involved, but it is primarily emotional and is given cognitive content by teaching or preaching or by the authority of social pressure. Only if conversion is due to a personal revelation is it based on a direct cognitive claim. In the third case the authority accepted as evidence is that of the person claiming to have had the revelation, or more likely, the authority of a tradition or a literature handed down from the past. Religious belief, then, uses authority as a source of evidence which is not permissible in a rigorous determination of empirical knowledge; and when a personal revelation is accepted as evidence, the body of conclusions is not natural knowledge. A body of philosophic beliefs is a philosophic science only in so far as what purports to be known is known by the "unaided light of natural reason."

The tendency of systematic theology to become an orthodoxy witnesses its reliance upon authority as a source of evidence. Although the acceptance of authority and revelation is enough to characterize systematic theology as a body of belief and not knowledge, the use of the rules of inference in religious beliefs offers further reasons for rejecting the knowledge-claim. The applied logic wherein empirical conclusions are drawn from empirical premises demands that the rule of cognitive relevance be observed. The rule is that all concepts in the conclusion be derived from concepts or combinations of concepts in the premises. In deductive inference the generality of the concepts of the conclusion is no greater than that found in the premises. In inductive inference the concepts of the conclusion are more general and therefore of greater extension than the concepts or combinations of concepts in the evidence, but the greater extension must be either justified by the application of the mathematics of statistical probability or verified by the perceptual observation of events deduced from the generality. If the conclusion is reached because of its human value or its volitional or emotional import, the logical rule of cognitive relevance has been transgressed.

To recognize that a body of religious beliefs is not to be called empirical knowledge does not disparage religious beliefs. There are human values that surpass and elude the grasp which is predominantly cognitive. It is the *belief* of this author that knowledge must be supplemented by rational belief when dealing with these values, whether they be, for example, of poetry, of nobility of character, of reverence, or of devotion. But knowledge in the literal, cognitive sense of the word must not be confused with what can be called knowledge only metaphorically, and the volitional and emotional aspects of these values do not yield knowledge in the literal sense.

Belief must outrun knowledge also because it is not always possible to act or decide on the ground of knowledge alone. Often there is not time enough to establish knowledge; often one cannot get enough knowledge. This is especially true in cases at law where a decision must be reached within a reasonable time. A judicial decision should be based on all the evidence that can be gathered, but it cannot be treated as a research problem. When it is necessary to act one must often act on belief, but it must be reasonable belief, compatible with what knowledge there is.

It is also the belief of the author that what is worthwhile in human life is often better and more fully attained if man *knows* in the literal sense as much as he can about his environment, about himself and about his interactions with the environment. Theoretic knowledge leads to understanding which is not only worthwhile in itself—its application yields many other things that are worthwhile. Therefore, the conditions of theoretic knowledge must be rigorously adhered to, and we must not confuse knowledge with beliefs that are not knowledge.

It is not one of the conditions of knowledge, however, that it be deduced or deducible from theoretically certain premises. The assumption that it can be established only deductively has vitiated much of the epistemology since Descartes. It underlies many of the contemporary theories of perception which look for an immediately given that is itself knowledge and is both certain and capable of being propositionally reported in its immediate certainty. The sense-datum theory and the theory of protocol sentences to be found in early logical positivism both seem to have been motivated by reliance upon the deductive model. From the point of view of this study, there is no theoretic certainty in perceptual experience, and even if there were, it could not be propositionally reported in its pristine condition. Conscious experience, even of the most rudimentary sort, is interpretative. That to which the interpretation is applied (that is, the intuitive flux or any part of it) is not an uninterpreted perceptual experience. There is no uninterpreted perceptual experience. All perception involves interpretation.

When intuitive data become the content of perception they are interpreted by means of rudimentary identifications and recognitions, that is, proto-generalizations; and when the perception is reported, even to one's self, it is in terms of coordinating concepts and relationships. These coordinating concepts and relationships, when elaborated, become a conceptual scheme. If there are no intuitive data, there is no content for the conceptual scheme, that is, there is nothing to report. But if there is something to report, the very possibility of reporting puts the data in terms which go beyond their own immediacy.

Knowledge is gained by induction more often than by deduction, and while the processes of confirmation and criticism are more often deductive than inductive, they are not and cannot be restricted to deduction alone. Concrete procedures either of gaining or of confirming knowledge usually employ a combination of the two.

CHAPTER VIII

Induction

Most beliefs are based on induction from past experiences. Some of them are general to a greater or less degree while others pertain to particular events. Some of them are well taken and some are not. Some are worthy of being called knowledge and some are not. Although these beliefs are based on the perception of particular events or facts, they are theoretical in form, and even if they pertain to anticipated future events, they are inductive if they are based on pattern or regularity alleged to be displayed in experience.

This is the setting for the so-called problem of induction. Systematic, theoretic, empirical knowledge relies largely on induction; but how are generalities to be obtained from particular data, and is there any guarantee that they are reliable? Hasty generalizations are as prevalent today as they were when Francis Bacon inveighed against them and they are still worthless. How can it be assured that induction will produce reliable knowledge and not error? Bacon's attempt to answer this question led to the statement of his methods of induction. Mill later elaborated these into his inductive canons. Such methods, however, are not directed at the basic problem of induction, and the question that they are designed to answer is not the basic issue. They assume that induction under correct conditions is a knowledge yielding process, and they attempt to formulate the conditions. Thus, they assume that

149

some inductive inferences are valid, and they direct themselves to the problem of separating the valid from the invalid ones. This is primarily a logical problem and leaves unanswered the epistemological question: How do we know that the generalizations based on the experience of particular facts are themselves, under any conditions, worthy of being called knowledge?

Following suggestions gleaned from Hume's philosophy, other persons have stated the problem of induction: "How can we know causation?" or "How can we know that predicted future events will take place?"[1] These are highly confused ways of stating the problem. Causation is a special kind of relation and is not involved in all inductions. And the prediction of future events depends on the prior establishment of generalities obtained from the observation of particular events.[2] If these generalities are not worthy of being called knowledge, then the prediction itself is not knowledge.

In Chapter VII it was noted that knowledge is subject to its own criteria: man not only knows, but can know that he knows. If one believes that induction yields empirical knowledge, and if that belief is rationally founded on evidence and is progressively confirmed by new evidence, it itself is knowledge, and one knows that induction yields knowledge. This assurance is not a pleonasm, for there are forms of qualified skepticism and of fideism which hold that although induction works for ordinary practical purposes, there are no adequate criteria establishing that it yields genuine theoretic knowledge.

1. For example, Jerrold J. Katz, *The Problem of Induction and Its Solution* (Chicago: University of Chicago Press, 1962). At the beginning of his Preface, Katz states the principle of induction as "the rule we use to make inferences about unknown events from a sample of data drawn from experience."

2. Of course Katz acknowledges generality in referring to a rule. On page four of his text he states the paradigm of inductive inference in terms of generality and speaks of "inductive predictions and generalizations."

The theoretic knowledge-claim, according to these doctrines, amounts to no more than a habit of thought or an act of faith. In particular, both the skeptical and the fideistic positions challenge that one can *know* that scientific method is a reliable and adequate source of empirical knowledge.[3]

Unless a rational basis can be formulated for holding that inductive inference yields knowledge, either theoretic skepticism or fideism is the final epistemological position for science. Deductive inference raises no problem provided that one does not inquire into the source of the knowledge of the premises of deduction. The rule of relevance and the rules of deductive inference ensure that nothing is asserted in the conclusion that cannot be found to have been implicitly asserted in the combination of the premises; that is, no concepts appear in the conclusion that are not in the premises, and the extension of these concepts is fully determined by the combined extensions of the concepts of the premises. Unless one raises the question of the source of the premises, however, the conclusions of deductive inference yield no empirical knowledge. If the conclusion is to yield empirical knowledge, at least one of the premises must contain an empirical generalization, and there is nowhere to get this except by induction.

The evidence from which empirical inductions are made is particular experiences, and a greater degree of generality

3. Hume's "mitigated skepticism" of sec. 12, pts. 2 and 3 of the *Enquiry Concerning Human Understanding* is of this sort. For an example of fideism, see M. Polanyi, *Science, Faith and Society* (London: Oxford University Press, 1946) p. 59. Perhaps Katz is to be counted among the fideists. He holds that induction can be neither validated nor vindicated, but that nevertheless "The laws of nature are of a certain order of complexity, and some of the rules, but not others, are capable of discovering such laws, or adequate approximations of them, within a reasonable number of trials" (op. cit., p. 115). He does not prove this, however, and on p. 22 he says "there may be nothing to justify our preference for inductively established conclusions, but there may be a great deal to be said by way of explaining why we persist in the inductive faith."

appears in the conclusion than is to be found in the evidence. This greater generality may be expressed in the form of the conclusion, as when it is judged that all crows are black because multitudes of crows have been seen and each one was black; or it may appear as a new concept, as when Kepler, on the evidence of many observed positions of the planet Mars, judged that its orbit was *elliptical;* or when a geologist, on the evidence of many observations of New England landscapes, introduces the concept 'glaciation'. In each of the two latter cases, the concept is a generality based on separate percepts, and it connects the percepts.

The greater generality of the conclusion in inductive inference will be taken in the present chapter to be the heart of the epistemological problem of induction. What is the warrant for calling the conclusion at which inductive inference arrives knowledge? How can one say that one knows generalities on the evidence of the knowledge of particular instances? This way of putting the question does not state the strictly *logical* problem which concerns the criteria for establishing the difference between correct or incorrect, valid or invalid inductions, but the present discussion is not primarily concerned with the logical problem.

The confused state of the theory of induction at the present time is probably due to its having been treated in the history of philosophy primarily as a problem of logic. Although it has been so treated, epistemological considerations have often played a predominant role and have been confused with the strictly logical problem. Epistemology asks whether the generalities induced from particular, perceived experiences constitute genuine knowledge; logic asks for a formal statement of the norms of inductive inference. The solution of the logical problem is highly technical and lies in the mathematical relations between the composition of samples and the composition of whole populations, and in the theories of sampling and probability that systematically articulate these relations. This strictly logical problem cannot be said to have been satisfactorily solved at the present time. Epistemological issues are often involved in the discussion of probability, too, and these hinder the solution of the strictly logical problem. But as more becomes known in the domain of sampling and frequency, the logical and the epistemological problems can be more easily disentangled.

There has been a persistent tendency in discussions of induction to assimilate induction to deduction, to "justify" induction deductively, or even, in extreme cases, to show that induction is an implicit or disguised form of deduction. If such attempts are directed at the epistemological problem, they are radically misconceived, for epistemologically induction and deduction are opposite and complementary processes. From the standpoint of pure logic, however, the case is not so clear. There is nothing inconsistent in the assumption that the ordering relations of valid inductions can be displayed in a formalized structure in which they are deductively arranged and systematized. Such a formalized structure, however, has not yet been elaborated to the satisfaction of all students of the subject.

Returning to the strictly epistemological problem, we repeat that induction is the process of acquiring theoretic (general) knowledge about the particulars of experience. Thus, the first question is: how can the nature of such knowledge be formulated in accordance with the view of the nature of knowledge of particulars stated in the present study? The answer requires a review and elaboration of some of the points in Chapters III and IV. Particulars are known through perception, but the goal of induction is systematic, theoretic knowledge, and this is known rationally, not through perception. The belief that a generality holds of particular facts must be based on adequate evidence or else it is not knowledge. An investigation of the nature of the evidence and how it operates to yield knowledge is indicated.

If particulars were known in absolute separateness, there

would be no intelligibility, for intelligibility depends on relatedness. Aside from intelligibility, however, particulars could not be known at all if they were absolutely separate. They are known by reference to interpretation, and this is recognition, identification in terms of parts of the flux not present. *Knowledge* of any part of the flux in absolute separateness is a contradiction in terms. A particular is an event (episode) in the flux that is singled out by a mind, another event (episode) in the flux. Events are not discrete. The flux is a continuum, inclusive of all its parts, and each part is inclusive of lesser parts, but the parts, considered as parts of the *continuum,* have no fixed boundaries. When one part is singled out, it may be regarded as a whole relative to *its* parts. Beyond this relative meaning of 'whole' and 'part' the present usage does not go. It neither assumes nor implies any metaphysical doctrine of the nature of wholeness.[4]

Perception singles out an event in the flux, and each event is a whole relative to its parts. In point of time knowledge starts with perception, but every percept has parts, and the process whereby we distinguish parts is analysis. Analyzing is the most fundamental and one of the most important cognitive activities. Without it no farther cognitive step is possible, because without parts there are no structural relationships, and without structural relationships there is no intelligibility or understanding.

When the mind in an act of perceiving singles out an event in the flux, it does so by reference to other events in the flux, recognizing and identifying by means of proto-generalizations. Particulars of perception, then, do not exist in absolute separateness. They exist as particulars by virtue of being cut out of the flux, and they are cut out by reference to what they have in common with other events, though there is no assumption of absolute identity of what they have in common.[5]

4. *See* p. 25.
5. *See* p. 52.

There is no evidence that a perceived whole can be analyzed in only one way. The analysis depends on purpose. If a perceived whole seems to be composed of rigidly fixed parts, that is because unduly rigid habits of perception lend their fixed patterns to the way in which the perceptual object is regarded. In the aesthetic attitude, the parts apprehended may be very different from those apprehended in the practical attitude. Most adults perceive in the practical attitude most of the time, and it is only for this reason that fixed parts sometimes seem to be given.

Analysis itself is only an extension of the selective activity of perception. Perception contains a focus of attention, and attention is selective; there are parts in what is perceived, and on reflection there is consciousness of the parts. The important thing is that although there are parts, it is not foreordained exactly *what* parts. The whole exercises a negative determinism over the parts in so far as nothing can be a part which is incompatible with the whole or with other parts. Analysis is responsible to the whole, for the parts must be parts of this whole, they cannot be irrelevant to it; but there is nothing to indicate that a whole can be analyzed into only one set of parts and there is plenty of evidence the other way. Every time a person "changes his mind" about something he perceives, or every time he discriminates something in the field of perception that he did not discriminate before, the analysis is different.

A persistent error in theories of perception has been to regard perception as primarily synthetic—as a synthesis of separately given sensations or impressions or sense-data into a whole of perception. The psychological theory of atomistic sensationalism of the nineteenth century led into a blind alley. Nevertheless, many recent theories of perception ignore the psychological "lesson." The only synthetic process in perception is interpretation, and this is not synthetic in the ordinary sense of putting together antecedently separate parts. It is synthetic only in the sense of assimilating present perception to previous perceptions.

It would be equally an error, however, to suppose that perception is a process in which a whole without parts is first perceived and at a subsequent moment parts are found in it. Whole and parts are relative to each other, and there could be no moment of perception of a whole before a subsequent analysis into parts. Concrete perception is of a whole composed of parts or of parts constituting a whole—there is no essential difference in meaning between the two expressions.

Analyzing is the first step in a continuum of inductive procedures. Other steps, in increasing complexity, are prescinding, generalizing, and abstracting, but each step grades continuously into those on each side of it, and an indefinite number of substeps could be elaborated. What are here called steps might be better envisaged as dimensions of inductive procedure rather than as a linear progression, but either alternative is analogical. For simplicity of exposition I shall introduce them as steps, but the processes of induction are continuous. The names here used are of little importance, and one can use whatever name one wishes as long as the principle of the inductive continuum is preserved. I have dealt with analysis and shall proceed to the exposition of prescinding, generalizing, and abstracting.

When parts have been distinguished in perception, prescinding can come into play. To prescind is to isolate for purposes of thought one of the parts found by analysis. Prescinding treats the part as if it were separate from the context wherein it is found. It is thinking of one part without reference to other parts. To prescind means to cut something out—it takes one of the analyzed parts from its concrete context, that is, from the whole of perception, not actually but in thought. The part is not perceived by itself; it may not be the sort of thing that can be perceived by itself, but it is thought of without reference to its context. Whenever one thinks of the red or the blue or the yellow of a visual object or field, for example, one prescinds. Red or blue or yellow is not perceived without spatial extension, but a specific hue can be held in thought without respect to its extension, shape or anything else in the perceptual context where it is found. The specific quality is prescinded from the percept.[6]

A great deal of free play is exhibited in the mind's ability to prescind. What product of analysis the mind fixes upon to think of separately sometimes seems quite arbitrary, but often it is determined by purpose. Perhaps it would be better to say that it is an expression of purpose. Perhaps 'purpose' means only the description in terms of expected events of the kind of analysis and prescission carried out. The important thing to notice is that *any* of the products of analysis can be prescinded. On the basis of a single analysis, alternative aspects can be prescinded. In addition, alternative analyses may give rise to greatly diverse schemes of prescission. It makes no sense to ask which scheme is correct. Each is relative to the analysis upon which it is based, and any analysis is correct that can be consistently and coherently made and that is responsible to the whole analyzed. There are multitudes of ways to prescind from any complex whole of perception, and within the limits of legitimate analysis, many alternative schemes of prescission will result.

There is no entity ontologically independent of mind which is either the object of the process of prescinding or its resultant. A prescission, that is, what is prescinded, is literally a part of perception singled out as an object of thought or attention. It is not usual, however, for thought to stop with prescinding, for that which is prescinded is usually taken up without delay into a generalization. Generalizing is the next

6. C. S. Peirce carefully distinguished prescinding from abstracting, CP, 2.428. I am not holding Peirce's doctrine that prescinding requires imagining, however, as my reversal above of his illustration of color and extension at the bottom of p. 260 and top of p. 261 of vol. 2 of CP shows.

inductive procedure. Concepts are general. When it is noticed that what has been prescinded from one context can be prescinded also from another or other contexts, a simple qualitative generalization is made, and the present quality is a symbol for qualities experienced at other times but not now present.

A language difficulty that has been noted before appears here and illustrates the distinction between prescinding and generalizing. Noticing the red or blue or yellow of a visual percept is a case of prescinding, but strictly, it is only *this* red or *this* blue or *this* yellow that is prescinded. 'Red' ordinarily is the name not of a prescission but of a concept, and concepts are general. Ordinary language does not distinguish between prescissions and low-grade qualitative generalizations, and it need not, for there is no absolute boundary between the two. The difference is a difference of degree; proto-generalizations are present throughout.

Simple qualitative generalizations are relatively concrete, but other generalizations may be more abstract. For example, 'color' is a generalization of higher order than is 'red',[7] it names a more abstract concept for different kinds of qualitative generalization; it covers the different visual qualities, red, blue, yellow, and others.[8] 'Color' does not name what red, blue, and others have in common. They have nothing qualitative in common. Neither does 'color' name what is not red or blue or others. 'Color' is a class name (I shall call it a generalization of kind as distinct from a qualitative general-

7. Cassirer makes this distinction in his discussion of Lotze. *See* Ernst Cassirer, *The Philosophy of Symbolic Forms,* vol. 1, p. 283.

8. Of course 'red' may be taken as a generalization of all the more specific shades of red, and so on for the others. This is a case of the language difficulty mentioned. What is named is only a cut in the continuum. There is no sheer dividing line in consciousness between what is absolutely specific and what is not. There are different degrees of specificity and generality.

ization) and is of the nature of a variable. It indicates one of the specific visual qualities but does not indicate which.

Generalizations of kind are classes of higher order than are simple qualitative generalizations. They are classes of classes. Some classes have as members things with a quality in common. Other classes have as members the qualitative classes, and these classes of higher order are more abstract since they are further from the concrete source of experience. Of course the more abstract classes such as the generalizations of kind can be dealt with only by means of symbols, of which verbal and mathematical symbols are most important.

The grasp of a new class of higher order by an act of symbolization is the inductive leap that ranges from the "aha" response of a dull mind to the scientist's flash of genius. Not all generalizations are equally fruitful, and sometimes it takes a flash of genius to make prescissions and to formulate coordinations between previously made generalizations that lead to illuminating abstractions. Both the prescissions and the generalizations are formulations of the mind, as was emphasized by William Whewell in his controversy with John Stuart Mill over induction more than a century ago: ". . . that in which the particular things are found to agree, is something formed in the mind of him who brings the agreement into view."[9] Mill, however, could not comprehend the meaning of such a statement, for, in his methods of induction, the initial analysis (and it is a completely rigid one) of the particulars from which an induction is to be made is uncritically assumed. Mill was devoted to the blackberry bush fallacy.

Generalizations are based on prescissions that are common to more than one context. 'Special' or 'specific' in the sense in which it is contrasted with 'general' means 'existing in only one instance' or 'present in only one context'. 'General' means 'present in many contexts'. Each context is itself specific, that

9. Wm. Whewell, *Of Induction With Especial Reference to Mr. J. Stuart Mill's System of Logic* (London: John W. Parker, 1849) p. 42.

is, different in its wholeness from all others. It is only in ana-lyzing and prescinding that clear-cut similarities between dif-ferent contexts emerge and generalizations can be formulated, first qualitative generalizations and then generalizations of empirical kinds.

The proto-generalizations of Chapter III, the simple recog-nitions and identifications implicit in the economy of response to intuitive data, are not full-blown inductions; they are nec-essarily vague. This vagueness is one reason for distinguishing them by the term '*proto*-generalization'. Inductive knowledge proceeds from the vague and the tentative, from imperfect grasp, to the relatively more precise and sure, to a more ade-quate grasp. It is a self-correcting process. Steps are tentatively taken. In the light of later steps, the first steps are modified or discarded, and then, in turn, the later steps are modified, and this process goes on and on. Analysis, prescission, and gener-alization are not performed in one-two-three order, but inter-act with each other, and from the interaction there emerges a more complex inductive procedure, functional abstraction.

Analysis can operate on wholes of thought as well as on wholes of perception. Out of the previous results of the induc-tive process, new wholes of thought are constructed, and new relations will emerge between parts of the new wholes. To quote Whewell again, "To hit upon the right conception is a difficult step; and when this step is once made, the facts assume a different aspect from what they did before: that done, they are seen in a new point of view; and the catching this point of view, is a special mental operation, requiring special endow-ments and habits of thought."[10]

The present theory holds with Whewell that fully developed induction is this "special mental operation." When the per-ceptual world is put into simple order by means of qualitative generalizations and generalizations of empirical kind, a larger, more inclusive whole becomes available for analysis. Rules of

10. Whewell, *Of Induction* . . . , p. 29.

relatedness tying together different parts of the ordered world can be formulated, and patterns of change emerge. Serial relations can be defined, and different series can be correlated. Thus, the concept of a function of a set or series of events is reached, and since rational relations and rules of relatedness are highly abstract, the formulation of such relations and rules has been called 'functional abstraction'.[11] Functional abstraction is necessary to produce the inductive knowledge lying at the foundations of both mathematics and natural science.

The concept of number is an example of functional abstraction. It may well be that counting arose from tallying, and these operations are close to the simple ordering of concrete, perceptual experience; but counting is more than prescinding a qualitative similarity from an aggregate of perceptual objects, and things counted are not necessarily of an empirical kind. Counting is ordinal, and an important new concept is grasped when it is realized that cardinal number is an abstract order *exemplified* by instances of counting, and that in its own nature it is the formulation of abstract relationships according to a rule. The formulation according to a rule frees the mind from dependence on counting, and as soon as a suitable symbolism has been devised, numbers can be manipulated and the concept extended indefinitely without reference to perceptual aggregates.

Induction in the natural sciences uses the method of functional abstraction when it introduces into a context under investigation a new explanatory concept such as Kepler's ellipse or the concept of glaciation mentioned before. Kepler was able to coordinate his knowledge of spatial relations and the results of Tycho Brahe's observations of the positions of the planet Mars in such a way as to suggest the generalization

11. *See* Ernst Cassirer, *Substance and Function,* chap. 1. Cassirer is treating of concept formation whereas I am treating of the larger processes of induction, but the formation of highly abstract concepts is an inductive process.

that planets move around the sun in elliptical orbits. The concept of the elliptical orbit was a brilliant functional abstraction from the data at hand. In a somewhat similar way, a geologist may be able to establish a functional relationship between many different characteristics of a landscape, such as U-shaped valleys, hanging valleys, cirques, polished boulders, scratches on bedrock, drumlins, and arrive at the induction 'glaciation'. Robert Boyle, in his experiments with gases in the seventeenth century, measured the volumes of a gas when subjected to different pressures. The changes in volume could be reduced to an ordered series, and the changes in pressure to another series. The two series could be correlated and the statement of the law of inverse proportion of volume and pressure resulted. Scientific laws are functional abstractions often of great complexity and generality.

An illustration of a relatively complex case of functional abstraction available to persons having only an elementary knowledge of physics may be found in a consideration of Ohm's law. In the first place, the concept 'electricity' is not a simple qualitative generalization. There are no perceptual qualities that are prescinded and generalized to comprise the concept. The concept of current electricity was arrived at slowly through the use of a model from hydrodynamics to comprehend several series of observed changes in phenomena on the analogy of water flowing through a pipe under pressure.[12] Some of the observed phenomena (such as the production of work, heat, electrolysis, shock strength) were gathered together in a concept of "current flowing," and a unit of measurement (the ampere) was devised. Other phenomena were gathered together and a unit of "pressure" (the volt) was determined. Other phenomena were assimilated to constrictions or other impediments in the pipe and gave rise to a unit of resistance (the ohm). Now the whole concept of current elec-

12. The use of perceptual models in science will be discussed later. *See* pp. 210–213.

tricity could be clarified by the observation of the functional relation between current, pressure, and resistance. The numerical value of any one of the three terms could be stated as a ratio between the other two. The ordinary statement of the law is that the amount of current is equal to the pressure divided by the resistance. With exact measurement, the concept could be given a mathematical model that further clarified it and made it more definite.[13] There is still no perceptual grasp of electricity except in analogical terms. The definition of the concept today consists wholly in the mathematical terms wherein the functional relationships are expressed. The concept of electricity itself is a functional abstraction, and Ohm's law is one of the ways in which it is expressed.

In summary, the procedures of induction are analyzing, prescinding, generalizing, and abstracting (functional abstraction). This classification is itself analytical, not temporal or psychological. Although some measure of analysis of perception must precede the others, the processes do not necessarily occur in successive order, but interact with each other as has been pointed out. The processes are psychological but this does not make the explanation merely psychological. Gaining knowledge is itself a psychological process, and its analysis might be expected to involve other psychological processes, but epistemology does not set up the categories of the science of psychology. The present analysis of induction is rational, not psychological.

This account has taken its point of departure from perception because inductive knowledge begins in point of time with the act of perceiving. As it proceeds, however, it becomes more complex. New inductions are based on previous inductions and interlock with other inductions. This is the case both in common sense and in the sciences. In so far as induction yields precise theoretic knowledge, the generalizations

13. For mathematical models, *see* pp. 203–205.

involved must be precise. This ideal is difficult to achieve in empirical knowledge, for there are no precise limits or boundaries in the flux. It requires an adept mind to set limits that are precise, clear, and consistent, and always to adhere to them in different contexts. The generalizations made in the course of ordinary, commonsense inductions will only more or less approximate the ideal. Exact measurement in the sciences makes analysis and generalization more precise, however, and as a result, functional abstractions can be systematically ordered into comprehensive theory. Functional abstractions are always highly general.

Theoretic knowledge, as contrasted with perceptual knowledge, is a systematic structure of generalizations. It is true that there is a minimal conceptual (theoretic) element present in all perceptual knowledge; and even in direct perception, proto-generalizations are necessary. Commonsense class concepts of the external world (embodied in common nouns) are necessary to veridical perception. Perceptual knowledge is intuitive data mediated by concepts, while theoretic knowledge is a systematic structure of concepts wherein perceptual content is referred to (if at all) only by symbolism. There is a theoretic thread running throughout, and it is this theoretic thread that not only makes induction possible but also "justifies" it epistemologically. The induction of generalities that can be systematically structured is the enlargement and completion of what makes knowledge possible in any case. If induction is not a legitimate epistemic procedure, there is not only no knowledge of any kind, there is no perception or even consciousness.

Inductive generalizations are worthy of being called knowledge when they are based on adequate evidence. The evidence consists of percepts and constellations of percepts comprising facts; and it is adequate when the facts can be analyzed and prescinded from in such a way as to bring out common elements. A generalization is warranted to the extent that the facts can be shown to have a common element[14] or that the generality is a functional abstraction. Such generalizations, however, are not universal.

Two questions remain: the question of universality and the question of the applicability of induction to predicting future events. These two questions are not unrelated, for complete universality includes reference to future instances. The remainder of this chapter will consider these questions. Some readers may note that I have not considered the question of the truth of inductions. The omission is deliberate, for whenever the problem of induction is approached from the direction of truth, the discussion becomes a web of confusion. This is because by definition truth cannot be erroneous, whereas inductions—quite valid ones—are often in error. Knowledge can accommodate induction, however, for knowledge is fallible. *After* we have discovered error we may no longer call it knowledge, but the discovery of error is based on new evidence. Knowledge has been here defined as relative to the evidence. When more or other evidence is discovered, what was knowledge previously may no longer be such relative to the new evidence, but it may have been genuine knowledge relative to the evidence then pertaining. These conditions do not apply to truth, and it is confusing to introduce questions of truth at the present stage of the inquiry.

Induction cannot yield complete universality because when generalizations are universal, they are intended to apply to unexamined instances (including future ones) as well as to examined ones. Nevertheless, empirical knowledge must be cast into universal forms if strict deductive inferences are to be based upon inductive generalizations, for at least one of the premises of deduction must contain a universal statement,

14. It must be constantly held in mind that the commonality of the present theory is based on commonality of reaction and not on identity in different instances. *See* p. 52.

and the method of verification of hypotheses in the sciences requires deduction. Strict universality is not obtained from induction alone, however, but from a combination of induction with definition by stipulation. There is an element of conventionalism in all universal empirical statements. Conventionalism does not solve or dissipate the problem of induction.[15] But it is combined with induction to yield universal empirical premises.

When one says "All men are mortal", the property 'mortality' is attributed to men by observation, but not to all men. There are billions of men who have not died. A surprisingly large proportion of all the men who ever lived are still alive.[16] It is nevertheless known that all men are mortal because 'man' is defined by reference to terminating physiological processes. The physiological processes are known to terminate, again partly by induction and partly by definition; but unless it is stipulated that what does not involve these processes will not be classified as a man, it is not known that all men are mortal. Inductions on several levels are involved, but they are systematically interrelated by the stipulation of the definition. This is as it should be according to the present theory, for definitions are made by the mind, they are not given in discreteness in the flux. They are made in the process of ordering the flux and grasping it in knowledge and understanding. 'Man', being the name of a class and going far beyond a qualitative generalization, is a functional abstraction, and in order that its application should be clear, it must be sharply defined and the stipulation understood that nothing but what fulfills the definition is to be a member of the class. Thus, according to the present theory, there legitimately can

15. *See* G. H. von Wright's chapter entitled "Conventionalism and the Inductive Problem," *The Logical Problem of Induction*, sec. ed. (Oxford: Basil Blackwell, 1952) chap. 3. *See also* Ernest Nagel, *The Structure of Science*, pp. 179–83.

16. Population experts estimate that between a quarter and a third of all men who ever lived are now living.

be universal, empirical propositions, but to a blackberry picker such as John Stuart Mill there cannot.

This, perhaps, can be further illustrated by a crucial example: "All birds are feathered." If some animal were discovered now that did not have feathers—not even vestigal ones —but had all the other anatomical and physiological characteristics of a bird, the taxonomist would have to decide whether or not he would keep 'feathered' in the definition. If he did, the universal "All birds are feathered" would still be empirical knowledge and the new specimen would be labeled a non-bird. If he did not, "All birds are feathered" would go the way of "All swans are white" (although it is doubtful that the latter statement was ever regarded as a genuine universal by anyone but authors of logic textbooks).

The foregoing examples are oversimplified, but they bring out the connection between induction and definition in the formation of empirical universals. An empirical universal is not a simple analytic statement, for genuine inductive generalities are involved. Empirical defintions are made in terms of concepts inductively arrived at, and the stipulation in the definition is by no means arbitrary, for it must serve the empirical purpose of coordinating this induction with others, and so of introducing order and coherence into experience.

Furthermore, in the actual practice of the sciences, the decision to make some characteristic or characteristics definitive is not made until it becomes necessary. Each possibility will be considered tentatively in order to follow out the implications of each one. It may be possible to hold the definition hypothetically for some time before a decision must be made. Not only is this true of definitions, it is also true of the conditions under which experiments are to be performed when a tentative induction is being tested. The experimental conditions must be inductively established, but again it sometimes becomes necessary to regard them or some of them as definitive. When Boyle performed his experiments on volume and pressure of gases, he did not stipulate that the temperature remain constant, but later, from further inductions on gases, it was seen that this condition must be made definitive. Different inductions had to be connected and some of them made definitive before universality could be achieved.

The way in which a characteristic or property may be made definitive and yet stated hypothetically is illustrated by the way universal propositions of the form 'All A are B' are expressed logically in quantified form 'For every x, if Ax then Bx'. Here, A is not categorically predicated of x. The proposition says only that if anything is A, it is B, or in terms of illustrations, "If anything is a man, it is mortal" or "If anything is a bird, it is feathered." All the consequences that follow from the categorical form of the proposition follow also from the hypothetical form.

The universality of an induction applies to all instances, future as well as present or past, and in this connection, it is sometimes asked "How do we know there will be a future?" The question, in this form at least, is pointless. One does not know that there will be no future, and even if there will be no future, one will not know that, so what is one talking about? Perhaps the question is intended to ask "How can it be known that there will be events or physical objects in the future similar to those of the past and the present, so that inductions from past events will apply to the future?" It is, perhaps, to answer this question that the Principle of the Uniformity of Nature has sometimes been held to be a postulate necessary to justify induction. The Principle, however, is an unwarranted ontological assumption. If it is genuine knowledge, it is based on evidence and the evidence itself would have to be inductive. If it is not genuine knowledge, it cannot be an adequate foundation for other knowledge. It is merely an *ad hoc* hypothesis.

The major difficulty with the Principle of the Uniformity of Nature, according to the present thesis, is that it makes the ontological assumption that "nature" is composed of discrete events, facts, ready-made and fully definitive each in itself

without reference to the selective and interpretative activities
of a mind. The Principle requires a rigidly structured (even a
fully deterministic) world in which to operate, and such structure obtains only between parts that are fully definitive and
discrete. Fluid parts do not yield rigid structure. Knowledge
of a world in which the Principle held would be the result of
observing and registering ready-made facts, and the activities
of mind would be restricted to inspecting and expressing the
connections between these facts—connections which are
always the same under the same conditions. If facts were fully
definitive, each in itself, "nature" would not be a continuum.
A continuum is not an aggregate of discrete units.

Passage is an aspect of intuitive data. The highly conceptualized *time* in which events, past, present, and future, are
located is a very different matter. As has been pointed out,
the *concept* of time is obtained from the interpretation and
grasp of intuitive data, and is a result of the process of abstraction.[17] This is not the place to attempt to solve the metaphysical problem of time. Suffice it to say for present purposes that
past facts and present facts are relative to cuts made in the
continuum. Future facts also will be relative to cuts or else
there will be no future facts. Facts are discrete only in so far
as cuts have been made and definitive limits and boundaries
have been introduced into the continuum. Hence, the question
of the application of induction from past experience to future
events becomes the question of whether it will be possible to
continue to cut the flux and apply concepts to it as it has been
cut and concepts applied in the past.

The answer of this study to the question just posed is that
it is not only possible to continue, but that it is impossible to
cease altogether making such cuts and applying concepts as
in the past. To stop making all cuts would be to stop reacting,
and this would entail death. To stop making cuts *as in the*

17. *See* p. 75. Precisely ordered time is an elaborate functional
abstraction.

past would be to avoid all the proto-generalizations of past life. Hence the future will be subject to the same sort of cuts as in the past or else it will be subject to none unless one starts all over again with new proto-generalizations, and this one *cannot* do. One would have to free oneself from all memory, from all learned language, and from all social inheritance. No individual who has learned a language invents his own conceptual scheme. The skeletal framework of the conceptual scheme which anyone holds comes from the past. The only approximation toward a uniformity of nature lies in the way the flux has been ordered and grasped.

The prediction of future events on the basis of the knowledge of past events is made through the mediation of generalities. There is no possible inference from particular to particular. But as there is no determinateness of future events (or any events, for that matter) without reference to generalities, the point is hardly worth making. In order for future events to be determinate, the flux must be cut and concepts applied, but the applied concepts must, in the main, be those that are available for application—and their formulation comes from the past. The concepts can be and are modified as one gains more knowledge, but if there are to be any determinate future events at all, their definition will depend in part on past experience. Thus, if valid inductions from past experience are not applicable in the prediction of future events, there will be no precise future events. If one tried to assume a future that is not continuous with the past and the present, it would not be a future to *this* present with its past. What is discontinuous with *this* present could not appear in *this* present. The notion of future events to which no inductions from the past could be applied is a self-contradictory notion.

Contemporary man can predict and control nature better than could the ancients (or better than could the nineteenth century, for that matter) because he *knows* more about nature. Yet this does not mean that he is more adept at picking ready-made generalities from ready-made facts. It means that he has become progressively more adept in reducing experience to order by formulating high-level generalizations which themselves can be fitted into inclusive and articulated structures that enable him to grasp the infinite variety of the flux and to find his way around in it. Prediction and control are criteria of the adequacy of our grasp of the flux and our ability to deal with it.

If the content of experience is a continuum, it can be cut in an indefinite number of ways. Categories are based on a selection of possibilities of division. If an experienced future is to be continuous with the past and the present, some of the same selections and generalizations must be made. The selections are the basis for regularities, and *some,* at least, of the regularities will be discoverable in the future. The "justification" of induction, then, lies in the consideration that unless generalizations based on past experience are applicable to the future, there will be no *determinate* future in any intelligible sense of the term. It is also true that if they are applicable, there is a predictable future.

Which generalities are more reliable and which are less in the prediction and interpretation of experience is to be discovered by the calculus of probabilities in those cases where specific correlations can be cast into a form where a valid estimate of relative frequency can be made. In the case of the more inclusive generalizations of scientific or philosophic theory, the reliability is established by the method of hypothesis.

CHAPTER IX

Hypothesis

Induction yields generalities, but the knowledge of generalities is hypothetical, not categorical. It is the knowledge of conditions and results, not of unconditional states of affairs. All theoretic knowledge is knowledge of generalities, and thus all theoretic knowledge is hypothetical. The term 'theoretic knowledge' is here used in contrast to 'perceptual knowledge' in the way pointed out in Chapter VIII.

Perceptual knowledge comes as close to being categorical as any human knowledge can be, yet it is not absolutely categorical because of the theoretic thread that runs through the interpretations and proto-generalizations involved in even the simplest perceptions. Perceptual knowledge is conditioned by what cuts are made in the flux. Nevertheless, a valid distinction of degree can be made between the observation of fact (particulars with space-time locus) on the one hand and knowledge comprising relatively high degrees of generalization and abstraction on the other. The present chapter will deal with theoretic knowledge in the latter sense.

Hypothetical knowledge is not necessarily stated in the form of an hypothetical proposition, but for purposes of analysis it is better and more clearly so stated. An hypothetical proposition is one of "If . . . , then . . ." form; for example "If p, then q" where 'p' and 'q' stand for any subsidiary propositions. The if-clause is called 'the protasis' and the then-clause 'the apodosis'. The if-clause is often called 'the antecedent' or even 'the hypothesis' and the then-clause 'the consequent' or 'the conclusion'. 'Protasis' and 'apodosis' are here preferred because they are completely unambiguous, having no use other than reference to the if-clause and the then-clause respectively of an hypothetical proposition. To call the if-clause 'the hypothesis' is undesirable because then the whole proposition and part of it are called by the same name, encouraging a false application in scientific method and leading some scientists incorrectly to suppose that the if-clause by itself is the hypothesis that science tries to establish.

In the form 'If p, then q' neither p nor q is asserted, only a relation between them is asserted. This relation is ordinarily called 'implication'. In it, one may have q without having p, but one may not have p without having q. This is all that the hypothetical proposition asserts. Hence, the form of the hypothetical proposition stating a scientific law is *not* 'If particulars $a, b, c, \ldots$ are observed, then the generalization G holds as a universal law'. If this were the form, generalities could be picked off accumulations of fact, and science would be a huge blackberry picking expedition. Whenever one observed particular events, one could know deductively that a specified generalization holds. One cannot have $a, b, c, \ldots$ without having G. In other words, the generality could be *deduced* from the observation of particular events. This is exactly what cannot be done. There were multitudes of falling apples, stones thrown into the air and falling back to earth, and observed planetary motions before Newton's time, but the law of gravitation cannot be deduced from them.

The form of the inductive hypothesis is the reverse of that considered above. It is 'If the generalization G holds, then $a, b, c, \ldots$ can be observed as particular events'; or 'If G holds, then $a, b, c, \ldots$ can be subsumed under it as instances'. Inference is the movement of thought from the known to the relatively unknown. *Deductive* inference is based on the relation of implication: deductively, one infers q, the apodosis of the hypothetical proposition, from *p,* the protasis. But *inductively,* one infers the generalization, the protasis, from the particular instances, the apodosis. Deductive inference from premises is implicative, but inductive inference from particular evidence is counter-implicative. This is usually expressed by saying that inductive inference is nondemonstrative. In the inductive hypothesis, one can have *a, b, c,* . . . without having *G,* but one cannot have *G* without having *a, b, c,* . . .[1] This correctly renders the inductive situation. If one has already observed *a* and *b,* one may say that the generalization explains them. If one has not observed *c,* one says that the generalization predicts it, and one looks for it. If one observes it, then to that degree the generality is confirmed.

The generalization cannot be proved in the strict sense of the word 'proof', however, and all inductive knowledge falls short of certainty. Since the form of the inductive hypothesis is 'If *G,* then *a, b, c,* . . .', any attempted proof of *G* on the basis of the observations of *a, b, c,* . . . would assert the consequent. This is always a fallacy. Hence, the observation of particulars never proves a generalization. The generalities of theoretic knowledge are not established with absolute certainty, but they are confirmed as the hypotheses of which they are parts are verified.

The objection may be raised that the generalities of mathematics and logic are highly theoretic and they are certain. This objection, however, rests on being somewhat vague about where the certainty in mathematics and logic resides. A closer inspection in the light of recent advances in logic shows that it resides not in the postulates, not in the rules of procedure, and not in the theorems of the system, but in the relations between all of these. The only certainty is that the conclusions

---

1. The statement of the paradigm is simplified for schematic emphasis. *G* may be several generalizations or a system of interrelated generalizations, and additional semantic rules of application are often necessary to yield the particulars.

are bound up with the premises. If the postulates are assumed and the rules rigorously adhered to, the theorems follow with logical necessity; but the postulates are adopted unproved and they possess no self-evidence. If other and nonequivalent postulates are adopted, different theorems follow, but they follow with the same rigorous necessity as the elaboration of non–Euclidean geometries has shown. The only restriction on the postulates is that they be consistent with each other.

The full import of the logical discovery of the nature of postulate sets did not make itself felt to the natural scientists until the shock of the revolution in physics beginning in the first part of the twentieth century. Then it was seen that the relation between the fundamental laws of natural science and the observations that confirm them is analogous to the relation between the postulates and theorems of a mathematical or logical system.[2] The major criterion of postulates after their consistency is that they yield a body of acceptable theorems. Similarly, in science, the major criterion of fundamental laws is that they yield instances that can be verified by observation. To use an expression that arose in the Academy shortly after Plato, the hypothesis must "save the appearances."

Many writers on science distinguish between a scientific hypothesis and a scientific law. The terms 'law', 'theory', 'hypothesis' can all be used in a wider or a narrower sense, but formally, there is not a great deal of essential difference. To one who uses the words in the narrower sense, a *law* is an inductive generalization which has received a high degree of confirmation, while a *theory* is a broad explanatory scheme usually embodying many laws arranged in deductive order. Writers committed to this usage usually restrict the term *hypothesis* to a working hypothesis or a generalization not

2. *See* R. D. Carmichael, *The Logic of Discovery* (Chicago and London:Open Court Publishing Co., 1930) pp. 86–87. *See also* R. B. Braithwaite, *Scientific Explanation* (Cambridge: at the University Press, 1953) pp. 22ff.

well confirmed. There is no harm in the narrower usage as long as it does not lead to the misunderstanding that the high degree of confirmation of a law establishes it independently of the hypothetical statement in which it is imbedded. From the point of view of the kind of knowledge involved, all scientific laws are theoretical and all theory is hypothetical.

The primary purpose of the laws, or theories, or hypotheses, of natural science is explanatory. Science seeks to understand natural phenomena by relating them to each other and so to the "scheme of things." This is accomplished by constructing a conceptual scheme the empirical concepts of which are generalizations of wide scope that can take the particulars of experience as instances within an acceptable margin of approximation.[3] Particulars are intelligibly related to each other by means of generalizations, and more restricted generalities are subsumed under wider generalities. A pattern of relationships is thus established, and when all-embracing generalities are reached in any field of natural phenomena and are well confirmed, a deductive system is established and the explanatory task of science is well performed.

The present chapter will be primarily directed to the discussion of four topics concerning the hypotheses of natural science: (1) How are hypotheses formed? (2) What are the major criteria of an acceptable hypothesis? (3) How are hypotheses verified? (4) Precisely what is established by the verification of an hypothesis in natural science? Finally, there will be a brief discussion of the more speculative hypotheses of philosophy.

(1) Hypotheses are ordinarily formed by induction. Under some circumstances, when an hypothesis of wide scope has already been formed and has received some measure of confirmation, a lesser hypothesis may be deduced from the wider

---

3. *See* pp. 94–96. *See also* H. N. Lee, "Conceptual Models in Knowledge," *Tulane Studies in Philosophy* 17 (1968): 101–113.

one. For example, after Torricelli had formulated the hypothesis of atmospheric pressure and had offered some confirmation of it, Pascal made the deduction that the pressure would be less at higher altitudes than at sea level, and proceeded to have this lesser hypothesis tested by experiment.[4] It is possible that there was some deduction in the formation of Torricelli's original hypothesis, for the laws of hydrostatics were already known, but Torricelli left no detailed report of how he came to his formulation.

The widest hypothesis must be formulated by induction, for there is nothing more general from which to deduce it, and induction characteristically enters into most hypotheses. Induction does not follow logical rules but comes as a result of insight and imagination. An inductive generalization is a creation of the mind. Analyzing and prescinding are necessary but not sufficient. Close observation and skill in handling the facts from which an induction is made are of utmost importance, and acquaintance with rules such as those of Bacon or Mill may sometimes help. Seeing an analogy with past inductions, perhaps in a different field, is often fruitful, but as Conant says, "Few if any pioneers have arrived at their important discoveries by a systematic process of logical thought. Rather, brilliant flashes of imagination or 'hunches' have guided their steps—often at first fumbling steps."[5] A detailed description of how hypotheses are formed would be psychological, not logical, and the description is in the province of one of the most difficult of psychological fields, the psychology of creative imagination.

(2) The major criteria of a good hypothesis are first of all that it be consistent and lead to consistent conclusions; then

4. *See* J. B. Conant, *Science and Common Sense* (New Haven: Yale University Press, 1951) p. 75. It is of little moment that Conant prefers the term 'conceptual scheme' to the term 'hypothesis'.

5. Conant, *Science and . . .* , p. 71. A further analysis of hypothesis formation may be found in Donald S. Lee, "Scientific Method as a Stage Process," *Dialectica* 22 (1968): 31–32.

that it be precise and clear; that it be fruitful both of predictions and of other hypotheses; and that it be as simple as it can be while "saving all the appearances."

Consistency is a logical criterion. Since the purpose of an hypothesis is to display logical relations, the hypothesis must first of all be logical. It is sometimes difficult, however, to see whether or not a generalization involves a self-inconsistency, especially if the generalization, through abstraction, is far removed from concrete experience. Unless the hypothesis is expressed in terms that are verbally inconsistent (and it is not apt to be so expressed), inconsistency appears only when it is seen that the hypothesis leads to incompatible deductions. For example, Galileo argues that the hypothesis that heavier bodies fall faster than lighter bodies (of the same material and in the same medium) is self-inconsistent by presenting a "short and conclusive argument" wherein "from your assumption that the heavier body moves more rapidly than the lighter one, I infer that the heavier body moves more slowly."[6] This situation is similar to that in pure logic where inconsistencies in the postulates usually show up only in the deductions from the postulates.

It is also desirable that an hypothesis be consistent with other hypotheses, even in other fields of science, if the other hypotheses are well confirmed. This is not a ruling criterion except from the point of view of the wider hypothesis of the unity of science. The latter is a speculative hypothesis, and more will be said later concerning them. Nevertheless, especially if the fields of science are related, such as mechanics and electromagnetics, it is highly desirable that the hypotheses in the two fields be consistent with each other. It might be possible to establish a wider hypothesis that would subsume both sets of laws, and this would often greatly increase the verification of the separate laws. They would then be deducible from the wider laws which have support other than the support for

---

6. *Dialogues Concerning Two New Sciences* (New York: Dover Publications, First Day, pp. 62–63, n.d.).

them. Thus they would receive the indirect support of everything that tends to confirm the wider hypothesis.

The criterion that an hypothesis should be both precise and clear is both a logical and a material one.[7] Unless it is precise and clear, the deductions to which it leads are neither specific nor rigorously supported. Hence, the degree to which it is verified or verifiable cannot be determined. Many biologists reject the vitalistic hypothesis in biology for this reason. To take the example of Driesch's entelechy, it is not apparent exactly what is being assumed or what kind of experiments and observations would tend to confirm it. To the degree that the concept of a vital force is not itself clear, deduction will be confused and clear-cut verifications cannot be obtained.

A good hypothesis is fruitful both in the way of producing experiments and observations and in leading to other hypotheses. Torricelli's above-mentioned hypothesis of atmospheric pressure was highly fruitful. It led not only to Pascal's hypothesis and the experiments that tended to confirm it, but also to Boyle's experiments and to the statement of Boyle's law. On the other hand, the funicular hypothesis to explain the variations in the height of the column of mercury in a barometer was sterile. It led to no further experimentation or hypothesis. Boyle briefly argued against it, but it was not put down by argument: it died a natural death because nothing could be done with it. If one granted that there could be such a thing as an invisible elastic membrane, one could explain the phenomena by this means, but it would not lead one to find out more or to make any new inductions.

The phlogiston theory, formulated in the early eighteenth

7. For the remainder of this chapter, I shall use the terms 'material' and 'materially' to refer to empirical content in contrast to form. They will not be used to refer to physical matter or in the sense that 'material' is used in the term 'material implication' in Whitehead and Russell's *Principia Mathematica*. The usage referring to empirical content is adopted because there are no adjectival or adverbial forms of the noun 'content'.

century, is now rejected and almost forgotten, but it was a very fruitful hypothesis. Although its proponents continued to hold it too long into the nineteenth century, it served a useful purpose. It brought together under one generalization such diverse phenomena as burning, the respiration of animals and the calcination and purification of metals. In so doing, it gave rise to experiments connecting these phenomena and led to hypotheses concerning different kinds of "fixed airs," thus leading to further experiments in the chemistry of gases ('gas' since Van Helmont). It was so fruitful that it led to knowledge that eventually brought about its own overthrow, a triumph for any hypothesis. Lavoisier's theory of oxidation proved to be not only in closer relation to the observed facts but it was of wider scope, and after a protracted struggle the phlogiston theory was dropped. It had served as a good hypothesis in terms of fruitfulness, but that service had now ended.

Simplicity is a criterion of a good hypothesis (if other criteria have been met or closely approximated) not only because scientists must get their work done and so must not take unnecessarily complicated ways of going about it, but because the simpler an hypothesis is the better it accomplishes its purpose in the scheme of empirical knowledge (provided that it meets the other criteria and "saves the appearances"). The function of an hypothesis is to explain natural phenomena in the sense of enabling us to understand their interconnections and relations so that they can be seen to form an orderly pattern. A complicated explanation does not explain as well as a simpler one provided they both explain the same phenomena. Hence, a simpler hypothesis is a better hypothesis, *ceteris paribus*.

There is no single reliable index of simplicity, for the simplicity wanted in an hypothesis is relative to a combination of ease and completeness of grasp. It is to be expected that what would seem to be relatively simpler under one set of conditions might not be so under a different set. No rigid definition or rule of simplicity is required. Simplicity is not a major criterion, but can be applied only after the other criteria have been met or approximated as closely as conditions will permit. It operates only in choosing one out of several competing hypotheses all of which can be confirmed to the degree where the difference in confirmation does not make a decisive choice between them. It is desirable that the concept of simplicity be made as clear and precise as possible without sacrificing its proper function in understanding. To insist on arbitrary rules of application such as counting the elements or relations or something else in a system and saying that the smaller numbers always indicate greater simplicity is to rob it of its use as a criterion of hypotheses.[8] It is also desirable to be able to order degrees of relative simplicity. In cases amenable to mathematical treatment this can be done with tolerable adequacy. If the cases are not amenable to mathematical treatment, exactness cannot be achieved anyway.

To make simplicity a criterion of good hypotheses, even a secondary criterion, would be wholly unwarranted if generalizations were *there* in the structure of an already rigidly structured nature. If nature were rigidly structured, the use of hypothesis in science would be to find and describe its ready-made order. But to use the words of William Whewell, "Man is the *Interpreter* of Nature; not the Spectator merely, but the Interpreter."[9] If the scientist were merely the spectator his use of the criterion of simplicity, even as a subsidiary criterion, would be rashly presumptive. It would assume that a nature the order of which is independent of him is nevertheless so ordered as to make his work easier.

(3) Confirmation of an hypothesis is offered when the relation of implication between the generalization, the pro-

8. For an advance toward a clearer concept of simplicity without making it rigid, *see* J. G. Kemeny, "The Use of Simplicity in Induction," *Philosophical Review* 62 (1953): 391–408.

9. Wm. Whewell, *Of Induction . . . ,* p. 34. Whewell's italics.

tasis, of the paradigm and one or more facts stated in the apodosis is shown to hold, provided that the fact is not one of those that entered into the induction of the generalization. The implication must extend to the statement of new or previously unrelated facts. The observation of such facts or the demonstration that they (if already known) are related to the other known facts by means of the generalization tends to confirm the hypothesis. All the facts together cannot prove the hypothesis, but they can offer strong enough confirmation to enable us to say that the hypothesis is verified and is scientific knowledge. No one observation offers strong enough evidence to establish the hypothesis although conditions can sometimes be set up that make an observation "crucial."[10] For example, it was deduced from the general theory of relativity that the path of light is affected by a gravitational field. It was calculated, using known laws, that during a total eclipse of the sun the apparent positions of stars in line of sight near the sun should be displaced outward. The Royal Astronomical Society in 1919 sent an expedition to observe and obtain photographs of a total eclipse, and it was observed that the stars were so displaced. This observation offered strong confirmation of the theory. Observations of other eclipses, using better instruments and affecting the observed positions of other stars have since further confirmed it. An hypothesis is held to be verified by the convergence of many instances of confirmation provided that no strong disconfirming instances have been observed.

The deduction of instances the observation of which tends to confirm an hypothesis is, of course, much more complicated than the paradigm used above would indicate. The paradigm, when applied to the illustration of the previous paragraph is "If the general theory of relativity is a universal law, then the

10. Of course, no crucial experiment can *prove* an hypothesis. For illustrative instances, see Philipp Frank, *Philosophy of Science*, pp. 193–99.

apparent positions of stars seen near the sun during an eclipse
will be displaced outward." The paradigm does not give any
of the details necessary to make the deduction. In order to
deduce instances from a universal, particular or initial conditions must be stated as an added premise or premises. The
generalization is tentatively taken to be universal; the particular premise or premises give it existential content, and a
particular conclusion can be tentatively stated. Even this
description is still a great simplification, for the protasis of
the paradigm may be complex and may lead to the conclusion
through lesser but already well established generalizations.
In the illustration the mass of the sun and hence its gravitational field, and the speed of light entered into the deduction.
But the relation of implication is transitive and reference to
mediating considerations can be omitted for paradigmatic
purposes.

All the known apparatus of deduction available in mathematics or logic can be used in deducing instances from the
generalization. In the case of the physical sciences where meas-
urements are of prime importance, elaborate mathematical
tools are often required. The use of mathematical methods
complicates the procedures but not the principles of the
deduction of instances. Where the instances have never been
observed, their deduction takes the form of a prediction. A
newly observed fact, observed as a result of prediction, offers
a spectacular confirmation of an hypothesis. The discovery
of the planet Neptune, coming as a result of an hypothesis
to account for the observed perturbations of the motions of
other planets, was a spectacular added confirmation of the law
of gravitation. Prediction and the ability to control based on
prediction are not the chief aims of pure science (its main
purpose is to explain), but prediction is a fundamentally
important step in the verification of hypotheses.

It is often held that the observation of instances contrary
to what is predicted (negative instances) overthrows an
hypothesis. The situation is never as simple as this, however.

It is argued that *modus tollens* requires that if the apodosis is false, then the protasis is false, and thus one negative instance shows that the implication of the paradigm does not hold. To argue in this fashion overlooks the purpose of the hypothesis, which is to explain and order phenomena. An imperfect explanation is better than none at all especially if it is fruitful of producing new experiments and observations. As Conant says, "A conceptual scheme is never discarded merely because of a few stubborn facts with which it cannot be reconciled; a conceptual scheme is either modified or replaced by a better one, never abandoned with nothing to take its place."[11]

The observation of a negative instance may point to other things rather than to the falsity of the protasis. Hidden assumptions often lie in the statement of the theory and an error in these assumptions may lead to the deduction of wrong conclusions. There are many possible sources of error in the deduction of instances. Other theories may be called on in making the deductions or in making the observations themselves, such as the laws of optics in making astronomical observations, or the laws of the interpretation of the use of instruments in any line of experimentation, and errors in using these laws may be the source of the negative instances. All these possibilities must be explored before it can be said that the observation of a negative instance overthrows an hypothesis. Even after they have been considered and rejected, if the hypothesis has been strongly confirmed by other observations, it may still be held until a better one is produced. All through the life of the phlogiston theory it was known that the calx weighs more than the metal which is obtained from it or from which it is obtained although according to the theory it ought to weigh less. The theory was not abandoned because of this flaw. It was abandoned only after a better

11. Conant, *Science and* . . . , p. 173.

theory was developed, one which among other things, could account for the accretion of weight.

Many years of careful observation and measurement established that the perihelion of the planet Mercury advances at a more rapid rate than that predicted by Newtonian theory, but the negative instance did not overthrow the theory. It was recognized to indicate something wrong with the theory, so that an alternative generalization should be sought. When the theory of relativity was shown more closely to predict the observed advance, the partial success was held to be a confirmation of relativity.

(4) The careful examination of the question "What is established by the verification of an hypothesis" has sometimes been overlooked. It is often uncritically assumed that the verification establishes the independent truth of the generalization or law, that is, of the protasis. Those who hold that the mind is a "spectator merely" of nature assume that it is the task of natural science to find and describe in general terms a rigid and immutable structure of nature, and that the verification of hypotheses yields knowledge of this structure in the statement of the law or generalization making up the protasis of the hypothesis. Such persons commit the blackberry bush fallacy. If verification were to consist in establishing the empirical truth of the protasis, skepticism would have to be the ultimate position of science, for to suppose that the independent truth of the protasis can be established or even made probable by any amount of observation is to commit the fallacy of asserting the consequent.

Skepticism is to be avoided, but so also is the fallacy. Both can be avoided, for there is no evidence for the belief in a rigid and immutable structure of nature. That belief is expendable. Nature is a selection from the intuitive flux, and mind is a part of nature. The detailed, definite structure of nature is due to the interpretative activity of mind. The ultimate material content is intuitive, but the form and structure are conceptual and theoretic. The truth, independent of mind, of the law or generalization which is the protasis of the hypothesis of science is not to be sought.

What verification establishes is that the hypothetical proposition *as a whole* applies to the actual world of experience. The deduction of the apodosis from the protasis establishes only a *logical* relation, and pure logic does not determine what is actual. Verification establishes that the relation holds *in the actual world,* that is, actual experience is ordered, and therefore understood, in terms of the hypothesis. It establishes that *these* are the laws by means of which to order and understand the world of facts, at least until better laws or new facts are found.

It is in the actual application of the logical, deductive relations between generalities and observable facts that the explanatory task of the natural sciences consists. Through those relations the understanding of objective nature is achieved. Natural laws and theories hold but only within the whole context of the explanatory process. It is an illusion fostered by the mistaken analogy of 'law' in 'natural law' that the generalities of scientific theory are supposed to have some sort of status prior to and independent of the facts of which they are generalizations. To the contrary, a scientific generalization or law has no status whatever—has no meaning whatever—except in terms of the specific instances of which it is a generalization.

If the foregoing is held firmly in mind, the bothersome problem of how the observation of instances can establish the truth or even the probability of a law or theory disappears. The independent truth or probability of the generalization which stands as the protasis of any scientific hypothesis cannot be established; it does not need to be established: the law or theory has no such independent status. It is not apparent how there could be a clear and precise empirical generalization independent of the instances to which it applies. The meaning of a generalization (functional abstraction) consists in relations among specific instances or previously obtained generalizations or functions, and there is no meaning without reference to them.[12]

An hypothesis in natural science is verified when a high degree of probability is attained that the law or generalization of the hypothetical proposition actually serves to order and relate large bodies of fact in the world of experience. The observed confirmations make up a very small sample of all that is to be related. On this view, verification depends on the relative frequency of confirmation and poses no problem beyond those of the frequency theory of probability. When a valid estimate of the frequency of confirmation approaches unity, the hypothesis is verified. Each confirming observation increases the relative frequency with which the law or generalization is shown to be the correct ordering principle. Of course, each test and each confirming instance is not of equal weight. Continued testing of instances of the same sort of fact has little weight, for such repetitive testing establishes the relation between the generalization and only the same arbitrarily selected group of facts. A fair sample of all the different kinds of fact must be made in order to test the scope of the generalization. If new facts in different fields of observation can be predicted and the predictions confirmed, a relatively heavier weight is assigned to these cases. Negative instances have a heavier weight than affirmative instances because the relative frequency of confirmation must be very high. Exact rules for weighting different confirmations have not been worked out, however, as controversies over the verification of new hypotheses testify. Yet in special cases a great enough weight can sometimes be assigned to make an experiment a crucial one.

Verification of an hypothesis should, however, not be confused with its acceptability. Consequently, its acceptability is not the same as its probability. The acceptability depends on

12. *See* Ernst Cassirer, *Substance and Function,* pp. 17 and 21.

all the criteria of a good hypothesis taken together, including the criterion of relative simplicity if that is applicable. If there should be two hypotheses both yielding the same probability, one could still be better than the other on the basis of other criteria, and thus more acceptable for the purposes of knowledge. All hypotheses are fallible, that is, they may be shown by an accretion of new facts to be in error, but until they are so shown they are knowledge on the available evidence if they meet the criteria.

It may be objected that in an hypothetical proposition the apodosis can be deductively inferred from the protasis only when the protasis by itself is true. This, of course, is correct, but is irrelevant as an objection to the present theory of verification. The rule is relevant within a system of strict logic where the objective is to make an independent assertion of the apodosis so that it becomes a theorem of the system. In the hypothesis of science, however, the material content of the apodosis is found by experience, it is not established by inference from the protasis. If one knew the generalization G to be true by itself, there would be no occasion to test the deductions $a, b, c \ldots$, provided that the inference was correctly drawn. On the contrary, no one supposes that the truth of $a, b, c \ldots$ is obtained by deduction. The only way to find whether $a, b, c \ldots$ are true is by observation.

In scientific deduction, the affirmative truth-value, not the material truth, of the protasis is assumed for the purposes of the deduction in hand. The assumption is tentatively justified because the protasis is an inductive generalization from experience. If, nevertheless, the assumption is incorrect, deductions that cannot be confirmed will show up sooner or later, because contradictory conclusions can be drawn from a protasis of negative truth-value.[13] Thus, the method of hypothesis is self-

---

13. As usually stated, though not quite accurately, "A false proposition implies any proposition."

correcting in its assumption of the affirmative truth-value of the protasis. This does not prove the protasis by itself to be categorically true, but it does show that, when the hypothesis is verified, the assumption of the truth-value of the protasis *within the pattern of implication* is justified, and the hypothesis as a whole is materially true, that is, it applies within the empirical world.

Philosophic knowledge is not essentially different from scientific knowledge in so far as its hypothetical nature goes. Philosophic method uses both induction and deduction as does scientific, and there is no more certainty to be achieved in philosophy than in science, in spite of the dogmatic assurance of many philosophers. Philosophy purports to be about experience and makes deductions from inductive generalizations with material content. It orders experience, but differs from science in that it is not confined to natural phenomena either in formulating inductions or in making deductions from them. It includes the experience of values, such as beauty, moral goodness and right, holiness, usefulness, and so on. No kind of purported experience is excluded by definition from philosophic examination. Thus, philosophic hypotheses are more widely speculative than are the hypotheses of natural science and their verification is not so closely tied to the observation of fact, but they are not independent of the observation of fact.

Philosophers have not always followed the hypothetical method but have often been dogmatic, assuming with a naiveté unbecoming a philosopher that the ordering and explanatory principles whereby they interpret experience are absolutely true and brook no alternative. The great masters such as Plato have seen more clearly and more philosophically, but their many disciples become more dogmatic. No wonder that dogmatism has been so often assumed in the method of philosophy, for only in the twentieth century has the hypothetical nature of scientific knowledge been widely acknowledged, and the full appraisal of the method has awaited the acknowledgement.

The acceptability of the postulates of a mathematical or logical system depends on the theorems that are deduced from them. The acceptability of the laws and theories of science depends on the observation of facts that can be subsumed under them. Similarly, the acceptability of philosophic doctrines depends on what can be deduced from them, but in regard to the verification of the deductions philosophy lies between logic and mathematics on the one hand and natural science on the other. The observation of facts is irrelevant to mathematics and logic. Only considerations of intrasystematic consistency are relevant. On the other hand, the observation of facts is of first importance in the verification of scientific theories. Philosophic generalizations must also be true to the facts of experience, but must often go beyond or behind these facts. They must order all experience and in so doing go beyond perception. It has already been pointed out that value experiences must be included. Science deals primarily with the cognitive aspect of experience whereas philosophy takes into consideration also the affective and conative aspects.

Thus, the verification of philosophic hypotheses depends on a wide consideration of the coherent and systematic relationships that can be established between *whatever* data experience can offer, but the actually occurring facts are not irrelevant as they are in mathematics and logic. The postulates of mathematics and logic yield theorems that deal with abstract possibility, and the postulates are justified by the theorems. Similarly, philosophic principles are justified by the theorems they yield, but among the theorems must be those that afford understanding of *this* world of conscious experience. Scientific theories yield theorems that apply only to the observation of natural phenomena in this world. The fundamental generalizations of mathematics and logic are postulates with their accompanying rules of procedure; the fundamental generalizations of natural science are its widest laws and theories; the fundamental generalizations of philosophy are categories whose systematic application reduces all experience to order and makes it amenable to understanding.

CHAPTER X

Science

In the previous chapter, William Whewell was quoted with approval as saying that the natural scientist is the "interpreter, not the spectator merely" of nature. The view that he is the spectator merely was closely bound up with the doctrine, widely held in the nineteenth century, that the natural sciences are merely descriptive. Of course the doctrine does not hold that sciences comprise only descriptions of facts. It holds that science finds generalizations and laws, but that these themselves are descriptions of the structure of nature and of the ways in which nature works. Nineteenth-century scientists were prone to the blackberry bush fallacy. They supposed generalizations and laws to be inherent in nature because they assumed nature to possess a ready-made structure—a structure in which logical relationships as well as the more concrete relationships of time and space are wholly determinate, independent of mind. Most nineteenth-century scientists and not a few philosophers on into the twentieth century held this view of the descriptive character of natural science.[1]

1. The above statement applies only in part to Mach and to phenomenalists. Phenomenalism tends to make perception or sensation or some mental process that depends on them (according to the strength of the Idealistic tendency in the phenomenalism) definitive of nature, but in the latter part of the nineteenth century the phenomenalists were in the minority among the scientists.

The view that the nature investigated by the scientist has a precise and detailed structure of its own is an expression of Cartesian dualism in which physical nature, although somehow known by mind, is a substantial reality wholly independent of mind. If it is such a reality, the delineation or definiteness of nature belongs only to nature. In this case, the only function that mind or cognitive activity can have in the pursuit of natural science is to find, to collate and systematically to arrange all the details of the structure—in short, to describe it.

The theory of classical mechanics was elaborated within the Cartesian metaphysics and offers the best illustration of the view that nature in itself is a completely articulated structure, and that natural science finds and describes this structure. Classical mechanics starts with bodies or particles which have absolute boundaries and absolute position, and it assumes that these constitute the substantial nature of the physical universe. They are essentially extensive and are disposed in space. Temporality is indicated in the motion of the particles. They have velocities and accelerations by means of which their motions are relative to each other in an inertial system or inertial frame; but all the different inertial frames must be related to each other to allow for invariance of the laws of motion. The result is absolute space, an unmoved, timeless and homogeneous container of all bodies and all motions and all inertial frames.[2] Since motion is measured in time, absolute space is itself somehow contained in another homogeneous container, absolute time. In this view time is of little importance, however, as it becomes merely a measure of the relative changes of positions of bodies in space. Bergson was justified in complaining that classical physics "spatializes" time.

The fundamental laws of optics were assimilated to the mechanistic picture, and when they, in turn, were absorbed into the laws of electromagnetics, even the latter could be

---

2. *See* Ernest Nagel, *The Structure of Science,* pp. 207–11.

assimilated with tolerable success. During the latter part of the nineteenth century, experimental findings began to cast doubt on the adequacy of the theory, but the important thing to notice at this place is that it is an elaborate theory. Physicists and philosophers alike tended to assume that the theory was a true picture, in the literal sense of the word 'picture', of the nature which is the object of the physicists' investigations, and that when they knew the structure of the theory, they knew the structure of an independent nature. They assumed that 'reality' is defined by the observations of experimental physics. The theory was held to be a *description* of what is there in a fully determinate, ready-made nature in which all the theoretic principles are inherent and waiting to be picked off by the scientist who is sufficiently diligent, keen, and discerning, and who does not mind the thorns.

It is, of course, true that the bodies and states dealt with in classical mechanics can all be successfully defined; even position at an instant or velocity at an instant can be defined; but the classical view tends to forget that the definitions involve a high degree of functional abstraction. It also tends to forget that the abstracting and defining process is highly interpretative and conceptual. According to the present view the person who thinks that the theory of classical mechanics is descriptive is hypostatizing his conceptual distinctions and definitions. He is committing what Whitehead called the fallacy of misplaced concreteness in that he is reading the abstractions of his theory as if they were concrete entities. He is also committing what might be called the fallacy of misplaced *discreteness* in that he puts the discreteness of his concepts into a ready-made external nature. Abstracting and defining are by no means merely descriptive. They enter into the construction of inductive generalizations and hypotheses which, when verified, put the data under investigation into order and make them amenable to understanding.

Epistemological difficulties inhere in the view that the theory of classical mechanics describes an unconditionally external structure. Most of these difficulties stem from the assumption that one can know that the structure of a theory is like the structure of reality in spite of the consideration that one knows the reality only by means of the theory; that is, no reality is given in independence of the theory with which to compare the theory. Such reality is not given in perception. None of the fundamental entities of classical mechanics are perceived. The fundamental entities are matter, motion, space, and time. Space is either occupied or unoccupied by matter. It is an inert, homogeneous receptacle, and somehow must itself be in time another inert, homogeneous receptacle; but one does not perceive any such receptacles. Extension and duration may be prescinded from percepts, but the prescinded qualities are not the receptacles of mechanics.

There is, according to the theory, a precise configuration of matter at an instant, but such a configuration at an instant is not perceived. A particle may have a velocity or even an acceleration at an instant; but not only does one not perceive any such velocity or acceleration at an instant, the conditions under which they could be perceived cannot be stated.

If nothing is known independent of a theory with which to compare the theory, the correspondence of the theory to a purported reality cannot be established. If the theory of classical mechanics literally describes anything, what it describes and how it can be said to be descriptive is not made clear. The unevidenced belief in an antecedently structured state of affairs, no matter how strongly it is held, is not knowledge. To say that there *must* be such a state of affairs because the theory of mechanics works is unwarranted special pleading. There are other possible explanations as to why the theory works, for instance the one put forward in this study.

Another inadequacy of the view that mechanics is descriptive may be found in the consideration that the theory removes all qualities except bare extent and impenetrability from external nature.[3] Perceived nature is, however, first of all qualitative. There were very good reasons in the seventeenth century for isolating those aspects of nature that could be measured. The aspects not amenable to measurement at that time were constantly getting in the way of the development of the functional abstractions at the roots of emerging scientific concepts. They were put out of the way by defining them as secondary qualities and putting them in mind where they could not interfere with the developing science since mind was conceived to be a separate reality. They were taken back into physics later when sound and light and heat were successfully correlated with details of mechanical theory, but they were taken back shorn of their qualitative actuality. This is as it should be from the point of view of mechanics, but it only further emphasizes that mechanics is a highly abstract theory and cannot be said in any literal sense of the word to describe experienced nature. If nature should happen to be, without anyone being able to know it, the sort of structure which mechanics purports to describe, then secondary qualities and their attachment to this nature would be an impenetrable mystery. This is how Descartes and Locke left them.

Advances in physics in the latter part of the nineteenth and first part of the twentieth centuries cast doubt on the adequacy of many of the concepts of classical mechanics and showed that, even from a narrowly scientific point of view, the theory could no longer be held to describe an immutable structure of nature. The concept of statistical mechanics arising from the theories of thermodynamics; the observed deviation in the advance of the perihelion of Mercury; the indications of the constant velocity of light were some of the developments taking place in the last part of the nineteenth century that did not fit into the theory. Further developments in the twentieth

3. *See* Iredell Jenkins, "The Postulate of an Impoverished Reality," *Journal of Philosophy* vol. 39 (1942).

century included: the impossibility of establishing absolute rest or of establishing absolute simultaneity at a distance; the absorption of space and time into the space-time of the theory of relativity, and the subsequent dethronement of Euclidean geometry; the statement of the quantum theory, and the development of quantum mechanics and wave mechanics; the rapid expansion of subatomic research; experimental findings in radioactivity; the Heisenberg principle of indeterminacy— these and other advances in physics made it impossible to regard classical mechanics as a description of a preexistent and immutable structure of nature.

It is the contention of this study that contemporary physics can be better assimilated into the view that scientific theory is a means of putting principles of order into the flux and articulating the structure of these principles than into the view that scientific theory is a description of an already ordered universe with an inherent and immutable structure of its own. The scientist is the interpreter of nature not merely the spectator.

The nature that is the object of the investigations of natural science is more adequately regarded as a process than as a structure of things or states. Process receives formulation in what the mind does with it, and the mind is a part of the process. For example, contemporary physicists have concerned themselves with the problem of whether electron beams are composed of particles or of waves. The present suggestion is that the paradoxical appearance of the problem comes from the persistent tendency to regard the scientific interpretation as a description of a fully formulated state of affairs. This tendency dies hard. I am not advocating the view that what is to be explained is produced by mind. The process taking place in the experiment is what is to be explained. It is part of the flux, and mind does not produce it, but mind *does* function in its articulation. The electron beam is a process which is well interpreted in terms of particles under some conditions but under others is better interpreted in terms of waves. Either is an interpretation and the interpretation is in terms of a concept drawn from "middle-sized experience," but the process being interpreted is not middle-sized. Any concept of middle-sized experience may be expected to fit the process only roughly if at all.

Nature is not a product of mind, but its definitive structure is. It is a result of the way mind reacts to the intuitive flux. The *content* of the knowledge of nature is composed of selections from the flux. Mind, by means of analysis, prescission, generalization, and abstraction, orders this content and builds it into a theoretic structure. The structure is not something already there to be inspected and investigated by the scientist; it is built by the scientist and is the achievement of all the scientists working together.

This study in its (speculative) hypothesis of the flux and the interpretative nature of perception has endeavored to lay the foundation for this view of scientific knowledge. Its doctrines of the nature of fact, of evidence, of knowledge, of induction, and of hypothesis further elaborate the view. Science aims at establishing a body of knowledge. This knowledge is theoretic; it is made up of generalizations which put precisely determinate relations and order into the flux, thus affording grasp and understanding.

Natural science investigates natural phenomena, and natural phenomena are perceived facts. But facts are *events,* they are not states of affairs or static or quasi-static *things.* A state of affairs or a thing abstracts from time, but contemporary physics has no space without time or time without space. Space-time itself is a functional abstraction constructed from events, and events are selections from the continuum of process. Thus, to speak in terms of the abstraction, a fact has a locus-moment in space-time, and this is *definitive but not descriptive of* fact. To use Whitehead's term, nothing in nature has simple location.[4] Or as Louis de Broglie says "Exact localization in time and space is a sort of static idealization

4. A. N. Whitehead, *Science and the Modern World,* p. 81.

which excludes all evolution and all dynamism."[5] Events are defined by cutting the flux and they do not carry their own boundaries with them. A cut in a continuum does not find a boundary, it makes one. The exact localization by means of which we deal with facts in space-time depends on where these cuts are made. Thus facts are conditioned by the process of which they are parts.

Natural phenomena are objects of perception in the sense that whatever could not be perceived under statable conditions is not a natural phenomenon. Thus, natural phenomena are objects or events that are perceivable in principle. They are not made up of sensations or of percepts, nor are they constituted by being intended or meant. They are delineated by concepts, but their contents are the intuited data that are the contents of perception; natural phenomena are episodes in the flux. Only as the intuited contents are formulated and assimilated by a mind are they consciously experienced and known. The mind itself is an episode in the flux and thereby is natural, but it is not a natural phenomenon. Neither one's own mind nor any other minds are directly perceived. Mind is not a perceptual object. It is neither a thing nor a place; it is a process. Mind is the name for a type of behavior of the organism—behavior that centers on perceiving, consciously reacting with foresight, and reflecting. In all of these activities, symbolism is essential because in all of them stimuli not actually present enter into the response. Mind is conscious and then self-conscious as a result of social interactions.[6]

Natural phenomena are facts in space-time in the qualified sense that they are the objects of veridical perception after the criteria of veridical perception have been established. And the space-time involved is not necessarily the highly abstract concept of physics but is the voluminousness and passage of

5. Louis de Broglie, *The Revolution in Physics,* p. 15.
6. *See* G. H. Mead, MSS, chap. 2, especially his concepts of "taking the role of the other" and "the significant symbol."

unreflective experience. There are no absolutes in the nature investigated by science. Facts are physically conditioned by the frame of reference in which they are taken. They are epistemologically conditioned by the conceptual frame by means of which they are known.

For example, the reason that the denial of absolute simultaneity in the theory of relativity seems paradoxical is that it is difficult to get away from the notion of the universe at an instant. If there is any such thing as the universe at an instant, then everything in it is absolutely simultaneous at that instant. This view not only negates time but it negates process. If the nature investigated by natural science is a process conditioned by the conceptual frame by means of which it is known, then there is no instant at which it is complete or completely delineated. Parts of nature influence other parts, and influencing is temporal. There is duration in the flux but no universal instant. The concept of a universal instant, beside being epistemologically suspect, is a concept that has proved unfruitful in science, and when it is given up, absolute simultaneity goes with it. There is no paradox here. Paradox appears only because an unsatisfactory and unfruitful concept is taken to be a literal description of an absolute state of affairs in nature.

The concepts by means of which the physicist deals with his subject matter come primarily from one of two sources: ordinary perception or mathematics. The explicit recognition of these two types of concepts has given rise to the method of elaborating a theory in the form of models. A perceptual model often illuminates an abstract statement of the theory; or a mathematical model is used to establish abstract relationships between perceptual data that are far removed from direct perception.

The objects of the world within which the physicist begins his investigation are uncritically delineated and defined by the proto-generalizations of raw perception and by the "natural" classifications of commonsense perception, that is, by the classifications embodied in socially inherited language. These serve only to delimit the field of investigation, however, and as the scientist pursues his task, special interpretations of data become increasingly important. The interpretation, although still in perceptual terms, may be guided by the systematic theory in which the experiment is enmeshed or the observation made. For example, what is perceived in a Wilson cloud chamber? On the level of least interpretation, it is a rapidly moving and gradually disappearing white streak; on the level of more interpretation, it is a chain of minute water drops; on a still higher level of interpretation, it is the vapor trail of an electron or some other charged particle. The physicist performs the experiment in order to observe paths of particles. Sometimes he is wont to forget that this is a highly conceptual interpretation of perceptual evidence.

Another example may be found in the observation of Brownian movements. Here a microscope intervenes in the observation. As one looks through the microscope, one sees dark spots floating around, but as Philipp Frank says, "A collection of mere statements about dancing spots is not science."[7] The theory of optics applied to the microscope allows the physicist to interpret the spots as minute particles not so much larger than the molecules of the gas in which they are suspended but that one can be visibly (microscopically) displaced by the impact of a large number of gaseous molecules all acting in the same direction.

The examples illustrate that the concepts used in the interpretations of observed phenomena may come from ordinary experience and be applied to observations by means of a perceptual model. Without interpretations, there is no science or even scientific observation. Without at least a dim model, there are no physical interpretations. A region of ordinary macroscopic experience is singled out and the observed events are perceived and classified initially by analogy to this model.

7. Philipp Frank, *Philosophy of Science*, p. 2.

It is only by the use of a perceptual model that either the very small or the very large, that is, microscopic events or astronomical events, can be assumed to be *like* the middle-sized events of ordinary perception. The use of a perceptual model is based on the assumption of an analogy, it does not establish the analogy.

The heuristic value of perceptual models has often proved great. Perhaps the best known recent case is the Rutherford-Bohr model of the atom. But as a perceptual model is always based on an analogy, it must be used with circumspection. Two systems that are analogous in some respects may be widely divergent in others. The later history of the Rutherford-Bohr model illustrates this point too.

Without some sort of a model by means of which to make conceptual interpretations of simple perceptions, advanced research in physics would not be apt to get very far, for science is theoretic and theoretic knowledge is interpretation in conceptual terms. Scientific theory is interpretation in highly systematic general concepts. There is a danger, however, that the scientist who is confined too closely to his perceptual model will not formulate new generalizations. Martin Deutsch says, "If one is too strongly attached to one's preconceived models, one will of necessity miss all radical discoveries. . . . On the other hand, if one is too open-minded and pursues every hitherto unknown phenomenon, one is almost certain to lose oneself in trivia."[8]

In addition to perceptual models, physics also uses mathematical models. The construction and use of mathematical models is quite different, for they are based not on analogy but on abstraction. A mathematical model deals with its field quantitatively, hence, abstractly, and the physicist who reads the structure of his mathematical model as if it were the struc-

8. *See* his essay "Evidence and Inference in Nuclear Research" Daniel Lerner, ed. *Evidence and Inference,* (Glencoe, Ill.: Free Press of Glencoe, 1959) p. 102.

ture of the field of his investigation before he started to investigate it is committed to an impoverishing reductionism. Nevertheless, the mathematical models are more important to physical theory than are the perceptual models, for the mathematical models furnish the framework for much of the deduction of consequences that leads to predictions. Mathematical models furnish the concepts of precise measurement, correlations and functional relationships, and they provide deductive schemata.

A mathematical model may or may not itself be interpreted by a special perceptual model from some field of experience to which the mathematics can be directly applied. For example, Maxwell's theory of the electromagnetic field was highly mathematical, but he endeavored to give it at least a quasi-perceptual model in the concept of the electromagnetic ether.[9] On the other hand, it is difficult if not impossible to represent Schrödinger's Psi-function in a simple or direct perceptual model.[10] One who is not a mathematician understands only obscurely physical theories expressed in terms of mathematical models, but his lack of understanding is irrelevant to the status of the scientific knowledge involved.

The use of models, either perceptual or mathematical or both, is not only heuristically valuable, it is necessary to the grasp of the data under investigation. Some sort of model is necessary because the theoretic nature of science consists of interpretations of data in terms of systematically ordered concepts. Interpretation in the last analysis means assimilation to what has been already experienced. When experience gives rise to knowledge, and when knowledge achieves a high degree of generality, the concepts involved become highly abstract. A mathematical model deals precisely with abstract concepts. A perceptual model furnishes the concepts whereby to interpret

9. *See* M. Capek, *The Philosophical Impact of Contemporary Physics* (Princeton, N.J.: Van Nostrand, 1961) p. 84.

10. *See* Nagel, *The Structure* . . . , p. 306.

observed phenomena and provides schemata of classification. In short, a good model, whether perceptual or mathematical, displays the data in a way significant to the task of physics, and often a new model enables one to see the data in a new way.[11]

Physicists have concerned themselves for many years with the question "Is the ultimate entity of physical theory a particle or a wave?"[12] This problem is, in great part, that of finding an all-embracing model, either perceptual or mathematical, by means of which to assimilate the experimental findings. With the adoption of the concept that light is composed of beams of photons, particles were brought back into the theory of light, but because of interference phenomena, waves were not abandoned. De Broglie says, "It was necessary to assume willy-nilly that the picture of waves and the picture of corpuscles had to be used one after the other for a complete description of the properties of radiation, and the relation between frequency and energy that Einstein had put at the base of his theory of photons clearly indicated that this duality of aspect for radiation was intimately connected with the very existence of quanta."[13]

Waves and particles are concepts coming from gross perception. Each furnishes a perceptual model, but the two are incompatible. With the almost contemporaneous development of quantum mechanics (1923) and wave mechanics (1925), the duality of particle and wave was extended to the electron. Quantum mechanics and wave mechanics are both built on mathematical models, but different kinds of equations are used, and an all-embracing mathematical model has not yet been found.

With the above considerations in mind, Bohr stated his

11. *See* Michael Scriven's essay in *The Validation of Scientific Theories*, Philipp Frank, ed. (Boston: Beacon Press, 1958) p. 138.

12. Some physicists and philosophers have naively formulated this question "Is the ultimate entity in nature a particle or a wave?"

13. Louis de Broglie, *The Revolution in Physics*, pp. 158–59.

principle of complementarity. This is somewhat of a make-shift, but it serves its purpose. It may not be possible to find a model in terms of "middle-sized" objects that gives satis-factory interpretations of data observed by the physicist when his experiments deal with what he has reason otherwise to interpret as subatomic events.

The same sort of situation manifests itself in the difficulty that the ordinary person has in assimilating the Heisenberg principle of indeterminacy; the model obtained from gross perception is not adequate to the minute scale of the events. If, in ordinary experience, one glances quickly at not too rapidly moving objects, one sees them with what appears to be sharp outlines and in definite positions. A moving object is photographed, and if the time of exposure is short relative to the distance moved, the photograph appears to give a pre-cise configuration of the object at the instant of exposure. Of course, it may be that the edges of the object are blurred, but the blur is so minute that it does not appear to gross percep-tion. After all, if the blur appears, one can make the exposure time a little shorter. Thus, the concept of a precisely defined object at a precise position at an instant is formed, and it goes unnoticed that this is an abstraction. Although the blur may be there, it cannot be perceived; gross perception does not handle minute differences. But when the physicist deals with the minute scale of subatomic theory, he can no longer pretend that the blur is not there. The only way to have absolute posi-tion is to stop the motion. Nevertheless, Newtonian mechanics found it convenient to work with precise boundaries in instan-taneous position, but scientists and philosophers alike have been wont to forget what a high-level abstraction it requires. It is not the business of philosophy to tell scientists what con-cepts they should or should not use; but it may be the pre-rogative of philosophy to remind scientists that they should not confuse their abstractions and interpretations with con-crete descriptions.

Some philosophers, far from exercising this prerogative,

have seized upon the principle of indeterminacy as ground for making sweeping inferences about fields of human inquiry far removed from physics, as if the principle were a pronouncement about the ultimate nature of reality. Such extrapolations are unwarranted. The epistemological import of the principle of indeterminacy indicates that the field of the physicist's investigations is the field of events cut from a space-time continuum. The physicist cannot stop his motion and have it too. If he has absolute position, he does not have velocity, and if he has velocity, he does not have absolute position. Zeno of Elea pointed this out, although he may not have believed it himself. The physicist can stop the flow of events conceptually, but only by making abstractions and interpretations. Scientific theory is built on these abstractions and interpretations. But in the object of the scientist's investigation, that is, in physical nature, there are only events, and events have fuzzy edges until the scientist makes them sharp by definition. No good reasons can be adduced for holding that the extremely minute events of subatomic theory must be like the events and objects of gross perception, but there is very good reason for human beings to try to conceive of them in this way. The attempt to do so, however, produces a perceptual model, not a literal description.

Then are there no atoms or electrons or subatomic particles? The question is highly ambiguous. If it means "Is subatomic theory a literal picture of a state of affairs unconditioned by knowledge," the answer is "no." There is no knowledge unconditioned by the conditions of knowing.[14] If the question means "Are subatomic particles or events part of nature," the answer is a carefully qualified "no," depending on what one means by 'nature'. They are not parts of nature in the sense in which nature denotes natural phenomena and is the field of ordinary experience which the scientist investigates. If the question means "Can the ontological indepen-

14. *See* Angus Sinclair, *The Conditions of Knowing.*

dence of subatomic particles or events be inferred from natural phenomena," the answer is "no." Interpretation and abstraction are not modes of inference. If the question means "Are subatomic particles or events sheer logical or mathematical constructs," the answer is "no." They are interpretations, and the logic and mathematics involved furnishes a model for the interpretation. If the question means "Is the concept of subatomic particles or events essential to the models, both perceptual and mathematical, by means of which those aspects of the flux called physical are grasped and understood in minutest detail," the answer is an unqualified "yes." There is, for example, a micro-character of events that is best grasped (within the context of present knowledge) by the concept 'electron'.

In spite of the manifest indebtedness of this study to Bergson, there is no rejection here of scientific concepts or any adherence to a doctrine that they distort reality. Concepts are selections, prescissions, generalizations, functional abstractions, but there is no occasion to suppose that these processes involve distortion. The only distortion comes when the scientist or the philosopher thinks of or treats his concept as if it were not a selection or abstraction but a literal recording of what is there. In this case, the distortion is not of reality but of the concept. Distortion occurs only when the delineation and definition of concepts is hypostatized and read into the events that are the objects of the scientist's investigation. Such hypostatization can be called the fallacy of misplaced *discreteness*. It was the majority of the scientists of Bergson's time, not Bergson, who committed this fallacy.

There are no absolute spatiotemporal boundaries in the flux, but the mind, in grasping the flux, draws boundaries, and that which is bounded is an event. The flux is ever changing quality, and ever changing quality is difference. The boundaries of events can be drawn in relation to qualitative differences in such a way as to give distinct qualitative character to the events. Proto-generalizations give rise to cuts or selections that mark this distinct qualitative character. Perception ensues, and when veridical perception has been distinguished from non-veridical, the events or facts called natural phenomena emerge. The inductive process takes over, and with the verification of inductive hypotheses, there is scientific knowledge.

In a previous chapter, the metaphor of nodes in the flux was introduced as an aid in explaining how selections that are not arbitrary can be made from the flux.[15] Recent advances in physics indicate that the concept of nodes may not be so metaphorical after all: it may be bound up with the body of knowledge in physical science. It may be regarded as an extrapolation to the broader epistemological situation of the concept in wave mechanics according to which what appears in some circumstances to be particles may, in other circumstances, be better interpreted as nodes or centers of intensity in a wave structure. Thus, the concept of nodes is part of a scientific model applied to the explanation of what is known. Cuts made in the flux by perception are not arbitrary, but are responsible to the flux.

So far this chapter has been concerned primarily with physics because physics well illustrates the nature of scientific knowledge, but physics or even natural science is not the only science. Any attempt to establish a systematic and orderly body of knowledge based on a rigorously critical use of evidence is worthy of being called a science, and there are rational and philosophic sciences as well as those that deal with natural phenomena. If the word 'science' is to be endowed with this broad meaning, it must be pointed out that not all attempts are equally successful. In so far as the knowledge achieved lacks systematic structure or is not adequately theoretic or in so far as it rests on insufficient evidence, the body of purported knowledge is not fully scientific. The ideal of science is most fully achieved in the rational sciences, is

15. *See* Chapter IV, p. 83.

achieved with widely varying degrees of success in the empirical sciences, and is very incompletely achieved in the philosophic sciences.

Knowledge is constructed on the basis of evidence, and the rational, empirical and philosophic sciences may be distinguished according to the kind of evidence admitted. The restriction on evidence demarcates the field of investigation. The only evidence admissible in the rational sciences, logic and mathematics, is rigorous consistency in the manipulation of symbols according to precisely defined meanings and stated rules of procedure. A minimum of symbols is adopted undefined initially, but these are defined in use by the postulates. The only restriction on the postulates is that they be consistent with each other. All symbols other than those initially taken and defined in use must be explicitly defined in terms of the originals. The postulates are the initial evidence for deduction, but as theorems are proved, each theorem may be taken as added evidence for further deductions. This procedure builds up a complex body of purely formal knowledge—knowledge of types of order without regard to what may exemplify the order.

Perceived facts are irrelevant to the rational sciences. Their admissibility as evidence demarcates the empirical sciences, natural and social, since perception of fact always has empirical content. The empirical sciences begin with facts and end with facts in the order of their inquiry, but in spite of this they are not primarily concerned with facts. They are concerned with *ordering* the facts by means of generalizations and conceptual schemes. Thus, the knowledge of order systems achieved in the rational sciences is relevant as evidence in the empirical sciences. The *scientific* nature of the empirical sciences is theoretic. Facts are their raw data and their means of verification. Even those sciences which have not yet advanced beyond classification are theoretic, because, as has been pointed out, classification is a theoretic procedure.

The task of the empirical sciences in their character as pure science is not to predict and control but to understand and explain natural phenomena. Prediction has an important role in the verification of hypotheses, but emphasis on control defines applied science, which is the use in practical affairs of the knowledge attained by pure science. The rational sciences may be applied too, and one of their most important applications lies in furnishing knowledge of system and order to the empirical sciences.

Among the natural sciences those parts of physics such as mechanics, where the facts can be successfully manipulated and isolated for observation, most fully achieve the ideal of empirical science. In some branches of physics, however, such as meteorology, the facts are difficult to isolate and almost impossible to manipulate, and in consequence the science has not developed to an advanced stage. In biology, the facts seem to be of great complexity, and there is difficulty in isolating them because they are essentially enmeshed in an organic context. Historical considerations complicate the data in evolutionary biology as they do also in many branches of geology. The nature and use of historical evidence will be considered in Chapter XI.

The social sciences are, on the whole, not as fully developed as are the natural sciences, not only because of the complexity of the data, but because questions of fact have not been as successfully distinguished from questions of value in the social sciences as they were in the natural sciences. Values are admissible as evidence in the philosophic sciences, but in so far as the social sciences are classed with the natural in allowing only observable facts as empirical evidence, values are excluded. Much of the theory of some branches of so-called social science consists of social philosophy. For example, Marxian theory both in economics and politics is based on a value interpretation of the facts of social conditions, and the value conditions often determine the relevance of evidence. In addition, the value interpretations are presented by Marx within a philosophy of science, and it is a philosophy of sci-

ence that has been long outmoded. Science, either empirical
or rational, does not present any "iron laws of necessity."[16]
Marxian theory is of immense influence in the world today,
but as a social philosophy, not as a social science. Many of the
adverse criticisms of Marxism by the social scientists, however, also include social philosophy along with social science.

The philosophic sciences (metaphysics, epistemology, axiology with its divisions into ethics, aesthetics, political and
social philosophy and similar investigations) must admit of
all the evidence of both the rational and the empirical sciences
and in addition must admit values as evidence. Partly because
the logic of value structures is not at present as fully developed
as is the logic of perceptual experience, the philosophic sciences are more speculative than are the empirical sciences.
'More speculative' means that neither the formation nor the
verification of hypotheses is well controlled.

The philosophic sciences admit as evidence all kinds of
experience because they attempt to integrate all knowledge,
including knowledge of values into one consistent system. In
carrying out this attempt they formulate categorial schemes
furnishing the fundamental concepts by means of which to
define and assess evidence for all knowledge. Thus, each of
the rational and empirical sciences has its philosophy, that is,
its special categorial scheme with which it operates to put
order into its field of investigation. For example, the difference between the formalistic, the logistic and the intuitionist
schools of mathematics is a difference in philosophies of mathematics. The theory of relativity and the quantum theory do
not overthrow Newtonian physics, but they do overthrow the
philosophy of Newtonian physics. The philosophy of each
specialized rational and empirical science is itself a philosophic
science, and metaphysics, epistemology and axiology attempt
to integrate the more specialized philosophic sciences into an

16. Preface to the second edition of vol. 1 of *Capital*.

inclusive scheme. The problem of the categories will be further considered in Chapter XII.

The rational, the empirical and the philosophic sciences are interdependent as it seems they ought to be if an all-inclusive categorial scheme is possible. The rational and the empirical depend on the philosophic for the criticism of categories; the empirical and the philosophic depend on the rational for the criticism of systematic and orderly articulation; and the philosophic depend on the empirical for the refinement of factual content. All the sciences, however, are theoretic in the sense that scientific method is the attempt to construct generalizations whereby the subject matter of each is reduced to order and thereby understood. The theoretic knowledge embodied in the rational sciences aims at the understanding of abstract order systems; that of the empirical sciences is aimed at the understanding of natural phenomena; while that of the philosophic sciences is aimed at the coordinating of all experience.

CHAPTER XI

History

That which is actual occurs in present, concrete experience. In this statement, 'present' is a characterization of experience, it is not the name of an instant in time in which experience occurs or in which actuality is to be found. In an unguarded moment, one might assent to the statement "Actuality is to be found in the present" without noticing the plain metaphor involved. In the metaphor the present is a receptacle which may or may not contain actuality. To take this literally would result in sheer nonsense. What would a present be that contained no actuality? What would one be talking about?

The term 'the present' refers to the "undifferentiated now"[1] of direct experience. The concrete present is the participation of a center of conscious experience in the flux, and hence is in passage and is temporal. It can be analyzed into a before and an after: novelty is constantly appearing, and what is no longer novel is disappearing; but the direct participation is undifferentiated until reflection divides it into what is appearing and what is disappearing.[2] It is often called 'the specious present', but this term is to be avoided at this place if it refers

1. The expression is G. H. Mead's. See MSS, p. 351.
2. The "undifferentiated now" is what I understand Peirce to mean by the percipuum when he distinguishes between the percept and the percipuum. *See* CP 7.643–649.

to a concept of psychology or if the use of 'specious' connotes what is not quite genuine.

The concrete present is not a knife-edge dividing the past from the future. It could be so regarded if there were a past and a future to start with; then the present could be a boundary between them, but there is no actuality in such a scheme. The view of the nature of time as a past and a future with a boundary between them is a high-level abstraction and may have a legitimate use in those branches of knowledge that are on a high level of abstraction, but it has no reference within concrete experience. What is consciously experienced is the ongoingness of events. Events pass, and their passage is process. Process flows. Time does not flow. The present does not flow in time. Events flow, and from this character of events we abstract the concept of time which finds application in physics and in history. Again to refer to Mead, the immediacy of passage is stretched out into a past and a future. "Memory and anticipation build on at both ends. They do not create the passage."[3] Conceptualized time is a characteristic not of direct experience but of experience as it is known. The concrete present is the undifferentiated now of unreflective experience. The abstract present is a bare locus in conceptualized time—time without past or future extremities.

The data of history are events that are assigned to a past locus in conceptualized time. Historical knowledge refers to past events, and the evidence for such knowledge is factual. Facts are characteristically known in perception, but perception is present, concrete, conscious experience. If, then, history deals with facts that occurred in the past, the question arises, how are these facts known; they are not known perceptually. Thus, the problem of historical knowledge is raised.

The problem is not that of the ontological status of historical fact, whether it is "made of a peculiar stuff . . . and is to be plumbed by a special organ of a nonintellectual, ultra-

3. Mead, PA, p. 66.

scientific sort."[4] It may be assumed that past facts are of a piece with present facts in so far as they were once present. The past is continuous with the present or it is not the past to *this* present. If it were not the past to this present, it would not be relevant and there could be no *knowledge* of it in this present. Nevertheless, the methods of investigating the facts of the past are different from those of investigating the facts of the experimental sciences because the facts of the past are not available to perception.

Some of the data of natural sciences such as evolutionary biology and geology refer to the distant past. From present evidence inferences are made concerning the past, and techniques for establishing knowledge of the past have been developed. If beliefs concerning past events are rationally based on adequate evidence and progressively confirmed by new evidence, they constitute knowledge. Thus, consistent with the position of the present study that the flux is continuous, that facts are selections and determinations of the flux, that all theoretic knowledge is based on evidence, that facts are evidence for empirical knowledge, and that such knowledge is scientific, it is reasonable to make the hypothesis that knowledge of past facts can be established scientifically. Past events are ontologically of a piece with present events, but they are not and cannot be perceived. Nevertheless, knowledge of the past can be scientifically established by means of present evidence with the help of valid inductive inferences.

Since process is continuous and temporal, there was a past; and that there was a past does not depend on knowing it. The epistemological problem lies in knowing in as precise detail and delineation as possible what were the events of that past, and the detail and delineation are not independent of the activities of mind. Knowledge is based on evidence, and all

4. The quotation is from Donald C. Williams, "More on the Ordinariness of History," *Journal of Philosophy* 52 (1955) p. 270, where Williams gently takes A. C. Danto and me to task for vacillating "between the propositions that history is odd and that it is ordinary."

the evidence for a past event exists in the present. The past does not exist in the present; the past depends only on process of which it is a part; but the concepts by means of which we grasp process exist in the present. The application of these concepts to the continuum of process takes place in the present, and it is this application that puts precise definition and delineation into process. Hence, the precise definition and delineation of past events is a function of the present. The view that the structure of past events is rigid and immutable in its own nature is of a piece with the view rejected in Chapter X that the precise structure of external nature is independent of the interpretative activities of mind.

The initial task of the historian or the historical scientist is to establish the knowledge of past events. This knowledge must be established differently than is the knowledge of present events in so far as present events can be perceived and past events cannot; but the pastness of events does not make them essentially different *as* events. Events are episodes of passage cut from the continuous flux, and are not given with boundaries as parts of their own nature. Events as such are not discrete, since they have no fixed boundaries within themselves. They are parts of the continuum and are conceptually cut from the continuum, that is, their boundaries are conceptually drawn. This is the case with past and present events alike. Events which are not discrete do not become so by becoming past. To suppose that they do is to suppose that the past is an aggregate of discrete entities. In this case, there is no continuity in the past unless it is further supposed that past events are contained within a continuous receptacle, time, empty in its own nature. This would reinstate absolute time as a metaphysical postulate, and as was pointed out in Chapter X, physical science has found absolute time to be an unfruitful hypothesis. It is both unfruitful and unnecessary as a metaphysical hypothesis.

Of course, if past events were those of human history, selections and determinations were made by those persons who participated in them or observed them. These determinations are carried into the evidence which those persons left as to the nature of the event. Present knowledge depends on the evidence. Thus, the determinations made in the past are not abrogated but are accommodated to the discovery of new evidence or are supplemented by the reinterpretations which accounts of the past are constantly undergoing in the light of their changing relations to each new present. These past determinations make the events of the past appear to be more rigid and fixed than are those of the present, especially if they are known well and in detail. In this case the relative determinateness of the evidence is read back into the events as if it belonged to them prior to the knowledge of them and independent of it. If the event of Caesar crossing the Rubicon was a selection from a continuum when it happened, it is still a selection from a continuum; but reference to it today depends on selections made in the past because it is known only on the basis of available evidences, and these evidences are to a large extent determined by past selections.

The present doctrine does not deny or reject the irrevocableness of the past, but it does reject the absolute immutability of the past. The past is irrevocable in the sense that it cannot occur again. The gross content of the past is the process that occurred which cannot be called back, but like all process it was and is fluid and subject to different determinations. Past events are relatively changeable to the degree that their precise determination and definition depend in part on relations to the present, and these relations change with each new present. Past events have meaning in the present, and these meanings are part of the precise nature of the past, but they are never fixed. The past is being constantly reinterpreted; each new present demands such reinterpretation. Time is not a misty future which condenses into a fluid present which, in turn, freezes into a rigid past. The past does not reduce to rigidity whatever comes within it. The flux does not cease to be a flux or cease having been a flux by becoming past. Mind is constantly making selections and interpretations in the past. It is in the light of these that the past is known.

The doctrine that the past is not immutable does not, however, justify those who would revise history for the sake of personal profit or of national glorification. Such persons are either knaves or charlatans, for the knowledge of history rests on evidence. The methods of obtaining and weighing evidence are impersonal even though carried on by personal agents. If some new evidence is found that challenges long-accepted historical interpretations, it must be investigated and pursued; but the incursion of special interests, personal or corporate, into the investigation removes it from the field of historical inquiry.[5]

If there is any cogency in the position of the present study that mind is a part of nature, there is no essential difference between those past events that are a part of *human* history and those that are not. Both kinds are known only from present evidence and both kinds are equally hypothetical. The perceptual evidence for events not of human history consists largely of physical traces, including traces of both animal and plant physiology such as are to be found in paleontology or in dendrochronology. Such evidences are supplemented in human history by artifacts, records, documents, written accounts, monuments, and memories. Much of the remainder of the present chapter will be concerned with human history because of the wider reach of its evidence. However, I shall not define history in human terms.

I shall use 'history' to refer to the course of past events without restriction to human history unless the context requires it. I shall use the word 'historiography' to refer to the process of ascertaining and recounting the course of his-

5. To take a familiar example from a previous generation, the controversy over whether Francis Bacon wrote the plays usually attributed to Shakespeare had little to do with the question of establishing historical knowledge.

tory and shall use 'historiographer' to refer to the person engaged in such a task. I shall call a person an 'historian' if he is also concerned with explaining and assessing events in their connection with the wider scope of human achievements and aspirations. Most historians are also historiographers and historians are necessarily concerned with human history, but I shall not restrict the term 'historiographer' necessarily to one who is concerned with human history. The problem of ascertaining the events of the past is the same in both the natural sciences and human history.

The task of the historiographer is to establish the knowledge of past events from present evidence. In the case of human history, this task is further complicated because one wants to know how the past events were delineated and defined by those persons who participated in them or observed them, but the delineation is carried in the evidence if humans had a hand in making it. This task is hypothetical because the knowledge is conditioned by the evidence. The historiographer, in seeking knowledge of a past event, is confronted by a present situation which he has reason to think may be evidence. He wants to assimilate the evidence into a connected account of a past continuous with the present in which the evidence is found. He does so by making an hypothesis (or applying one previously made) that if such and such an event occurred at such and such a locus in the physical past, then the trace or record or monument with which he is confronted is accounted for. A past event and a present situation are assimilated into an orderly whole of the course of events.

Contemporary history can be written by one who participates in the events recorded, as presumably Thucydides participated in and perceived many of the events of the Peloponnesian War. Even so, however, Thucydides had to rely on memories, reports of others, and documents when he did his actual writing. Thus, the materials with which he worked were not essentially different from those with which any historiographer must work. They were fresher than the evidences with which the historiographer who does not witness the events about which he writes must work because they came in larger part from his own memory. Without some reliance on memory there would be no historiography. Memory is notoriously fallible, however, and must be checked against other evidences. In addition, contemporaneous historiography cannot be adequately definitive because both the selection that goes into the constitution of fact and the selection of facts made by a writer who participated in the events he records reflect a single point of view which may be limited or biased. Contemporaneously written history, however, is invaluable as source material for later historiographers.

In spite of its unreliability memory is the source of all belief in past events. To one who has the memory it is compelling, but compelling only as belief. The question is how this belief is to be guaranteed as knowledge. Previously in this study knowledge has been defined as that portion of belief based on adequate evidence and progressively confirmed by new evidence. The memory of an event suggests a hypothesis, which when confirmed is worthy to be called knowledge. The memory can never be *directly* confirmed or disconfirmed, for it is of what is not and cannot ever be perceived. It can and does yield a hypothesis, however, that may be confirmed or disconfirmed. Other evidences confirming the memory can usually be found. If such and such an event took place, testimony of other observers may bear it out; records, documents, physical traces which confirm the event may be found.

It is a misinterpretation of the logic of historiography to say that the existence of the evidence implies the existence (or date or description) of the past event. If it did, the form of the hypothesis of historiography would be "If evidence *a, b, c, . . .* exists, then the event of history was so and so." In the hypothetical proposition, one cannot have the protasis without having the apodosis. Thus, one could not know the evidence without knowing the event. Historical knowledge is not so easily established. Present evidence is compatible with various things other than the event: a clever forgery, for example. This form of the paradigm would leave no place for new evidence which might establish a somewhat different event; and on principle new evidence cannot be ruled out. It would leave no place for reinterpretation of past events, and would assume that each event bore its own fully delineated structure within itself. It would make the knowledge of past events categorical as soon as any evidence was attained.

The paradigm of the hypothesis of historiography is, in simplified form, "If the event E occurred, then this trace or record or monument or memory is accounted for." The event is posited in the protasis of an hypothetical proposition to account for the existence of the evidence or some of it; that is, the assumption of the event assimilates the evidence into a connected whole of the course of events; it renders the evidence coherent and fits it into a connected account. The hypothesis is different from the hypothesis of natural science in that the protasis is not a generalization of which the evidences are instances. Thus, the relation it displays is not deductive implication. This is expressed in the apodosis by saying "the evidence is accounted for" rather than "the evidence exists."

No one event or series of events is connected with another event or series of events in the sense of accounting for it or explaining it except through the generalizations of a well ordered body of experience. In the simplified form of the hypothesis of historiography, it appears as if the hypothetical relation holds between two particular events, but of course it does so only because both events are taken as parts of an orderly and connected world wherein the generalizations of common sense or of empirical science hold. These generalizations are not explicitly stated by the historiographer unless his account of the connection between the past event and the present evidence is challenged. For example, carbon 14 dating involves both the theories of nuclear physics and of the absorption of carbon 14 atoms in animal or plant physiology. If these generalizations are unfamiliar, it is well for the historiographer to state them explicitly.[6]

Inference proceeds from the known to the unknown. The inference in the hypothesis of historiography, like that in the inductive hypothesis of science, proceeds from the apodosis to the protasis. The evidence is what is first known. Something in the evidence or in memory suggests a hypothesis. The historiographer then searches for more evidence, and as he finds it, the hypothesis is confirmed, overthrown or modified. The first hypothesis is usually incomplete and vague. Added evidence fills it out and makes it more definite. Finally, in the ideal case, that hypothesis which accounts best for all the available evidence is accepted. Needless to say, the ideal case does not always happen and some purported evidence has to be rejected, possibly because it is less congruent with the body of traditionally accepted historical knowledge, possibly for no better reason than that it cannot be assimilated to other evidence. In such cases, controversies between historiographers arise; but in any case, reinterpretation of the past is in order when new evidence is discovered or a new way of assessing old evidence is devised. For example, the discovery of carbon 14 dating confirmed the allocation of dates to some past events, but brought about a redating of others.[7]

Given suitable generalizations, the evidence follows from the hypothetically posited event, but this can be said only after the evidence is in. It is true that on rare occasions an historiographer can tell an archaeologist "Dig here and you will find such and such evidence," but the hypothesis would not be disconfirmed if the archaeologist did not find what he was looking for but found something else that could equally well be construed as confirming the original hypothesis. The his-

---

6. I have given an account of the use of generalizations in a particular case in "The Hypothetical Nature of Historical Knowledge," *Journal of Philosophy*, 51, 7 (1954): 213.

7. *See* Jacquetta Hawkes, "Stonehenge" *Scientific American*, vol. 188, no. 6 (June 1953).

toriographer usually must wait until evidence turns up or he must endlessly sift through likely sources for evidence. But the evidence, if it does turn up, confirms or disconfirms his hypothesis much as the predicted facts confirm or disconfirm the hypothesis of the natural scientist.

It must be remembered, however, that what is verified by the convergence of many bits of confirmation is not the existence of the past event, that is, the protasis of the hypothetical proposition. It is the hypothetical proposition as a whole that is verified here as in the case of the scientific hypothesis, as shown in Chapter IX. To suppose that any amount of confirmation establishes the protasis as an independent piece of knowledge is to commit the fallacy of the affirmation of the consequent. Evidence is not like scaffolding that can be discarded once it has performed its purpose, leaving the past event standing in bold independence. No event, past or present, has any such independence. Historiography does not establish past events (even though events are cut from the flux and do not come with their boundaries fixed); it seeks to establish *knowledge* of past events, and the knowledge lies in the *relation* between the protasis and the apodosis of the hypothetical proposition. Knowledge of history is never independent of the evidence. Knowledge of history is the construction of an account of past events ordered in temporal and logical relations to present events. Historical events are past and gone, and thus are irrevocable, but they are never finished as long as they are related to the present either in evidence or in meaning: they are not immutable.

In spite of its emphasis on the hypothetical nature of historical knowledge the present doctrine gives no comfort to the historical skeptic. If the skeptic points out that knowledge of the past cannot be secure because it rests on memory and memory is notoriously fallible; if he points out that memory cannot be directly verified because the past event does not happen again; if he points out that the reliability of the inference from historical evidence cannot be *proved* because any proof of it would involve the fallacy of affirming the consequent, then he must be reminded that all of these strictures apply not only to historical knowledge but to all theoretic knowledge. The very process of induction depends on having undergone past experience. If the induction is critically established, it depends on *knowledge* of past events. All generalization refers to the past, to parts of the flux not here and now as content of present perception. Without proto-generalization there would not be even perception. Briefly, if there is no knowledge of the past, there is *no knowledge,* and the historical skeptic becomes an absolute skeptic with nothing to talk about and no ability to talk.

When the historian attempts to show causal connections between events or facts of history, he is engaging in the same sort of generalizing task as are the natural or the social scientists, and if causal connections can be shown in science, they can be shown in history. Yet they are more difficult to establish in history because the required abstractions are more difficult to make and the generalizations are more difficult to verify. By causal connections I mean not merely recurrent sequences abstracted from events, but sequences wherein what precedes is *relevant* to what comes after. My understanding of causal relationship rests on Whitehead's concept of causal efficacy,[8] wherein the immediate past (the disappearing portion of the now that is passage) is perceived to be relevant to what it becomes. Causal efficacy is the conformation of the present to the immediate past. 'Relevance' and 'conformation' here mean that the continuity between the past and the present is not merely temporal, but that the proto-generalizations and concepts, the interpretative principles in the light of which perception takes place, carry over from the immediate past to the present. This continuation is what is meant by causal connection, and the connection is experienced.

Since the connection depends on the continuity of applica-

8. A. N. Whitehead, *Symbolism* . . . , pp. 39–43.

tion of interpretative concepts in successive portions of experience, a clear-cut concept of causal connection requires abstraction. This concept is extrapolated to the succession of other events in which similar relevancy is found, and thus a causal generalization is made. To say that the whole of one event in its historical uniqueness is the cause of a succeeding event in its historical uniqueness is to make an unwarranted application of causality, not only because events are separate from each other in historical uniqueness only by courtesy of a defining mind, but also because the actual connection is to be found only by virtue of conceptual analysis and abstraction. Causal relations are found only in selected characteristics or properties of successive events. Many of those who have argued against the possibility of establishing causal connections in history have done so because they saw that cause, being general, cannot be established between unique events. But the concept of cause in science applies only to abstracted characteristics or properties, and should not be expected to apply otherwise in history.

The abstraction of cause in history is, on the whole, more difficult to make and to verify than it is in natural science because the scientist can usually experiment with his material in a way that the historian cannot. The historian must find other events from which similar characteristics or properties can be abstracted; he cannot produce them under carefully controlled conditions. The similarities abstracted are often vague, and when they are, the causal generalizations based on them are equally vague. The natural scientist has the tools of measurement and mathematics to help him in making precise abstractions. The generalizing social scientist is developing the use of statistics for a similar purpose. But no way of using the precision of mathematical concepts or calculation has yet been discovered to help the generalizing historian.

The lack of precision in the historian's knowledge of causal connections makes the attempt to find universal laws of history a precarious undertaking. The data with which the historian making such an attempt must work are very limited.

He knows relatively few events of the past, and many of those he does know are selections made in the past by highly biased persons. His method in accepting as knowledge what he does accept is apt to be what Collingwood called the method of scissors and paste,[9] that is, reliance upon authorities, for the scope of his inquiry is too great for him to make a critical examination of all the evidence. Furthermore, the knowledge of his data is speculative to a greater degree than is that of the natural scientist, for his data are not open to direct inspection. The attempt to find universal laws in history almost inevitably results in a rigidly monistic interpretation of history. The laws are economic laws (Marx) or cultural laws (Toynbee) or quasi-biological laws (Spengler) or theological (Augustine) or geographic and climatic (Montesquieu) or laws of the development of Spirit (Hegel). Before such a single interpretation of history could be established, it would have to be demonstrated that one and only one analysis of the historical situation is correct. Such a demonstration is impossible if events are cut from a continuum; the assumption of a single analysis is unjustified. It can be made to appear reasonable only by a highly biased selection from all the events of known history.

The selection of events by the generalizing historian, especially the one who seeks universal laws, is governed by the appraisal of the importance or value of the events in the course of human affairs. To this extent his task is philosophical, and so much so that the writings of one who seeks universal laws are usually called philosophy of history. I am not suggesting that such attempts are poorly taken. Whatever insights a person with such breadth of learning as, for example, a Toynbee has are all to the good and may be of great value in illuminating the course of human events, but it should always be held in mind that they are highly speculative and should be accepted as established knowledge only in so far as they are verified.

9. R. G. Collingwood, *The Idea of History* (New York: Oxford University Press, 1956) p. 257.

Let Hegel or Marx or Toynbee make an hypothesis about a universal pattern of history. This hypothesis must be verified by reference to the events of history, and the knowledge of the events is just as hypothetical for the one man as for the other. Thus, the universal hypothesis is hypothesis compounded. Hegel's rationalism may give him grounds for asserting that there is a pattern and that it can be known, but when he wants to establish what it is, and that he knows what it is, he has to go to the same kind of evidence and the same kind of reconstruction of past events as does anyone else. Any hypothesis made about a universal pattern of history involves interpolation and extrapolation on a grand scale from very limited data. All hypotheses about the general course of events must go to empirical historiography for their confirmation, and if knowledge of individual past events cannot be theoretically certain, the knowledge of a universal pattern cannot even approximate certainty.

Although the attempt to find a universal pattern in history is not illegitimate, yet the highly speculative nature of the results of the attempt hardly warrant their adoption as the basis of a universal plan for attempting to decide or control the future course of human action. If the doctrines of some specific philosophy of history are held, there is no warrant for holding them in any other way than tentatively and hesitatingly. One may be pessimistic about the future of Western European civilization, but this pessimism is not rationally compelled by the results of Spengler's study. It is not one's duty to work for a proletarian revolution because Marx's dialectic of history purports to show that the revolution is a necessary result of a universal historical pattern.

The sweeping generalizations of the philosophies of history are somewhat arbitrary. The only reason that they seem precise and definite is that they are not examined too closely with the purpose of subjecting them to empirical verification. The timberline on a distant mountain range seems to be definite until one goes up to it, but if one does it cannot be located with any great approximation to precision. The huge masses of cumulus cloud above the horizon on a summer day are beautiful in their sharp contours and billowing details of light and shade, but when one tries to verify the apparent precision seen at a distance, one finds only nebulous fog with no sharp details or boundaries.

The process of gaining historical knowledge is a process of categorization. Although all that is experienced is experienced in the present, some of its aspects are referred to the past. This is a conceptualized past. Some of its aspects, by means of anticipation, are referred to a future, and the relation between past, present, and future yields the concept of an all-inclusive time. Thus, experience is organized by reference to the category 'time' with its subcategories 'past', 'present', and 'future'. Passage as experienced is not a category or a concept. Before and after as they occur belong to the realm of experience outside the realm of discourse, but the *concepts* of past and future belong to the realm of discourse. There is, in experience, a before and an after both included within a duration 'now'. By abstraction and generalization of these aspects of experience, concepts of the past, present, and future are formed and further generalized into the concept 'time'. This concept is of fundamental importance in organizing experience. The concepts are derived from experience; thus there is no mystery or miracle involved in their application to experience. As the freshness and vividness of the immediate past grow dim and retreat, they become memory images. Visual memory images must not be overemphasized; the images may be auditory, kinesthetic, tactile or of other kind. Within adult memory verbalized images are often predominant. The images are in the present but they are referred to the conceptualized past, that is, they are categorized and the foundation for locating events in a precisely defined historic past is laid. Past events are believed although no event can be experienced in a historic past. When this belief is established on the basis of evidence of other corroborating facts of present perception, the source of all natural knowledge, there is knowledge of the events of a historic past.

CHAPTER XII

Categories

Theoretic knowledge is characteristically human. There is evidence that many of the higher animals have acute and discriminating powers of perception surpassing those of man. Eagles are said to possess highly developed vision. Dogs and many other animals excel in the ability to discriminate and react differentially to odors. Deer and bats have acute hearing. In these cases the character of the response indicates protogeneralization, but there is little evidence of any reflective conceptualization. Behavior has been observed among anthropoid apes which is reasonably interpreted as involving simple sorts of prescission and generalization, but this behavior ordinarily takes place only when the animal is confronted with direct perceptual data.

Conceptualization is a symbolic process. Something presently experienced is taken to refer to something not presently experienced. When the symbol refers to what present experience has in common with previous experiences, the reference is general and conceptual. A concept, in the simple case, is the general reference of a symbol. There is no such substantial *thing* as a concept. The noun form is used for convenience to name a *process* of conceptualization, that is, a mode of generalized symbolic reference. The symbol means the generalized abstraction to which it refers. Thus, the terms 'concept', 'generalization' and 'meaning' have been used interchangeably throughout the discussion and one or the other has been chosen on each occasion of its use for purposes of emphasis.

It is not assumed that the symbolic reference of conceptualization need be a conscious or a reflective process. To the contrary, it emerges from the need for an economy of response in reacting to different intuitive data in similar ways, establishing aspects of those data that are repeated, recurrent, and recognizable. Action comes first, reflection follows. It is to be presumed that animal perception marks the behavioral recognition of that which is repeated or recurrent. Such behavioral recognition has here been called proto-generalization and has been asserted to be the foundation of all natural knowledge. Proto-generalization is a response to *present* data, however, and thus occurs only upon confrontation. As soon as there is *veridical* perception, symbolic reference goes beyond confrontation. The object of veridical perception is veridical in so far as it is a part of a coherent whole with all of which one is not confronted. The other side and the inside of a physical object are relevant to the percept of such an object, but one is not and cannot be confronted with either one. As the symbolic process progressively becomes more independent of confrontation, logical relations are recognized and symbolized in language. Then it is said that the concept is held in mind.

A preponderance of the symbols used in the process of conceptualization is verbal. The social inheritance of language accounts for the commonsense ways of cutting the intuitive flux. Those who learn a language of a common language stem are assured of living in the same commonsense perceptual world. The skeletal aspects of the commonsense world, the world of ordinary, unreflective perception, are blocked out in the concepts of one's native tongue, and the fundamental lines of the interpretation of the intuitive flux are laid down. Even those persons who are born deaf and acquire no spoken language, nevertheless, if they are intelligent, acquire the basic concepts of interpretation through the language of gesture or whatever means of communication is established.

As soon as the fundamentals of the interpretation of the intuitive flux are acquired, a categorial scheme is formed even though it be vague and confused and inadequate to the purpose of understanding. Categories are concepts of wide generality whereby the concepts of lesser scope are ordered and related. Concepts constitute the ordering element in experience, for conceptualization is symbolic reference to the connectedness and relatedness by means of which different portions of the flux are grasped. Rudimentary conceptualizations, that is, proto-generalizations make possible orderly perceptual experience. Critical concepts based on prescission, generalization, and functional abstraction carry the order farther. A critical categorical scheme produces a well ordered experience and yields understanding. Understanding is achieved when it is shown how each part or aspect of experience is related to all other parts or aspects.

All knowledge contains a conceptual factor, and it is by virtue of this factor that it is to be called knowledge at all. Theoretic knowledge is of relatively high degrees of generality—knowledge based on critical, reflective concepts. It produces a logically related scheme of categories, which scheme yields understanding. The goal of knowledge is understanding. It has often been assumed by men of affairs that the goal of knowledge is successful practical action. It may be that for man as engineer or military commander or manufacturer the goal is practical action, but for man as philosopher or scientist it is understanding. Successful practical action takes place in the commonsense world or in the world of science. What these worlds are and how they are related and, further, how successful action is related to them calls for understanding. Sometimes successful action is the *criterion* of understanding, but the sign whereby one can tell when one has understanding is not to be confused with what understanding is as a cognitive process.

Knowledge itself is action and understanding is action, but this is to use the word 'action' in a different sense than when speaking of successful practical action. Knowledge and understanding are actions in the sense of being processes. They are activities wherein one episode in the flux reacts to others. Successful practical action is a very special kind of action. It assumes a world of commonsense or a world of scientific objects and is always determined by a specific purpose.

If successful practical action can be a criterion of knowledge, it can be so only on the assumption that all conscious experience in either the present or the future, including all the consequences of present choices, is in principle capable of logical formulation in a structure of delineated and articulated relationships. The present theory gives grounds for this assumption. The assumption is justified because one cannot know that which is incapable of conceptual formulation and one is not even aware of that which is incapable of the rudimentary order of proto-generalization.

If knowledge is action, the Greek ideal of knowledge as contemplation must be given up or modified. It is true that the Greeks also knew that knowledge is discovery; but if it is discovery of what is already there in complete definition,[1] the discovery is merely the introductory step to contemplation. After the discovery is made, the results may be contemplated. If, however, knowledge is action forever carving out its objects and continually interacting with them, the discovery is never finished and there is no final result. Modern science has shown that there is no finality of knowledge. Knowledge is not only action, but it is hypothetical in form, always seeking new evidence.

Knowledge is cognitive action carried on by the mediation of concepts; but if the concepts themselves are not generated from experience, it is an eternal miracle where they come from and how they are applicable. Of course, if by 'experience' one means only conscious or remembered experience, there is no

1. *See* H. H. Price, *Perception*, p. 15.

experience not mediated by concepts; but if one uses 'experience' in a more inclusive sense to mean participation in process, then concepts, beginning with proto-generalizations, are generated from experience, and their applicability is part of their own nature until the technique of abstracting them from any connection with any specific content has been mastered in logic and mathematics. Pure logical and pure mathematical concepts are nonempirical, and if they are to indicate anything empirical they must be connected with content again by means of a semantic scheme.

Orderly experience is interpretation of intuitive data by means of concepts. A highly ordered experience (that is, experience which is understood) involves the interpretation of concepts of lesser generality in terms of concepts of greater generality. Categories are concepts of greatly inclusive generality, but there is no sharp dividing line between categories and less inclusive concepts; what might be called a category in one context might not in another. For example, mass and velocity are categories of physics, but not categories of philosophy unless one adopts a philosophy of physicalism or of materialism. Choice and decision are moral categories, but they are not categories of metaphysics unless one adopts a voluntaristic metaphysics. Because of the relativity of categories, no list of *the* categories is called for. Alternative categorial schemes are always possible.

Categorial schemes are conceptual, and critical concepts are derived from the processes of analysis, generalization and abstraction. It is not to be assumed that only one analysis of a situation is correct and all others are incorrect, and that only one set of prescissions can be made from a single correct analysis. On the contrary, the evidence shows that alternative analyses and abstractions are always possible. Therefore, alternative categorial schemes are always possible. A categorial scheme is an overall hypothesis and cannot be established to the exclusion of others. No hypothesis can be established in any field to the exclusion of all others.[2] Even in logic alternative postulate sets may yield the same logical structure. A rigid set of categories is a sign of a closed mind. The list becomes a Procrustean Bed which all experience is made to fit. If the experience cannot be made to fit even by violence, it is thrown out.

No category is absolute, that is, absolutely absolute. 'Absolute' means 'unconditioned'. It is true that something may be unconditioned within a carefully delimited context, but this would be absolute relative only to the context. Thus, in spite of the verbal incongruity, a relative absolute may be significantly distinguished from an absolute absolute. The failure to recognize that this is only a verbal incongruity has engendered much obfuscation of issues throughout the course of the history of philosophy. There can be no absolute absolute within a continuum, for there are no parts of a continuum unconditioned by other parts. In particular, no category can be absolute. All categories are conditioned by the cuts whereby concepts are determined, and there are unlimited ways of cutting a continuum.

It has often been supposed by philosophers that at least one category, the category 'reality', is absolute. This notion needs further analysis. Is a category to be conceived of as the name of a distinction already set up in the nature of things; and do separate things belong in one category or another according to their own nature? On the assumption that this is what a category is, whatever is in its own nature absolute (unconditioned) belongs in an absolute category. Thus, if reality is absolute, the category 'reality' is absolute; but it follows deductively that if the category 'reality' is *not* absolute, then reality is not absolute, and any consideration

2. Speaking of the field of natural science, Ernest Nagel says "Contemporary analyses . . . have shown . . . that a theory is never uniquely determined by any set of empirical data, however numerous and varied these may be." *Sovereign Reason* (Glencoe, Ill.: The Free Press, 1954) p. 304.

challenging the absoluteness of the category challenges the assumption on which it rests, that is, the assumption that categories are names of distinctions set up in the nature of things— that they are characteristics of a pre-structured reality.

The view that any category is absolute is rejected in the present study and a different hypothesis offered because the rejected view carries with it an unresolved bifurcation of whatever is real into things and concepts. It makes knowledge not a process of interpretation but mere information about ready-made distinctions—information which sorts out fully formulated experience into ready-made classes whose nature is found by the inspection of a large number of instances. Such a view commits both the blackberry bush fallacy and the fallacy of misplaced discreteness. It engenders all the traditional problems of the classical nineteenth-century theory of induction. It does not fit into the theory of hypothesis as carried out in twentieth-century natural science. It is more appropriate to preevolutionary biology or prerelativity physics than to contemporary biology or physics since it makes classification the primary task of the natural sciences. It assumes a copy-correspondence theory of truth in holding that the structure of knowledge must copy the structure of a reality that is uninfected by knowledge, though the uninfected reality is neither given nor to be found.

If the rejected view of the nature of categories were held, categories could not be applied to a continuum, for a continuum does not contain any ready-made distinctions. Furthermore, no continuum could be generated, for a continuum is not to be obtained from discrete parts, no matter how tightly they are jammed up against each other. Thus, there can be no genuine continuity if 'reality' names an absolute category. The present study holds that 'reality' when used in this sense is a term without philosophic meaning. It is a term to conjure with, not one with which to solve genuine problems of the understanding.

To say this is far from saying that there is no useful sense in which 'reality' can be predicated. Reality is whatever is subsumed under the right category. Everything is real in some sense or other, and the task of categorization is to find the right sense. The right category is the category that does what a category is supposed to do, that is, to introduce order into experience. For example, one has a perceptual experience of flying. This cannot be assimilated into orderly experience under the category 'physical process', but it can be assimilated under the category 'dream.' One has real dreams. If one narrates as a dream what one did not have as a dream, there is still something real—a real prevarication. There are real imaginations, real fantasies, real illusions, real hallucinations. Experience is orderly to the degree that it can be placed in a category that coherently relates and assimilates it to the rest of experience.

There is also a more fundamental philosophic sense in which 'reality' may be used. Reality is whatever *can* be categorized. This would be a matrix-reality, however, and not a delineated reality.[3] The sole ontological assumption of the present study is that this matrix-reality is process—is the intuitive flux. All categories arise from it and are applied to it, yielding knowledge of it. If it would be said that 'matrix-reality' names a category, it would be a completely ubiquitous category and thus without special significance. Nothing can be known of matrix-reality until concepts are derived from it and applied to it but it is not unknowable. To the contrary, it is not only knowable but is all that is knowable. 'Process' names a definite category, however, for matrix-reality may be and usually has been interpreted in the history of philosophy not as process but in some other way, for example as substance.

Categories and classes are "there" in reality, but not absolutely. They are always relative to some conceptual scheme for grasping matrix-reality, and are conditioned by the scheme.

---

3. A dictionary definition of this sense of the word 'matrix' is: "that within and from which something originates, takes form, or develops."

Other categories and classes are possible relative to some other conceptual scheme. There are more ways than one of interpreting and grasping reality. Some ways are better than others, and the method of hypothesis offers means for testing and comparing to determine the better ways. There are no such things as *the* categories of reality.

The sciences, rational, empirical, and philosophic, are attempts to gain knowledge, hence they must use the tools of the knowledge process, namely concepts. Concepts are definitive; they are formulated in definitions, and definition is limitation. Each concept, in so far as it accomplishes its task in knowledge, is clear and precise; it has discrete boundaries so that what falls under it and what does not is fully determined. Concepts, then, furnish the discrete element in experience. Both the continuous and the discrete must be accounted for since both are in experience. The intuitive flux is a continuum. It contains no boundaries except as cuts are made in it. The cuts give rise to concepts, and the application of concepts to the flux marks discrete distinctions without which there is no knowledge. The master plan of the application of concepts is a categorial scheme.

Whitehead observed that cosmology must take account of both the continuity and the atomicity of nature.[4] This study points out that cosmology can do so indirectly through epistemology. If the source of atomicity can be traced to the way that nature is conceptually grasped by making selections and divisions within the original experience of continuity, then both the continuity and the discontinuity are taken into account, but the continuity is ontologically primary. The same nature cannot be both continuous and discontinuous in the same respect at the same time.

4. Whitehead, *Process and Reality,* p. 365. I have argued elsewhere that Whitehead's cosmology does not unambiguously do so. *See Tulane Studies in Philosophy* 10 (1961): 59–70.

Being a cognitive enterprise science deals with its subject matter conceptually, and concepts are discrete. It is to be expected, then, that the analyses science makes will seem to find discrete parts. The natural phenomena with which science deals are already divided by means of the selection exercised in perception, and the understanding of them further divides them by means of discrete, critical concepts; but this is no indication that the flux is composed of discrete units. Concrete experience is a continuum, but conceptual models are made up of discrete parts. Concrete experience never more than approximately fits the conceptual models whereby science understands its subject matter. So-called errors of observation often are due, at least in part, to the inaccuracies of the fit. The discrepancies become proportionately larger in subatomic theory, and the perceptual models taken from middle-sized experience, the models by means of which the conceptual models are applied to subatomic data, can never be taken completely literally.

Logic and mathematics, being purely conceptual, also analyze their subject matter into elements. Even in the formulation of a logical or mathematical theory of continuity, the analysis is into conceptual elements, but the discrete concepts can be applied to the continuous content by providing that the elements themselves are not discrete. The elements of a linear continuum can be interpreted as infinite classes, each having no last term, and therefore no boundary within itself.[5]

Parallel to Whitehead's fallacy of misplaced concreteness,[6] and of equal importance, is the fallacy of misplaced discreteness. The analysis of knowledge always finds discrete elements. This is as it should be; knowledge is conceptual and concepts are discrete. But this affords no warrant for assuming that that which knowledge is about is composed of discrete elements. The fallacy of misplaced discreteness consists in hypostatizing

5. See E. V. Huntington, The Continuum . . . , p. 53.
6. Whitehead, Science and the Modern World, p. 72.

the discrete elements of knowledge and reading them back into that which knowledge is about—ultimately into the matrix-reality which is the source and ground of all knowledge—and supposing that there is a Reality composed of discrete units. An adult human being is ordinarily aware only of that which is assimilated into the commonsense conceptual frame. The concepts of the frame come to him ready-made, being part of the social inheritance of language. Thus, it is easy to assume that the ultimate content of knowledge comes in ready-made units too, such as Hume's impressions or the sense-data of more recent theories of perception. But so to assume is to commit the fallacy of misplaced discreteness.

The view of the nature of the philosophic enterprise widely held in the nineteenth century, that philosophy is analytic and synthetic, is based on the fallacy of misplaced discreteness. The view goes back to that part of the correspondence theory of truth which holds that, although empirical knowledge is always limited, each part of knowledge is a faithful mirroring of some part of reality, and that therefore the knowledge of reality can be attained by a synthesis of all the parts. The view assumes that parts in knowledge correspond to parts in matrix-reality, and that analysis can reach the ultimate parts of which matrix-reality is truly composed, and can (in principle) reach all of them. But there are no such parts. Analysis is selective and abstractive, for the whole that is analyzed is a continuum and affords unlimited possibilities of division into parts. Knowledge is composed of discrete parts, but a continuum is not so composed. To suppose that the continuum is composed of discrete parts because knowledge is, is to commit the fallacy of misplaced discreteness.

The task of philosophy is not analysis and synthesis. Synthesis as the nineteenth century conceived of it is no part of the task. The task is understanding; analysis plays an indispensible role in understanding, but in addition to analysis, prescinding, generalizing, and abstracting are essential because they lead to fully developed interpretation. Complex interpretation consists in grasping and applying relationships between the parts resulting from analysis and abstraction, but neither the grasp nor the application is a synthesis in the sense of putting parts together. Analysis is applied to what is taken from the intuitive flux and yields parts which can be subjected to further processes of generalizing and abstracting, but all the philosopher's horses and all the philosopher's men cannot put the continuum together again. The intuitive flux is infinite in the sense that infinite selections can be made from it, but all the philosophers together can make only a finite series of selections.

It may be noted by some critics that there has been no systematic treatment of truth in the present study. The omission is intentional. Truth is not a fundamental category of epistemology. Knowledge is the fundamental category, but knowledge is not to be defined in terms of truth. Knowledge is relative to the evidence, and in empirical matters the evidence is never all in; thus, knowledge is fallible and does not rest on truth. The concept 'truth' is useful in a nontechnical way, and it has not here been used technically. It is vague and ambiguous in that it means different things in different contexts. It could easily be given a precise definition by fiat, but any such definition would render most of its ordinary usages incorrect. For example, it is used differently in relation to perceptual than to theoretic knowledge; and in regard to theoretic knowledge, it is used differently in empirical than in rational sciences.

Strictly speaking, only the assertion or denial of a proposition in a judgment or a statement can be true or false. If this is held firmly in mind, many of the traditional problems of the nature of truth vanish. But even philosophers who are usually careful will sometimes ask a question such as "Is it true that the eclipse forecast for next year will take place as predicted?" The question is misput. Events, whether in the past, present or future, are not true or false; only the statement that asserts or denies the event is true or false. If the event is in the future, a statement about it is not now true or false. It becomes true or false as the event occurs or fails to occur.

Simply to say that a statement is true or false is elliptical. No statement is true except under specified conditions. To call a statement true without ellipsis requires that the conditions be specified. For example, to call a pure logical or mathematical statement true means that it can be shown deductively to hold within a stated system of primitive ideas, postulates, rules, and definitions. To call a statement of applied geometry true means that it holds not only within a stated postulate set but also within a semantic scheme of application to perceptual experience. To call an empirical statement of natural science true means that it holds within the refined conceptual scheme of perception which defines the field of the science. To call an ordinary empirical statement true means that it holds within the commonsense conceptual scheme whereby intuitive data are assimilated into the ordinary perceptual world. In every case, 'true' applies only to what fits within some particular categorial scheme; and this is why 'truth' is not a fundamental category of epistemology.

When the categorial scheme conditioning the truth of a statement can be assumed without a vitiating ambiguity, it is harmless to use the term 'true' in a nontechnical sense. When the categorial scheme cannot be assumed, recourse must be had to knowledge of conditions before the term 'true' can be used significantly. No truth is absolute; it is always conditioned by a categorial scheme and by knowledge gained through application of the scheme. Thus, truth may be said to be a semantic category, but it is not a fundamental epistemological category.

The fundamental categories of epistemology delineated in the present study are 'content' and 'form'. The content has been identified as well as it can be identified by calling it 'intuitive flux'. The form (order, structure) has been called 'the conceptual element in knowledge'. Content is that to which form is applied. No complete concept of the intuitive flux is possible, because any formulation is something done to the flux and is necessarily incomplete—other things can be done too. The flux is a continuum; it is that to which concepts can be applied; it is process; it is ever changing quality without absolute distinction; it is the source and ground of all knowledge; it is that from which the subject and object of knowledge emerge. All these and more are partial characterizations of the flux, and a characterization is the application of a definitive concept or set of concepts, but the flux is inexhaustible, there is no end to the concepts that may be applied to it. To say that the flux *is* any one of these characteristics or all of them put together is to commit the fallacy of misplaced discreteness and leads to the view that the flux is a synthesis of separately given parts.

Any conceptualization of the flux or all the conceptualizations together yield only a finite selection. No set of selections can be complete, for the flux is inexhaustible in possibilities of selections. This follows from its being a continuum, and the continuum is felt in the experience of passage. But there is no conscious experience of contentless passage. Conscious experience is of ever changing quality. To say all this is only to illustrate that knowledge is analytic and general. Nothing can be said about the flux except in conceptual terms, but the conceptual terms all have content. There is something in experience to which the conceptual terms apply. The assumption of this ultimate content is the ontological assumption lying at the root of epistemology; and this content is process.

Added to the categories of content and form is 'interaction', and interaction gives rise to the subcategories 'subjective' and 'objective', which appear under other names as 'mind' and 'environment'. Other subcategories are 'selection', 'interpretation', 'proto-generalization', 'analysis', 'prescisson', 'generalization', 'abstraction', 'theory', and 'logic'. Interaction between mind and environment yields the subcategories 'percept', 'concept', 'fact', 'evidence', 'belief', and 'knowledge'. It is of little importance whether or not other concepts, of less inclusive generality, are called categories; the distinction is a relative one. But the concepts that have been named are of highly inclusive generality in the ordering of experience. They are all conceived to be epistemological categories with the exception of the intuitive flux, which is introduced as the ontological counterpart of the epistemological category 'content.'

The above-named categories are not introduced as *the* list of epistemological categories. They are the result of one epistemological analysis, and other analyses are possible. They comprise a categorial scheme which is a speculative hypothesis concerning the nature of knowledge. The verification of such a speculative hypothesis consists in showing that it does what a categorial scheme is set up to do. A speculative hypothesis is not verified in the same way as is the purely systematic hypothesis of a rational science, for it is not sufficient to show that all its theorems follow deductively from a consistent postulate set. Its theorems are empirically oriented, and the hypothesis must succeed in ordering experience. Neither is a speculative hypothesis verified by observations and predictions as are the hypotheses of empirical science, for it does not restrict either its data or its verification to natural phenomena. It must encompass everything that lays claim to be experience. The hypotheses of empirical science operate to order experience within the categorial schemes already set up to define the fields of the sciences. The speculative hypotheses of the philosophic sciences criticize and coordinate all specialized categorial schemes.

The precise structure and interrelationship of categories can best be shown by a formalization of the scheme in a set of postulates and derived theorems. If such a formalization were attempted, it would undoubtedly be found that the present doctrine needs modification and adjustment. It would also undoubtedly be found that alternative formalizations could be made. If either of these situations were not found to be the

case, then the present doctrine would need modification anyway, for it leads to the conclusion that they would be the case.
Not only would a logical formalization be necessary, however,
but also the formalization of a semantic scheme of application, for knowledge has an empirical semantic reference in
every case except that of pure mathematics and logic. The lure
of the fallacy of misplaced discreteness would have to be constantly resisted, for there is an inherent incompatibility between
the present categorial scheme and a doctrine of a rigidly pre-
structured reality. C. S. Peirce pointed out that it is conceivable
that two persons should each have perfect knowledge which
conflicted, but he added that though conceivable, it is not possible "considering the social nature of man" if the two persons
"compare notes." He added, however, that in no case would it
be "sure knowledge" (theoretically certain), because sure
knowledge would be "not only perfectly to know, but perfectly to know that we do perfectly know."[7]

All knowledge, being organized within a categorial scheme,
is circular in the last analysis. This is not a flaw, but is of the
very nature of knowledge itself. Knowledge is relative to the
categorial scheme wherein it is organized; but the criterion of
a categorial scheme is that it should accomplish what it is set
up to accomplish, that is, it must produce order in experience,
and that highest type of order which is called understanding.
The circle is not a vicious circle unless it is too small and does
not take in everything it is supposed to take in. *Everything*
that lays claim to be accounted for must be accounted for; the
case is not to be won by refusing to look at some of the purported evidence. The sense in which all genuine knowledge
is circular is the sense in which it is systematic. Everything
that is known depends on everything else that is known. The
coherence theory of truth was not in error in pointing this out.
It was in error in holding that this is all that is involved in
truth and is definitive of it. The circle of knowledge must
always accommodate itself to the intuitive flux in which it is

7. Peirce, C. P., 4.62, 4.63.

immersed. Coherence must be fitted to the stubbornness of stubborn fact. The ultimate content of knowledge is not produced by the formal, conceptual, logical element in knowledge; it is just the other way around. The intuitive flux, selections from which are the ultimate content, produces the formal, conceptual element. Mind arises from the flux and initially can do nothing with it except to formulate conceptual schemes whereby to assimilate it into an orderly experience and to understand it. Now man has found that on the basis of this understanding, he can alter even the occurrence of the flux, and with the advent of knowledge in nuclear physics he has achieved the awful possibility of obliterating all knowledge and all mind from the flux.

Knowledge is not to be rejected or even to be questioned because it is circular in the sense of being systematic. Neither is it to be rejected or even down-graded because it is selective and abstractive. Selection and abstraction are necessary conditions, and without them there is no knowledge whatever. Bergson's relegation of scientific knowledge to what is merely useful is made possible only by his doctrine of mystical intuition in which the true knowledge of reality is non-cognitive and transcends the limitations by which conceptual knowledge is bound. This outcome of his philosophy belies the emphasis on continuity with which the philosophy begins. He has, in the end, two kinds of knowledge which are not continuous with each other: scientific, cognitive knowledge, and what he calls true philosophic knowledge. In an essay entitled "Philosophic Intuition," Bergson calls philosophy and science two ways of knowing.[8] In his *Introduction to Metaphysics,* however, he holds that the two ways are overcome in mystical intuition. But the mystic vision is admittedly rare and is the privilege of exceptional men.[9]

8. Henri Bergson, *The Creative Mind* (New York: Philosophical Library, 1946) p. 146.
9. *See Two Sources of Morality and Religion* (Garden City, N.Y.: Doubleday & Co., Inc., 1935) pp. 213, 236.

The present study points out that each person has his own conceptual scheme by means of which he orders and attempts to understand his experience. The conceptual scheme of each is in many respects necessarily like that of others, for, as Mead held,[10] a developed mind and a self are social products, and depend largely on communication, especially verbal communication, with others. It is also true, however, that the conceptual scheme of each is in some respects different from that of others, for it orders his own experience. Each person's conceptual scheme is the basis of his own philosophy, either a naive, commonsense one or a critical one. His philosophy becomes critical when the conceptual scheme is refined and reflectively elaborated into a systematic structure. If Bergson experienced the mystic vision, then his conceptual scheme must assimilate this experience, but his philosophy is not the experience. His philosophy is the elaboration of the conceptual scheme whereby he orders his experience as this scheme is presented in his writings. His *philosophy* is not the mystic vision.

Although everyone lives in what is in broad outlines the same world, no two persons live in precisely the same world in every definite detail. Every man is the center of his own experience and each experience is unique in its precise detail. There is a degree to which the religious person, the scientist, the artist live in different worlds. They live in the same world in so far as they communicate with each other and are each a part of the other's physical and social environment; but the precise details of the categorial scheme of each are constructed from his own experience. The philosopher, in attempting to construct a universal categorial scheme, must take this into account and his scheme must allow for it.

The general conditions of knowing are not different for the philosopher than for others. If all knowledge is fallible, so is the philosopher's. If all knowledge is conditioned by a cate-

10. *See* Mead, MSS.

gorial scheme, the epistemologist's knowledge of the nature of knowledge is too. If my study did not recognize this, it would commit what Angus Sinclair calls 'the epistemologist's fallacy', namely, the assumption that the strictures and limitations which it finds conditioning all other knowledge somehow do not apply to it.[11] To commit such a fallacy is a rather unsubtle form of special pleading. The present study avoids the fallacy in that it does not assert the categorial scheme whereby it attempts to understand understanding to be the only rationally possible or even the "true" scheme. But it is a scheme that calls for consideration in the light of what the natural sciences and logic have, in the past hundred years, contributed to the knowledge of the nature of theoretic knowledge.

11. Angus Sinclair, *The Conditions of Knowing*, pp. 41, 74.

"The merest hint of dogmatic certainty as to finality of statement is an exhibition of folly."

A. N. WHITEHEAD

INDEX

Prologue